Contents

Lesson 1

Lesson 2

Lesson 3

Lesson 4

Lesson 5

Lesson 6

Lesson 7

Lesson 8

Lesson 9

Lesson 12

Lesson 13

Lesson 14

Appendices

In memory of
Herman and Ethel Elbaum

Acknowledgments

I would also like to show my appreciation for the following teachers who reviewed **Grammar in Context:**

Caroline Cochran	Northern Virginia Community College, VA
Carol Dent	City College of San Francisco, Alemany Center, CA
Bill Griffith	Georgia Institute of Technology, GA
Kathi Jordan	Contra Costa College, CA
Ed Rosen	City College of San Francisco, CA
Rebecca Suarez	University of Texas, El Paso, TX
Ethel Tiersky	Truman College, IL
Karen Tucker	Georgia Institute of Technology, GA
Andrea Woyt	Truman College, IL
Anita Zednik	Northern Virginia Community College, VA

A special thanks to my family of friends for helping me get through it all: Jim M. Curran, Cornelius Hassell, Chay Lustig, Hal Mead, Alison Montgomery, Marilyn Orleans, Meg Tripoli, and Lydia York.

And many thanks to my students at Truman College, who have increased my understanding of my own language and taught me to see life from another point of view. By sharing their observations, questions, and life stories, they have enriched my life enormously.

A word from the author

It seems to me that I was born to be an ESL teacher. My parents immigrated to the U.S. from Poland as adults and were confused not only by the English language but by American culture as well. Born in the U.S., I often had the task as a child to explain the intricacies of the language and allay my parents' fears about the culture. It is no wonder to me that I became an ESL teacher, and later, an ESL writer who focuses on explanations of American culture in order to illustrate grammar. My life growing up in an immigrant neighborhood was very similar to the lives of my students, so I have a feel for what confuses them and what they need to know about American life.

ESL teachers often find themselves explaining confusing customs and providing practical information about life in the U.S. Often, teachers are a student's only source of information about American life. With **Grammar in Context, Third Edition,** I enjoy sharing my experiences with you.

Grammar in Context, Third Edition connects grammar with American cultural context, providing learners of English with a useful and meaningful skill and knowledge base. Students learn the grammar necessary to communicate verbally and in writing, and learn how American culture plays a role in language, beliefs, and everyday situations.

Enjoy the new edition of **Grammar in Context!**

Sandra N. Elbaum

Grammar in Context Unites Learners and Language

Students learn language in context, increasing their understanding and ability to use new structures.

Learning a language through meaningful themes and practicing in a contextualized setting promotes both linguistic and cognitive development. In **Grammar in Context,** grammar is presented in interesting and informative readings, and the language is subsequently practiced throughout the chapter. Students learn more, remember more and can use language more effectively when they learn grammar in context.

Students expand their knowledge of American topics and culture.

American themes add a historical and cultural dimension to students' learning. The readings in **Grammar in Context** help students gain insight into American culture and the way many Americans think and feel about various topics. Students gain ample exposure to and practice in dealing with situations such as finding an apartment, holiday traditions, and shopping, as well as practicing the language that goes with these situations. Their new knowledge helps them enjoy their stay or life in the U.S.

Students are prepared for academic assignments and everyday language tasks.

Discussions, readings, compositions and exercises involving higher level critical thinking skills develop overall language and communication skills. In addition to the numerous exercises in the student text and workbook, teachers will find a wealth of ideas in **Grammar in Context.** Students will have interesting, fulfilling, and successful experiences that they will take with them as they complete their ESL classes.

Students learn to use their new skills to communicate.

The exercises and Expansion Activities in **Grammar in Context** help students learn English while practicing their writing and speaking skills. Students work together in pairs and groups to find more information about topics, to make presentations, to play games, and to role-play. Their confidence to use English increases, as does their ability to communicate effectively.

Students enjoy learning.

If learning is meaningful, it is motivational and fun. Places, famous people, trends, customs, and everyday American activities all have an impact on our students' lives, and having a better understanding of these things helps them function successfully in the U.S. By combining rich, cultural content with clear grammar presentation and practice, **Grammar in Context** engages the student's attention and provides guidance in grammar usage and writing. And whatever is enjoyable will be more readily learned and retained.

Welcome to
Grammar in Context, Third Edition
Spanning language and culture

Students learn more, remember more and can use grammar more effectively when they learn language in context. **Grammar in Context, Third Edition** connects grammar with rich, American cultural context, providing learners of English with a useful and meaningful skill and knowledge base.

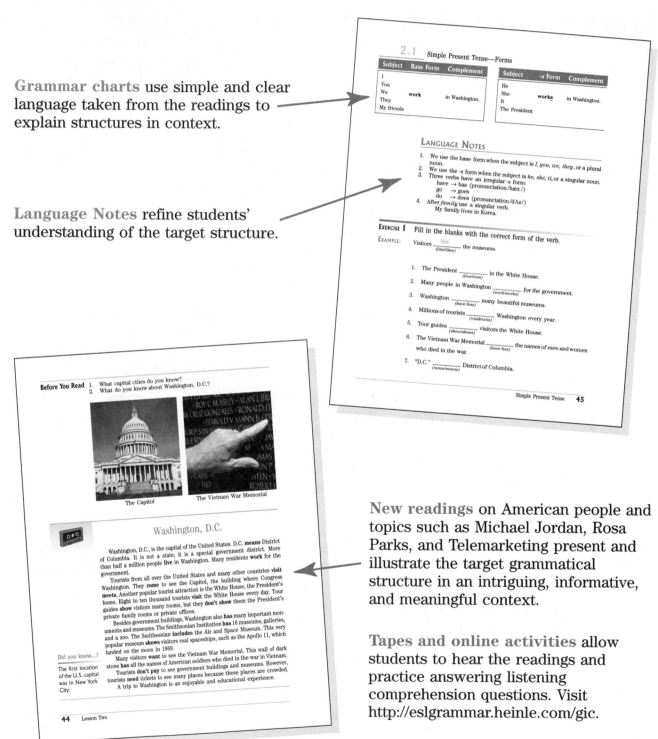

Grammar charts use simple and clear language taken from the readings to explain structures in context.

Language Notes refine students' understanding of the target structure.

New readings on American people and topics such as Michael Jordan, Rosa Parks, and Telemarketing present and illustrate the target grammatical structure in an intriguing, informative, and meaningful context.

Tapes and online activities allow students to hear the readings and practice answering listening comprehension questions. Visit http://eslgrammar.heinle.com/gic.

A wide array of exercises keeps the classroom lively and targets a variety of learning styles.

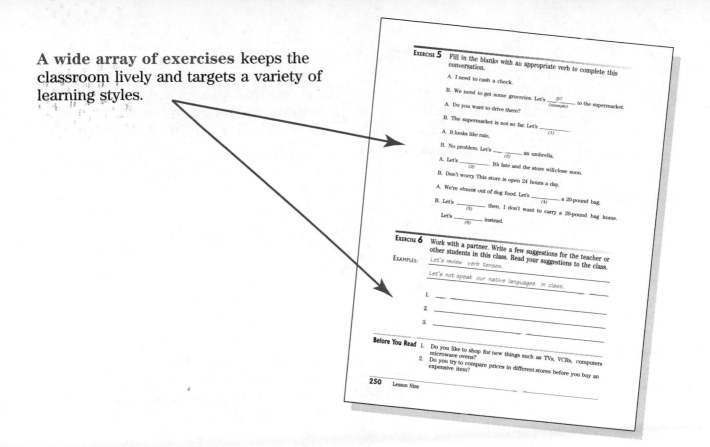

EXERCISE 5 Fill in the blanks with an appropriate verb to complete this conversation.

A. I need to cash a check.

B. We need to get some groceries. Let's ___go___ to the supermarket.
              (example)

A. Do you want to drive there?

B. The supermarket is not so far. Let's _____.
                                           (1)

A. It looks like rain.

B. No problem. Let's _____ an umbrella.
                       (2)

A. Let's _____. It's late and the store will close soon.
          (3)

B. Don't worry. This store is open 24 hours a day.

A. We're almost out of dog food. Let's _____ a 20-pound bag.
                                          (4)

B. Let's _____ then. I don't want to carry a 20-pound bag home.
          (5)
   Let's _____ instead.
          (6)

EXERCISE 6 Work with a partner. Write a few suggestions for the teacher or other students in this class. Read your suggestions to the class.

EXAMPLES: *Let's review verb tenses.*

           Let's not speak our native languages in class.

1. _____

2. _____

3. _____

Before You Read 1. Do you like to shop for new things such as TVs, VCRs, computers microwave ovens?
2. Do you try to compare prices in different stores before you buy an expensive item?

250   Lesson Nine

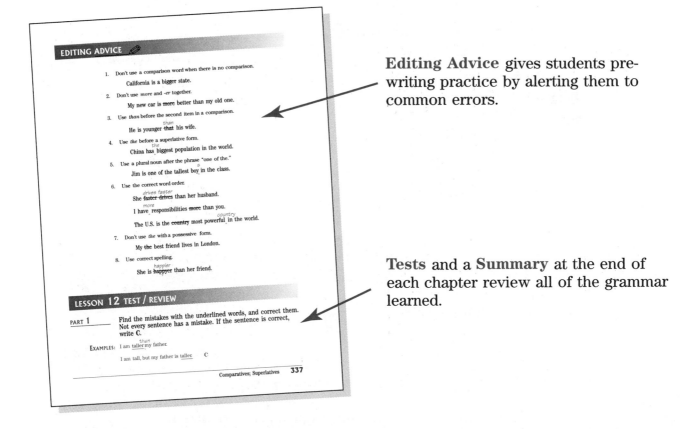

EDITING ADVICE

1. Don't use a comparison word when there is no comparison.
   California is a ~~bigger~~ state.

2. Don't use *more* and *-er* together.
   My new car is ~~more~~ better than my old one.

3. Use *than* before the second item in a comparison.
                        than
   He is younger ~~that~~ his wife.

4. Use *the* before a superlative form.
               the
   China has ~~biggest~~ population in the world.

5. Use a plural noun after the phrase "one of the."
                               s
   Jim is one of the tallest boy~~_~~ in the class.

6. Use the correct word order.
       drives faster
   She ~~faster drives~~ than her husband.
               more
   I have responsibilities ~~more~~ than you.
                         country
   The U.S. is the ~~country~~ most powerful in the world.

7. Don't use *the* with a possessive form.
   My ~~the~~ best friend lives in London.

8. Use correct spelling.
         happier
   She is ~~happyer~~ than her friend.

LESSON 12 TEST / REVIEW

PART 1 Find the mistakes with the underlined words, and correct them. Not every sentence has a mistake. If the sentence is correct, write C.

EXAMPLES: I am <u>taller</u> my father.
                  than

           I am tall, but my father is <u>taller</u>   C

                                    Comparatives; Superlatives   337

Editing Advice gives students pre-writing practice by alerting them to common errors.

Tests and a **Summary** at the end of each chapter review all of the grammar learned.

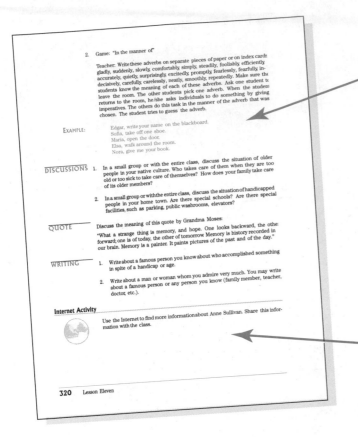

2. Game: "In the manner of"

Teacher: Write these adverbs on separate pieces of paper or on index cards: gladly, suddenly, slowly, comfortably, simply, steadily, foolishly, efficiently, accurately, quietly, surprisingly, excitedly, promptly, fearlessly, fearfully, indecisively, carefully, carelessly, neatly, smoothly, repeatedly. Make sure the students know the meaning of each of these adverbs. Ask one student to leave the room. The other students pick one adverb. When the student returns to the room, he/she asks individuals to do something by giving imperatives. The others do this task in the manner of the adverb that was chosen. The student tries to guess the adverb.

EXAMPLE: Edgar, write your name on the blackboard.
           Sofia, take off one shoe.
           Maria, open the door.
           Elsa, walk around the room.
           Nora, give me your book.

DISCUSSIONS 1. In a small group or with the entire class, discuss the situation of older people in your native culture. Who takes care of them when they are too old or too sick to take care of themselves? How does your family take care of its older members?

2. In a small group or with the entire class, discuss the situation of handicapped people in your home town. Are there special schools? Are there special facilities, such as parking, public washrooms, elevators?

QUOTE   Discuss the meaning of this quote by Grandma Moses:
"What a strange thing is memory, and hope. One looks backward, the other forward; one is of today, the other of tomorrow. Memory is history recorded in our brain. Memory is a painter. It paints pictures of the past and of the day."

WRITING 1. Write about a famous person you know about who accomplished something in spite of a handicap or age.

2. Write about a man or woman whom you admire very much. You may write about a famous person or any person you know (family member, teacher, doctor, etc.).

Internet Activity

Use the Internet to find more information about Anne Sullivan. Share this information with the class.

320 Lesson Eleven

Expansion Activities provide many fun opportunities for students to interact with one another and further develop their skills in speaking and writing.

New **Internet** activities encourage students to use technology to explore a wealth of online resources. Also available at http://eslgrammar.heinle.com/gic.

More Grammar Practice Workbooks

Used in conjunction with **Grammar in Context** or as a companion to any reading, writing, or listening skills text, **More Grammar Practice** helps students learn and review the essential grammar skills to make language learning comprehensive and ongoing.

- Clear grammar charts

- Extensive exercises

- Great for in-class practice or homework

- Follows the same scope and sequence as **Grammar in Context, Third Edition**

Lesson One

GRAMMAR
The Present Tense of *Be*

CONTEXT
The United States
Postcard from New York City
Conversation about Life in the U.S.

LESSON FOCUS
Be has three forms in the present: *am, is, are.*
Canada *is* north of the United States.
The U.S. and Canada *are* big countries.

New York City

Before You Read

1. Look at the map of North America. Find Alaska, Hawaii, and Puerto Rico.
2. Look at the map of the United States. Find the state where you live.

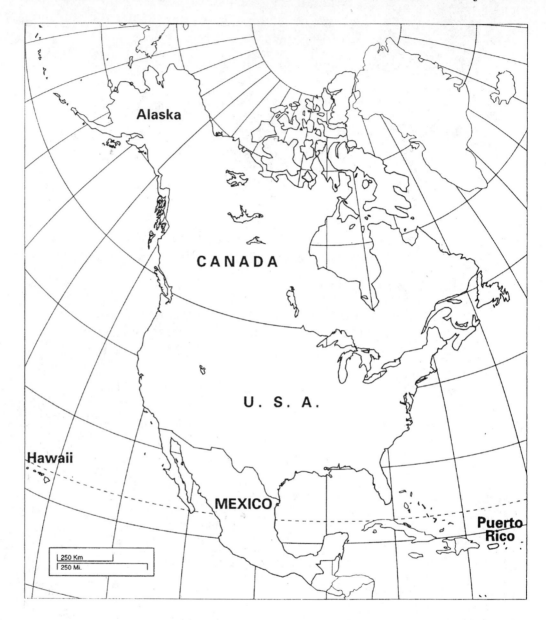

Read the following article. Pay special attention to the forms of the verb *be*.

The United States

The United States **is** a big country. There **are** 50 states in the U.S. Forty-eight states **are** on the mainland. Two states **are** far from the mainland: Alaska and Hawaii. Alaska **is** the largest state. It **is** northwest of Canada. Hawaii **is** in the Pacific Ocean. This state **is** a group of small islands.

Washington **is** a state. It **is** in the northwest. Washington, D.C., **is** not a state. It **is** a special government district. It **is** on the east coast. It **is** the capital of the U.S. The White House **is** in Washington, D.C. The White House **is** the home of the President.

Most states in the eastern part of the U.S. **are** small. Most states in the West and Southwest **are** large. The biggest city in the U.S. **is** New York. Other big cities **are** Los Angeles, Chicago, Philadelphia, and Boston.

Puerto Rico **is** not a state. It **is** a territory of the U.S. It **is** an island in the Caribbean Sea. Puerto Ricans **are** citizens of the U.S. The languages of Puerto Rico **are** Spanish and English.

The United States of America

AL	Alabama	IN	Indiana	NE	Nebraska	SC	South Carolina
AK	Alaska	IA	Iowa	NV	Nevada	SD	South Dakota
AZ	Arizona	KS	Kansas	NH	New Hampshire	TN	Tennessee
AR	Arkansas	KY	Kentucky	NJ	New Jersey	TX	Texas
CA	California	LA	Louisiana	NM	New Mexico	UT	Utah
CO	Colorado	ME	Maine	NY	New York	VT	Vermont
CT	Connecticut	MD	Maryland	NC	North Carolina	VA	Virginia
DE	Delaware	MA	Massachusetts	ND	North Dakota	WA	Washington
FL	Florida	MI	Michigan	OH	Ohio	WV	West Virginia
GA	Georgia	MN	Minnesota	OK	Oklahoma	WI	Wisconsin
HI	Hawaii	MS	Mississippi	OR	Oregon	WY	Wyoming
ID	Idaho	MO	Missouri	PA	Pennsylvania	DC*	District of
IL	Illinois	MT	Montana	RI	Rhode Island		Columbia

*The District of Columbia is not a state. Washington D.C. is the capital of the United States.
 Note: Washington D.C. and Washigton state are not the same.

1.1 Forms of *Be*

I	**am**	in New York now.
My father		in Boston.
He		a mechanic.
My sister	**is**	in Puerto Rico.
Boston		a city.
It		beautiful.
We		students.
You		a teacher.
Puerto Ricans	**are**	citizens of the U.S.
Chicago and Boston		cities.
They		big.

EXERCISE 1   Fill in the blanks with *is, are,* or *am.*

EXAMPLE: The U.S. ____*is*____ a big country.

1. Alaska _____ the largest state in the U.S.

2. Alaska and Hawaii _____ far from the mainland.

3. The states in the East _____ small.

4. Puerto Rico _____ an island.

5. Puerto Ricans _____ citizens of the U.S.

6. English _____ the main language of the U.S.

7. We _____ in the U.S.

8. I _____ a student in the U.S.

1.2 Uses of *Be*

Examples	Uses of *Be*
Washington, D.C., **is** beautiful.	Description
Washington, D.C., **is** the capital of the U.S.	Classification or definition
Washington, D.C., **is** in the East.	Location

(continued)

Examples	Uses of *Be*
We **are** from Mexico.	Place of origin
I **am** 25 years old.	Age
It **is** hot in Puerto Rico.	Weather
It **is** 6 o'clock.	Time

EXERCISE 2 Fill in the blanks to make **true** statements.

EXAMPLE: California is on the _____*west*_____ coast.
                                    (location)

1. Washington, D.C., is on the _____ coast.
                                    (location)

2. Chicago is a _____. Illinois is a state.
                    (classification)

3. Puerto Rico is an _____ with water all around.
                        (classification)

4. It is _____ now.
            (time)

5. It is _____ today.
            (weather)

6. The American president is about _____.
                                      (age)

7. The teacher is from _____.
                          (place of origin)

1.3 Word Order with *Be*

Subject	*Be*	Complement	Explanation
I	**am**	from Los Angeles.[1]	• The subject is first. The subject tells who or what we are talking about.
Los Angeles	**is**	a city.	
It	**is**	very big.	• The verb (*am*, *is*, *are*) is second.
Spanish	**is**	my native language.	• The complement is third. The complement finishes, or completes, the sentence with a location, classification, description, etc.
You	**are**	from Cuba.	
It	**is**	hot in Cuba.	

[1] Americans often say *L.A.* for Los Angeles.

EXERCISE 3 Put the words in the correct order to make a statement. Use a capital letter at the beginning and a period at the end.

EXAMPLE: big / the U.S. / is _____ *The U.S. is big.* _____

1. is / beautiful / San Francisco _____

2. is / Texas / a big state _____

3. hot today / it / is _____

4. the teacher / from / is / New York _____

5. years / my brother / is / 25 / old _____

6. a big country / Canada / is _____

7. in the classroom / are / the students _____

8. the map / on page 3 / is _____

9. my parents / in Germany / are _____

10. am / I / a student _____

1.4   The Subject

<u>Chicago</u> is very big. ↓ **It** is in Illinois.	<u>My friend and I</u> are in California. ↓ **We** are in Los Angeles.
<u>My sister</u> is married. ↓ **She** is very happy.	<u>My cousins</u> are in Mexico. ↓ **They** are in Mexico City.
<u>My father</u> is at work. ↓ **He** is busy.	<u>China and Korea</u> are countries. ↓ **They** are in Asia.

LANGUAGE NOTES

1. The **subject** can be a **pronoun**: *I, you, we, they, he, she, it.*

2. **Singular** means one. **Plural** means more than one. A plural noun usually ends in **-s**.
    SINGULAR: The *language* of the U.S. is English.
    PLURAL: The *languages* of Puerto Rico are Spanish and English.

3. *The United States* (*the U.S.*) is a singular noun.
    The U.S. is a big country. It is in North America.
    NOTE: Always use *the* before United States or U.S.
4. *You* can be a singular or plural subject. It uses the verb *are*.
    You *are* a student.
    You *are* students.
5. When the subject is "another person and I," use the plural verb *are*.
Put the other person before "I."
    John and I *are* good friends. (NOT: I and John . . .)
6. We use the subject pronoun *it* to talk about time and weather.
    It is hot in Hawaii.
    It is 6 o'clock now.
7. We use *they* for plural people and things.

    My friends are here. *They* are good to me.

    My books are here. *They* are on the floor.

EXERCISE 4   Fill in the blanks with the correct pronoun.

EXAMPLE: Canada and Mexico are countries. __*They*__ are in North America.

1. Florida is a state. _____ is in the Southeast.

2. _____ is warm in Florida.

3. New York and Boston are big cities. _____ are in the East.

4. _____ am a student.

5. The United States is a big country. _____ is between Canada and Mexico.

6. _____ is 4:30 P.M.

7. My parents are in California. _____ are in L.A.

8. You and I are students. _____ are in the classroom now.

9. _____ is cloudy today.

cloudy

10. Puerto Rico and Cuba are islands. _____ are in the Caribbean Sea.

EXERCISE **5**   Fill in the blanks with a subject.

EXAMPLE: _Los Angeles_ is a big city.

1. _____ is a city in the East.

2. _____ are states in the East.

3. _____ are citizens of the U.S.

4. _____ is the home of the President.

5. _____ is the language of Mexico.

6. _____ is the main language of the U.S.

7. _____ are big countries.

8. _____ are in the U.S. now.

9. _____ is warm in July.

10. _____ are ESL students.

Before You Read   1.   Name a place in the U.S. that you want to visit.
2.   What is your favorite city? Why?

Read the following postcard. Pay special attention to the contractions.

Postcard from New York City

Did you know...?

The Statue of Liberty was a gift from France in 1876 to honor one hundred years of independence for the U.S.

Dear Cousins,

    I'm on vacation. **I'm** in New York City now. **It's** the biggest city in the U.S. My **daughter's** with me. **She's** very happy here. **We're** both happy. The **weather's** nice this week. **It's** sunny and warm.

    New York's a very interesting city, but **life's** so fast here. People are busy. **They're** always in a hurry. And **traffic's** terrible.

    Some people say New Yorkers **aren't** very friendly, but New Yorkers are kind to me. When **I'm** lost, strangers are helpful.

    We're at the Statue of Liberty now. **It's** a beautiful monument.

    I'm tired now. More later.

Love,
Maria

1.5 Contractions with *Be*

Full Forms	Contracted Forms	Explanation
I am You are It is She is He is We are They are	**I'm** in New York City. **You're** at home. **It's** hot today. **She's** happy. **He's** busy. **We're** tired. **They're** on vacation.	We can make a **contraction** with a subject pronoun and *am*, *is*, and *are*. We take out the first letter of *am*, *is*, *are* and put an apostrophe (') in its place. We usually use a contraction when we speak. We sometimes write a contraction in informal writing.
My daughter is New York is Traffic is	My **daughter's** with me. **New York's** big. **Traffic's** terrible.	We can make a contraction with most nouns and *is*.

LANGUAGE NOTES

1. We don't make a contraction with *is* if the noun ends in these sounds: *s, z, sh,* or *ch*.
    The United States *is* a big country.
    The White House *is* in Washington, D.C.
    France *is* in Europe.
    New Orleans *is* a beautiful city.
    English *is* the language of the U.S.
    Long Beach *is* in California.
2. We don't make a contraction with a plural noun and *are*.
    Strangers *are* helpful.

EXERCISE 6 Fill in the blanks with the correct form of *be*. Make a contraction whenever possible. Not every sentence can have a contraction.

EXAMPLE: The United States ___is___ a big country. It___'s___ between Canada and Mexico.

1. Canada and Mexico ___are___ countries. They ___'re___ in North America.

2. Texas ___is___ a big state in the U.S. It ___'s___ in the South.

3. The White House ___is___ in Washington, D.C. It ___'s___ the home of the President. He ___'s___ busy now.

4. Texas and Alaska __are__ the biggest states in the U.S.
5. Los Angeles __is__ a big city. It __'s__ in California.
6. Puerto Rico __is__ an island. Puerto Ricans __are__ American citizens.
7. English __is__ the main language of the U.S. Spanish and English __are__ the languages of Puerto Rico. German __'s__ the language of Germany. French __is__ the language of France.
8. My daughter and I __are__ in New York City now. We __'re__ happy here.
9. Life __'s__ fast in New York City.
10. People __are__ busy. They __'re__ in a hurry.

EXERCISE **7**   Fill in the blanks. Make a contraction whenever possible. Not every sentence can have a contraction.

I __'m__ a student of English at City College. __I__'m happy
   (example)   *(1)*
in the U.S. My teacher __'s__ American. His name __'s__
                (2)   *(3)*
Charles Madison. Charles __is__ an experienced teacher. __He's__
                    (4)   *(5)*
patient with foreign students.

My class __is__ big. __It's__ interesting. All the students
        (6)   *(7)*
__are__ immigrants, but we __'re__ from many different countries.
(8)   *(9)*
Five students __are__ from Asia. One woman __'s__ from
           (10)   *(11)*
Poland. __It's__ from Warsaw, the capital of Poland. Many students
     (12)
__are__ from Mexico.
(13)
We __'re__ ready to learn English, but English __is__ a
    (14)   *(15)*
difficult language. I sometimes tell Charles, "You __'re__ a very kind
                                    (16)
teacher." Charles says, "__They're__ all good students, and I __'m__
                   (17)   *(18)*
happy to teach you English."

1.6   *Be* with Descriptions

Subject	*Be*	*(Very)*	Adjective
New York City	is	very	big.
People	are		helpful.
The weather	is		nice.
I	am		tired.

worry

LANGUAGE NOTES

1. We use a form of *be* with words that describe the subject. We use **adjectives** to describe. Descriptive adjectives have no plural form.
     New York is *big.*
     New York and Chicago are *big.*
2. Some words that end with *-ed* or *-ing* are adjectives: *married; tired; interesting; boring.*
     I'm *worried* about you.
     We're *tired.*
     New York City is *interesting.*
3. We use a form of *be* with a physical or mental condition.
     He's *hungry.*   We're *afraid.* (Pineapple)
     I'm *thirsty.*   They're *angry.*
     (sede)

EXERCISE 8 Complete each statement with a subject and the correct form of *be.* Write a contraction wherever possible. Make a **true** statement. Use both singular and plural subjects.

EXAMPLES:
My parents are _____ intelligent.
The teacher's very _____ patient.
Many people in my former country are _____ poor.

1. my shoes are _____ red.
2. The college's _____ expensive.
3. Many fruits are _____ cheap.
4. My book's _____ new.
5. (?) The president → The United States is rich.
6. many students are lazy.

7. my hair's _____ big.
8. The flowers are wonderful.
9. many exercise are difficult.
10. My boyfriend's _____ beautiful.
11. The Harvard's _____ famous.
12. Many people _____ young.
     in my country are young.

EXERCISE 9 Write a form of *be* and an adjective to describe each of the following nouns. You may work with a partner.

EXAMPLES:
This classroom *is clean.*
New York City *is interesting.*

1. The teacher _____

2. This city _____

3. This college _____

4. Today's weather _____

5. Americans _____

6. American food _____

1.7 *Be* with Definitions

Singular Subject	Be	A or An	(Adjective)	Singular Noun
I	am	a		student.
You	are	a		teacher.
New York	is	an	interesting	city.

Plural Subject	Be		(Adjective)	Plural Noun
New York and L.A.	are		big	cities.
We	are		foreign	students.

LANGUAGE NOTES

1. A **noun** is a person, place or thing. We use a noun after *be* to classify or define the subject.
2. We use the **article** *a* or *an* before a singular noun. We use *an* before a vowel sound. The vowels are *a, e, i, o, u*.
3. We don't use the article *a* or *an* before a plural noun.
4. We can put an adjective before the noun.

EXERCISE 10 Fill in the blanks with a form of *be* and a definition of the subject. You may add an adjective. Be careful to add *a* or *an* for singular nouns.

EXAMPLES:

California *is a state.*

Puerto Rico *is an American territory.*

1. Canada *is a state*

2. Alaska *is an American territory*

3. Blue *is a color*

4. Wednesday *is an Day week*

5. Christmas *is an Day*

6. Saturday and Sunday _____

7. The Pacific and the Atlantic _____

8. White and green _____

9. January and February _____

10. California and Illinois _____

EXERCISE 11 Add an adjective to each statement. Be careful to use *a* before a consonant and *an* before a vowel sound.

EXAMPLES: July 4 is a holiday.
July 4 is an important holiday.

1. August is a month.

2. Puerto Rico is an island.

3. Toyota is a company.

4. I'm a student.

5. Los Angeles and Chicago are cities.

6. John is a name.

EXERCISE 12 Fill in the blanks with the correct form of *be*. Add *a* or *an* for singular nouns only. Don't use an article with plural nouns.

EXAMPLES: The U.S. ___*is a*___ big country.
The U.S. and Canada ___*are*___ big countries.

1. California _____ state.

2. San Francisco and Los Angeles _____ cities in California.

3. Chicago, Los Angeles, and New York _____ big cities.

4. Puerto Rico _____ island.

5. Puerto Rico and Cuba _____ islands.

6. Thanksgiving _____ American holiday.

7. French and Spanish _____ languages.

8. France and Spain _____ countries.

EXERCISE 13 Complete each statement. Give a subject and the correct form of *be*. Add *a* or *an* for singular nouns only. Don't use an article with plural nouns. You may work with a partner.

EXAMPLES: ___*Russia is a*_____ big country.
___*Canada and Brazil are*___ big countries.

1. _____ nice person.

2. _____ good student.

3. _____ big company.

4. _____ expensive item.

5. _____ nice season.

6. _____ American holiday.

7. _____ warm months.

8. _____ small countries.

9. _____ South American countries.

10. _____ big cities.

11. _____ famous people. (NOTE: *people* is plural)

12. _____ American cars.

EXERCISE 14 Fill in the blanks to talk about this city. Make **true** statements. Remember to add *a* or *an* for a singular noun. You may work with a partner.

EXAMPLES:

Chez Paul is an _____ expensive restaurant in this city.

January and February are _____ cold months in this city.

1. _____ interesting place.

2. _____ popular tourist attraction.

3. _____ big stores.

4. _____ beautiful months.

5. _____ beautiful park.

6. _____ inexpensive restaurant.

7. _____ busy streets.

8. _____ good college.

9. _____ dangerous area.

10. _____ tall buildings.

EXERCISE 15 Fill in the blanks to make **true** statements. Put in a subject and a form of *be*. Read your answers to the class.

EXAMPLES:

Rock music is _____ popular in my country.

Politicians are _____ rich in my country.

1. _____ the biggest city in my country.

2. _____ rich.

3. _____ expensive.

4. _____ the language(s) of my country.

5. _____ necessary for a good life.

6. _____ a popular sport.

7. _____ hard to find.

8. _____ a common last name.

9. _____ a beautiful place.

1.8 *Be* with Location and Origin

Preposition	Examples	
On	The book is **on** the table. The cafeteria is **on** the first floor.	
At (a general area)	I am **at** school. My brother is **at** home. They are **at** work.	
In (a complete or partial enclosure)	The students are **in** the classroom. The wastebasket is **in** the corner.	
In front of	The blackboard is **in front of** the students.	
In back of/Behind	The teacher is **in back of** the desk. The blackboard is **behind** the teacher.	
Between	The empty desk is **between** the two students.	
Above/Over	The exit sign is **over** the door. The clock is **above** the exit sign.	

(continued)

Preposition	Examples
Under/Below	The textbook is **below** the desk. The dictionary is **under** the textbook.
Near/By/Close to	The sharpener is **by** the window. The sharpener is **near** the window. The sharpener is **close to** the window.
Next to	The light switch is **next to** the door.
Far from	Los Angeles is **far from** New York.
Across from	Room 202 is **across from** Room 203.
In (a city)	The White House is **in** Washington, D.C.
On (a street)	The White House is **on** Pennsylvania Avenue.
At (an address)	The White House is **at** 1600 Pennsylvania Avenue.
From	Mario is **from** Brazil. He is **from** Sao Paolo.

LANGUAGE NOTES

1. We use **prepositions** to show location and origin.
2. Word Order = Subject + *Be* + Preposition + Place

EXERCISE 16 Use a form of *be* and a preposition to tell the location of these things or people in your classroom or school.

EXAMPLES: My dictionary _____ *is in my bag.* _____
The students _____ *are in front of the teacher.* _____

1. This classroom _____

2. The clock _____

3. The teacher _____

4. The wastebasket _____

5. The light switch _____

6. The chalkboard _____

7. I _____

8. My books _____

9. The cafeteria _____

10. The school _____

11. The school library _____

12. We _____

1.9   *This, That, These, Those*

	Near	**Not Near/Far**
SINGULAR	**This** is my school. *Este*	**That** is my teacher. *Aquele*
PLURAL	**These** are my books. *Estes*	**Those** are tall buildings. *Aqueles*

LANGUAGE NOTES

1. We use *this, that, these,* and *those* to identify objects and people.

2. Only *that is* can form a contraction in writing: *that's.*

3. After we identify a noun, we can use subject pronouns.
    This is my school. *It's* on Wilson Avenue.
    Those are tall buildings. *They're* downtown.
    That's my teacher. *She's* a nice woman.

EXERCISE 17 Imagine that you are showing a new student the school cafeteria. Use *this*, *that*, *these*, and *those*, and a form of *be* to complete each statement. The arrows indicate if the item is near or far.

EXAMPLES:

This is _____ the school cafeteria. →

Those are _____ the clean dishes. ——————————→

1. _THESE are_ _____ the trays. →

2. _THis is_ _____ today's special. →

3. _THese are_ _____ the napkins. →

4. _Those are_ _____ the forks, knives, and spoons. ——————————→

5. _This is_ _____ the cashier. →

6. _Those are_ _____ the vending machines. ——————————→

7. _That's_ _____ the eating area. ——————→

8. _Those are_ _____ the teachers' section. ——————————→

1.10 Negative Statements with *Be*

Examples	Explanation
I am **not** married. Peter is **not** at home. We are **not** doctors.	We put *not* after a form of *be* to make a negative statement.
I'm not late. English **isn't** my native language. My friends **aren't** here now.	We can make contractions for the negative.

LANGUAGE NOTES

There is only one contraction of *I am not*. There are two negative contractions for all the other combinations. Study the negative contractions:

I am not	I'm not	—
you are not	you're not	you aren't
he is not	he's not	he isn't
she is not	she's not	she isn't
it is not	it's not	it isn't
we are not	we're not	we aren't
they are not	they're not	they aren't
Tom is not	Tom's not	Tom isn't

EXERCISE 18 Fill in the blanks with a pronoun and a negative verb. Practice using both negative forms.

EXAMPLE: The classroom is clean and big.
It isn't dirty. _It's not_ small.

1. We're in the classroom.
   We aren't in the library. _We're not_ in the cafeteria.

2. Today's a weekday.
   It isn't Saturday. _It's not_ Sunday.

3. I'm a student. _I'm not_ a teacher. My teacher is Odoir.

4. The students are busy.
   They aren't lazy. _They're not_ tired.

5. You're on time.
   You aren't early. _You're not_ late.

6. My classmates and I are in an English class.
   We aren't in the cafeteria. _We're not_ in the library.

EXERCISE 19 Fill in the blanks with a form of *be* to make a **true** affirmative statement or negative statement about the U.S.

EXAMPLES: The U.S. _is_ in North America.
The U.S. _isn't_ a small country.

1. Washington, D.C., _is_ a state.

2. Washington, D.C., _isn't_ the capital of the U.S. It _is_ on the East Coast.

3. The eastern states __are__ big. _aren't_

4. The western states __are__ big. _isn't_

5. The White House __isn't__ in New York.

6. New York __is__ a big city.

7. Alaska and Hawaii __aren't__ on the mainland.

8. Puerto Rico __is__ a state of the U.S.

9. Puerto Rico and Hawaii __are__ islands.

10. Florida __is__ in the South. It __isn't__ cold in the winter.

EXERCISE 20 True or False. Tell if you think the following statements are true or false. Discuss your opinions

	True	False
1. English is easy for me. F		
2. English is easy for children. T		
3. American teachers are very strict.[2] T		
4. This school is in a nice area. T		
5. This course is expensive. T		
6. All Americans are rich. F		
7. Baseball is popular in the U.S. T		
8. January and February are nice months. T		

EXERCISE 21 Fill in the blanks with a form of *be* to make an affirmative statement or negative statement about you, your native country, or your hometown. You may share your answers with a partner from a different country.

EXAMPLES: I __'m__ from the capital city.
I __'m not__ from a small town.

1. I _____ happy with the government of my country.

2. I _____ from the capital city.

3. My city _____ noisy.

4. American cars _____ common in my country.

[2] A *strict* teacher has a lot of rules.

5. Teachers _____ strict.

6. Most people _____ rich.

7. Gas _____ cheap.

8. Apartments _____ expensive.

9. Bicycles _____ a popular form of transportation.

10. Public transportation _____ good.

11. My country _____ rich.

12. A college education _____ free.

13. The president (prime minister) _____ a woman.

14. My hometown _____ in the mountains.

15. My hometown _____ very big.

16. It _____ very cold in the winter in my hometown.

EXERCISE 22 Use the words in parentheses ( ) to change each sentence into a negative statement.

EXAMPLE: My teacher is American. (Canadian)
He isn't Canadian.

1. Los Angeles and Chicago are cities. (states)
Los Angeles and Chicago aren't states

2. I'm from Mexico. (the U.S.)
I'm not from U.S.

3. The U.S. is a big country. (Cuba)

_____

4. Alaska is a big state. (Maryland and Delaware)

_____

5. We're in class now. (in the library)

_____

6. You're an English teacher. (a math teacher)

_____

7. Chicago is a big city. (Springfield)

_____

8. Chicago and Springfield are in Illinois. (Miami)

_____

9. January is a cold month. (July and August)

_____

10. You're American. (I)

_____

EXERCISE 23 Fill in the blanks with the affirmative or negative of the verb *be* to make a **true** paragraph.

My name ___is___ ___Mayllara___. I ___'m not___ from an English-
(example)   (your name)   (1)

speaking country. I ___'m___ a student at City College. I ___'m not___ in
(2)   (3)

my English class now. The class ___isn't___ big. My teacher ___is___
(4)   (5)

a man. He/She ___He's___ very young. The classroom ___is___ very
(6)   (7)

nice. It ___'s___ clean. My classmates ___is___ all very young
(8)   (9)

students. We ___aren't___ all from the same country. We ___are___ all
(10)   (11)

immigrants. I ___'m___ happy to learn English. English ___isn't___ very
(12)   (13)

easy for me. It ___'s___ a useful language.
(14)

Before You Read 1. Are all the students in our class about the same age?
2. Is your rent high?

Read the following conversation. Pay special attention to questions with
be.

Conversation about Life in the U.S.

A. **Are you happy with your life in the U.S.?**

B. Yes and no. Some things are good. Some things are not so good.

A. **What are some good things?**

B. I'm free. I'm free to say and do what I like.

A. **What are some problems?**

B. Rent is high.

A. **How much is your rent?**

B. It's over $700 a month for a one bedroom apartment. And medical care is so expensive.

A. **How much is a doctor's visit?**

B. It's over $100. But the visits are so short. I'm only in the doctor's office for 15 minutes. And doctors are cold. They're interested only in your disease, not in the whole person.

A. **Are you happy with education in the U.S.?**

B. Yes and no. Public elementary and high schools are free, but colleges and universities are very expensive.

A. **How much is the tuition at your college?**

B. It's over $50 per credit hour. And books are so expensive. But college classes are interesting. The students are from all over the world. And they're all ages. One man in my English class is very old.

A. **How old is he?**

B. He's 82.

A. Eighty-two? **Are you sure?**

B. Yes. He's an interesting man. He's a great student. In my country, most of the students are about the same age. They're young.

A. **What are some other differences between colleges in the U.S. and in your country?**

B. The teachers are very friendly and informal here. In my country, the teachers are strict and formal.

A. **What's your favorite thing about life in the U.S.?**

B. The people. They're friendly and helpful.

1.11 *Be* in *Yes/No* Questions and Short Answers

Statement	*Yes/No* Question	Short Answer
I am a student.	**Am I** a good student?	Yes, you are.
You are from France.	**Are you** from Paris?	No, I'm not.
He is late.	**Is he** absent?	No, he isn't.
She is married.	**Is she** happy?	Yes, she is.
It is cold today.	**Is it** windy?	Yes, it is.
We are here.	**Are we** late?	No, you aren't.
They are new students.	**Are they** from Mexico?	Yes, they are.

LANGUAGE NOTES

1. To ask a *yes/no* question with the verb *be*, we put a form of *be* before the subject.
2. We usually answer a *yes/no* question with a short answer. A short answer contains a pronoun.
    Is the teacher here today? Yes, *she* is.
3. We don't use a contraction for a short *yes* answer.
    Is Texas a big state? Yes, *it is*. NOT: Yes, it's.
4. We usually use a contraction for a short *no* answer.
    Is today Saturday? No, it isn't. OR No, it's not.
5. We usually end a *yes/no* question with rising intonation. Listen to your teacher pronounce the statements and questions in the above box.

EXERCISE 24 Look at the maps of the U.S. on pages 2 and 3 to help you answer these questions.

EXAMPLES:
Is Miami in Florida?
Yes, it is.

Is New York City the capital of the U.S.?
No, it isn't.

1. Is Texas a big state?
2. Are Puerto Ricans citizens of the U.S.?
3. Is New York City near the Atlantic Ocean?
4. Is Hawaii near Alaska?
5. Is Chicago the capital of Illinois?
6. Is Chicago a big city?
7. Is Puerto Rico an island?
8. Is Alaska an island?

EXERCISE 25 Close your book. The teacher will ask you some questions. Answer with a **true** short answer. If the answer is negative, you may add more information.

EXAMPLE: Is your book new?
Yes, it is.   OR   No, it isn't. It's a used book.

1. Is your hometown big?
2. Is Spanish your native language?
3. Is English hard for you?
4. Are you from South America?
5. Are you a citizen of the U.S.?
6. Are you married?
7. Are these questions difficult?
8. Is my pronunciation clear to you?
9. Am I a strict teacher?
10. Are all of you from the same country?
11. Are all of you the same age?

EXERCISE 26 Ask questions about this school and class with the words given. Another student will answer. Use the correct form of *be*.

EXAMPLE: school/big
A. Is this school big?
B. Yes, it is.

1. this school/near your house
2. it/near public transportation
3. the cafeteria/on this floor
4. it/open now
5. the library/in this building
6. it/closed now
7. this course/free
8. the textbooks/free
9. the teacher/strict
10. this room/clean
11. it/big
12. the chalkboard/black

EXERCISE 27 Ask questions with the words given. Another student will answer. Use the correct form of *be*.

EXAMPLE: you/a new student
A. Are you a new student?
B. Yes, I am.   OR   No, I'm not. This is my second semester here.

1. you/from Asia
2. you/a new student
3. your hometown/ big
4. you/from the capital city
5. you/an immigrant
6. you/happy in the U.S.
7. baseball/popular in your country
8. American cars/popular in your country
9. teachers/strict in your country
10. education/free in your country

EXERCISE 28 Ask questions about the U.S. with the words given. Another student will answer. If no one knows the answer, ask the teacher.

EXAMPLE: movie stars/rich
A. Are American movie stars rich?
B. Yes, they are. They're very rich.

1. American teachers/rich
2. a high school education/free
3. a college education/free
4. college books/free
5. medical care/free
6. doctors/rich
7. blue jeans/popular

8. houses/expensive
9. Americans/friendly
10. English/the official language
11. Japanese cars/popular
12. fast-food restaurants/popular
13. movie tickets/cheap
14. public schools/closed on Christmas

EXERCISE 29 Read each statement. Then write a *yes/no* question about the words in parentheses ( ). Write a short answer.

EXAMPLE: The post office is closed on Sunday. (this school) (yes)
Is this school closed on Sunday? Yes, it is.

1. July and August are warm months. (January and February) (no)

2. New York is a big city. (Chicago) (yes)

3. California is a big state. (Alaska and Texas) (yes)

4. Doctors are rich. (movie stars) (yes)

5. Washington, D.C., is in the East. (Washington state) (no)

6. New York is on the East Coast. (California) (no)

7. Chicago isn't a state. (Illinois) (yes)

8. Education in public schools is free. (education in private schools) (no) _____

1.12 Wh- Questions

Wh-Word	Be	Subject	Be	Complement	Short Answer
		Los Angeles	is	a city.	
	Is	Los Angeles		on the West Coast?	
Where	is	Los Angeles?			Yes, it is.
		Sacramento	is	the capital of California.	
	Is	Sacramento		in Southern California?	
Where	is	Sacramento?			No, it isn't.

Study the different question words:

Question Word	Question	Answer
Who = person	**Who** is your teacher?	My teacher is Ms. Weiss.
What = thing	**What** is your name?	My name is Linda.
	What is Christmas?	Christmas is a holiday.
When = time Use *in* for months and years. Use *on* for days and dates.	**When** is Christmas?	It's in December. It's on December 25.
Why = reason	**Why** is Mr. Park absent?	He's absent because he is sick.
Where = place	**Where** is China? **Where** are your books? **Where** are you from?	It's in Asia. They're on the floor. I'm from Hong Kong.
How = description, health	**How** is your life in the U.S.? **How** is the weather today? **How** is your mother?	It's difficult. It's warm today. She's fine.

LANGUAGE NOTES

1. A *wh-* question asks for information.
2. The *wh-* word + *is* can form a contraction.
    Where's your father?   *How's* the weather now?
    EXCEPTIONS:
    - We can't make a contraction for *which is*: → Which is your book?
    - We can't make a contraction for a *wh-* word + *are*: → Why are they late?
3. We usually end a *wh-* question with falling intonation. Listen to your teacher say the questions in the above chart.

EXERCISE **30** Fill in the blanks with the correct question word and a form of *be*.

EXAMPLE: _____What's_____ your name?
My name is Frank.

1. _____Where's_____ Los Angeles?
It's in California.

2. _____When's_____ your birthday?
It's in June.

3. _____What's_____ your teacher?
My teacher is Martha Simms.

4. _____What is_____ a rose?
A rose is a flower.

5. _____Why are_____ you late?
I'm late because of traffic.

6. _____where are_____ your sisters and brothers?
They're in my country.

7. _____Whow are_____ you?
I'm fine. And you?

8. _____Where's_____ the teacher's office?
It's on the second floor.

9. _____Where are_____ the restrooms?
The restrooms are at the end of the hall.

10. _____When is_____ Labor Day in the U.S.?
It's in September.

11. _____Why are_____ we here?
We're here because we want to learn English.

12. _____How is_____ the weather today?
It's cloudy and cool.

EXERCISE **31** Test your knowledge. Circle the correct answer to the following questions. The answers are at the bottom of the page.[3] (You may work with a partner.)

1. Where's Dallas?
   a. in California   b. in Texas   c. in Illinois

[3] Answers: 1b, 2a, 3b, 4c, 5c, 6b, 7b, 8c, 9a

2. When is American Independence Day?
   a. July 4   b. May 31   c. December 25

3. It's 8 a.m. in New York. What time is it in Los Angeles?
   a. 11 a.m.   b. 5 a.m.   c. 10 a.m.

4. On what day is Thanksgiving?
   a. on Friday   b. on Sunday   c. on Thursday

5. One of these is the name of a Great Lake. Which one is the name of
   a Great Lake?
   a. Mississippi   b. Missouri   c. Michigan

6. Where is the World Trade Center?
   a. in San Francisco   b. in New York City   c. in Los Angeles

7. What is the first day of summer?
   a. June 1   b. June 21   c. June 30

8. When is Labor Day in the U.S.?
   a. in May   b. in June   c. in September

9. What's the biggest state?
   a. Alaska   b. Texas   c. New York

1.13 Questions with *What* and *How*

What	Noun	*Be*	Complement	Answer
What		is	a verb?	It's an action word.
What	nationality	is	the teacher?	She's American.
What	kind of book	is	this?	It's a grammar book.
What	day	is	today?	It's Friday.
What	time	is	it?	It's 4 o'clock.
What	color	are	your new shoes?	They're black.

How	Adjective/Adverb	*Be*	Complement	Answer
How		is	your new job?	It's great.
How		is	the weather today?	It's cool.
How	old	is	your brother?	He's 16 (years old.)
How	tall	are	you?	I'm 5 feet, 3 inches tall.
How	long	is	this course?	It's 10 weeks long.
How	much	is	that painting?	It's $500.

LANGUAGE NOTES

1. A noun can follow *what*: *what time, what day, what color*
2. An adjective or adverb can follow *how*: *how big, how old, how much*
3. For height, Americans use feet (') and inches (").
   How tall is your father? He's 5 feet 8 inches tall. or He's five-eight.[4]
4. *How are you?* is often just a way to say hello. People usually answer, "Fine, thanks. How are you?"

EXERCISE 32 Fill in the blanks to complete the questions.

EXAMPLE: How _____old are_____ your parents? They're in their 50s.

1. What _____is_____ your husband? He's Mexican.

2. What _____time is_____ it? It's 3 o'clock.

3. What _color is your_ car _and brand is_ that? That's a Japanese car.

4. What _are that_ words _nice, beautiful_ tall, old, *new*, and *good*? They're adjectives.

5. What _color is_ your new car? It's dark blue.

6. How _old is your son_ ? My son is ten years old.

7. How _tall is your brother?_ ? My brother is 6 feet tall.

8. How _is your old_ ? I'm 25 years old.

9. How _much is that car_ ? That car is $10,000.

10. How _long is the movie_ ? The movie is 2½ hours long.

EXERCISE 33 Fill in the blanks to make **true** statements about yourself. Then find a partner from a different country, if possible, and interview your partner by asking questions with the words in parentheses ( ).

EXAMPLE: I'm from _____Bosnia_____ (Where)
A. I'm from Bosnia. Where are you from?
B. I'm from Taiwan.

1. My name is _____Odair_____. (What)
2. I'm from _____Brasil_____. (Where)

---

[4] See Appendix G for conversion from centimeters to feet and inches.

3. The president/prime minister of my country is _Luis Inacio_.
   (Who) *Who are the president/prime minister of you country?*

4. The president/prime minister of my country is about
   _____50_____ years old. (How)

5. The flag from my country is _green, yellow, Blue, white,_. (What color)
   south

6. My country is in _American_. (Where)
   (continent or region)

7. I'm _____5_____ feet, _____4_____ inches tall. (How tall)

8. My birthday is in _____may_____. (When)
   (month)

9. My favorite TV show is _move CNN_. (What)

10. My favorite color is _green, Blue_. (What)
    pentão

EXERCISE 34 Read each statement. Then write a *wh-* question with the words in parentheses ( ). Answer with a complete sentence.

EXAMPLE: Miami is in Florida. (Los Angeles)
Where is Los Angeles? It's in California.

here is whashington Dc?
e is the capital the U.S.?
re are Los Angeles San Francisco.
ere

1. Paris is in France. (Washington, D.C.)
   Washington is in U.S.A. in the U.S.

2. The capital of England is London. (the capital of the U.S.)
   The capital of U.S is Whashington.

3. Miami and Orlando are in Florida. (Los Angeles and San Francisco)
   Los Angeles and San Francisco are in california.

4. Alaska is a state. (Philadelphia)
   Philadelphia is a city.

5. Canada is in North America. (Peru)
   Peru is in south America.

6. Poland is in Europe. (Ethiopia and Nigeria)
   Ethiopia and Nigeria are in Africa.

7. Korea and Japan are in Asia. (Colombia)
   south
   Colombia is in American.

8. The Mexican flag is green, white, and red. (what color/the American flag)
   The American flag is red, white and Blue.

9. Igor and Boris are Russian names. (what kind of names/James and William)

James and William are American names.

10. It's 6 o'clock in New York. (what time/L.A.)

_____

EXERCISE 35 Read the following telephone conversation between Cindy (C) and Maria (M). Fill in the blanks.

C. Hello?

M. Hi, Cindy. This is Maria.

C. Hi, Maria. _____How are you?_____
    (example)

M. I'm fine. This is a long-distance call. I'm not home now.

C. Where _____are you now_____?
    (1)

M. I'm in New York City. I'm on vacation.

C. _____Have you visited the Statue Liberty_____?
    (2)

M. Oh, yes. It's very interesting. The Statue of Liberty is here.

C. How _~~weater are did~~ there now_ ?
    is the weater (3)

M. It's sunny and warm.

C. _Are you alone to New York_ ?
    (4)

M. No, I'm not alone.

C. Who _are ~~gone~~ with ~~you~~_ ?
    (5)

M. My daughter is with me.

C. _How old is she_ ?
    (6)

M. She's 12. She's very interested in the U.S.

C. It's six-thirty in Los Angeles. _What time is it_ in New York?
    (7)

M. It's nine-thirty.

C. I'm happy to hear from you. Thanks for calling.

M. I'll see you when I get home.

SUMMARY OF LESSON 1

1. Uses of **Be**

   Description: Chicago **is** big.

   Identification/Classification: This **is** Chicago. It **is** a city.

   Location: Chicago **is** in Illinois.

Place of origin: The teacher **is** from Chicago.
Age: I **am** 25 (years old).
Physical or mental condition: He **is** hungry. I **am** thirsty. She **is** worried.
Time: It **is** 6 p.m.
Weather: It **is** warm today.

[handwritten: Com side, Aflito]

2. Subject Pronouns
    I   we   he   she   it   you   they

3. Contractions
    Subject pronoun + form of **be**: I'm, you're, he's, she's, it's, we're, they're
    Subject noun with **is**: the teacher's, Tom's, Mary's
    Is or **are** + **not**: isn't, aren't
    Wh- word + **is**: what's, when's, where's, why's, who's, how's

4. **This/That/These/Those**
    [handwritten: Este] **This** is an English book.
    [handwritten: Estes, Estas] **These** are pencils.
    [handwritten: Esta] **That** is a pen.
    [handwritten: Aqueles, Aquelas] **Those** are pens.

5. Articles **a/an**
    Chicago is **a** big city.
    Puerto Rico is **an** island.

6. Statements and Questions with **Be**

AFFIRMATIVE:	California is a state.
NEGATIVE:	Los Angeles isn't a state.
YES/NO QUESTION:	Is Los Angeles in California?
SHORT ANSWER:	Yes, it is.
WH- QUESTION:	Where is Chicago?

AFFIRMATIVE:	You are from Asia.
NEGATIVE:	You aren't from Europe.
YES/NO QUESTION:	Are you from China?
SHORT ANSWER:	No, I'm not.
WH- QUESTION:	Where are you from?

EDITING ADVICE ✏

1. Don't repeat the subject with a pronoun.

    My father ~~he~~ lives in Australia.

    [handwritten: Sujeito]

2. Use correct word order. Put the subject at the beginning of the statement.

    Cuba is small.
    ~~Is small Cuba.~~

3. Use the correct word order. Put the adjective before the noun.

   Cuba is a ~~country small.~~ *small country.*

4. Use the correct word order in a question.

   Where ~~he is~~ *is he* from?

5. Every sentence has a verb. Don't omit *be*.

   My sister *is* a teacher.

6. Every sentence has a subject. For time and weather, the subject is *it*.

   ~~Is~~ *It's* 6 o'clock now.

   ~~Is~~ *It's* very cold today.

7. Don't confuse *your* (possession) with *you're*, the contraction for *you are*.

   ~~Your~~ *You're* a good teacher.

8. Don't confuse *this* and *these*.

   ~~These~~ *This* is my coat.

   ~~This~~ *These* are my shoes.

9. The plural of the subject pronoun *it* is *they*, not *its*.

   Dogs are friendly animals. ~~Its~~ *They're* good pets. *Amigo / amistos*

10. Always use *the* before U.S. and United States.

    My sister is in *the* U.S.

11. Use a singular verb after *the United States*.

    The U.S. ~~are~~ *is* a big country.

12. Do not use a contraction for *am not*.

    ~~I amn't~~ *I'm not* an American. *que falta*

13. Put the apostrophe in place of the missing letter.

    She ~~is'nt~~ *isn't* here today. *virgula*

14. Use an apostrophe, not a comma, for a contraction.

    ~~I,m~~ *I'm* a good student.

15. Use the article *a* before a singular noun.

   New York is ^a big city. _[handwritten: a inserted with caret]_

16. Don't use *a* before plural nouns.

   July and August are ~~a~~ warm months.

17. Don't use the article *a* before an adjective with no noun.

   New York is a big.

18. Use *an* before a vowel sound. _[handwritten: ⇒ vogal]_

   Puerto Rico is ^{an} ~~a~~ island.

19. Don't make an adjective plural.
   My daughters are beautiful~~s~~.

20. Don't make a contraction with *is* after *s*, *z*, *sh*, or *ch* sounds.

   Los Angeles^{is}~~'s~~ a big city.

21. For age, use a number only or a number + *years old*.

   He's 12 ~~years.~~ *or He's 12 years old.*

22. Don't use a contraction for a short *yes* answer.

   Are you from Mexico? Yes, ~~I'm.~~ _[handwritten: I am.]_

23. Don't separate *how* from the adjective or adverb.

   How ~~is he old?~~ _[handwritten: old is he?]_

LESSON 1 TEST / REVIEW

PART 1   Find the mistakes with the underlined words and correct them. Not every sentence has a mistake. If the sentence is correct, write **C**.

EXAMPLES: ~~He,s~~ my brother. _[handwritten: He's]_

Chicago's a big city. **C**

1. New York and Los Angeles are <u>a big cities</u>.
   [handwritten: New York and Los Angeles are big cities.]
2. The <u>teacher's</u> not here today.
   [handwritten: the teacher isn't here today!]

3. She is'nt in the library. _c_

4. I amn't from Pakistan. I'm from India.
   I'm not from Pakistan. I'm from India.

5. The students they are very smart. modern.
   The students ~~they~~ _are very smart._

6. Alaska and Texas are bigs states.
   Alaska and Texas are big states.

7. We're not hungry. We aren't thirsty. sediento.
   We aren't hungry. We aren't thirsty.

8. It's warm today. _c_

9. I'm from Ukraine. My wife from Poland.
   I'm from Ukraine. My wife is from Poland.

10. My little brother is 10 years!
    My little brother is 10 years old.

11. French's a beautiful language.
    French's beautiful language.

12. It's 4:35 now. _c_

13. Your in the U.S. now.
    You're in the U.S. now.

14. These is a good book. THIS
    These are good books.

15. These are my pencils. _c_

16. Those dogs are beautiful. Its friendly.
    Those dogs are beautiful. They're friendly.

17. I live in U.S.
    I live in the U.S.

18. January is cold month. _c_

19. My father is a tall.
    My father is tall.

20. New York City and L.A. are bigs.
    New York City and L.A. are big.

21. Chevrolet is a American company.
    Chevrolet is an American company.

22. Is he from Peru? Yes, he's. _c_

23. Chicago it's a big city. _c_

PART **2**

Find the mistakes with word order and correct them. Not every sentence has a mistake. If the sentence is correct, write **C**.

EXAMPLES: I have a book (new)
She is 25 years old.   C

1. Is very long this book.
   This book is very long.

2. She has a car very beautiful.
   She has a very beautiful car.

3. Why you are late?
   Why are you late?

4. How old are you? _c_

5. What nationality your wife is?
   What nationality is your wife?

6. What color is your new coat? *colors* e
7. Why the teacher is absent? *ausente* e
   Why is the teacher absent.
8. Is your father a doctor? e

PART 3

Fill in the blanks to complete this conversation. Not all blanks need a word. If the blank doesn't need a word, write 0.

A. Where are you __from__?
      (example)

B. I'm from __0__ Mexico.
      (example)

A. Are you happy in __the__ U.S.?
                      (1)

B. Yes, I __am__. The U.S. is __a__ great country.
            (2)   *(3)*

A. __Are you__ from __a__ big city?
      (4)   *(5)*

B. Yes. I'm from Mexico City. It's __a__ very big city. This city
                                    (6)

   is __0__ big and beautiful too. But __it's__ cold in the winter.
        (7)   *(8)*

A. __Are you__ from Mexico too?
      (9)

B. No, my roommate __is__ from Taiwan. I'm happy in the U.S., but
                      (10)

   he __isn't__ happy here. He __'s__ *saudoso* homesick.
       (11)   *(12)*

A. Why __is he__ homesick? *saudoso*
        (13)

B. His parents __are__ in Taiwan. He __'s__ alone here.
                  (14)   *(15)*

A. How __old is he__?
        (16)

B. He's very young. He __is__ only 18 years __old.__.
                        (17)   *(18)*

A. What __'s__ his name?
          (19)

B. His name __is__ Lu.
             (20)

Write a contraction of the words shown. If it's not possible to make a contraction, put an **X** in the blank.

EXAMPLES: she is _____she's_____

English is _____X_____

1. we are ___We're___
2. you are not ___you aren't___
3. I am not ___I'm not___
4. they are ___They're___
5. this is ___X___

6. Los Angeles is ___X___
7. Mary is not ___Mary isn't___
8. he is not ___he isn't___
9. what is ___What's___
10. what are _____

Read the conversation between two students, Sofia (S) and Danuta (D). They are talking about their classes and teachers. Fill in the blanks.

D. Hi, Sofia. How's your English class?

S. Hi, Danuta. It __'s__ wonderful. I __'m__ very happy with it.
(example)   (1)

D. ___I___'m in level 3. What level __is you__ in?
(2)   (3)

S. I'__m__ in level 2.
(4)

D. My English teacher ___is___ Ms. Kathy James. ___she is___ a very
(5)   (6)

good teacher. Who ___are your english teacher___?
(7)

S. Mr. Bob Kane is my English teacher. ___He is___ very good, too.
(8)

D. ___He is___ an old man?
(9)

S. No, he __isn't__. He's ___a___ young man. He __have__ about
(10)   (11)   (12)

25 years ___old___. How ___old have your Ms James___?
(13)   (14)

D. Ms. James ___have___ about 50 years old.
(15)

S. How ___tall is Ms. James.___?
(16)

D. She's about 5 feet, 6 inches tall.

S. Is she American?

D. Yes, she ___is___. She's from New York.
(17)

S. ___Is your class big?___?
(18)

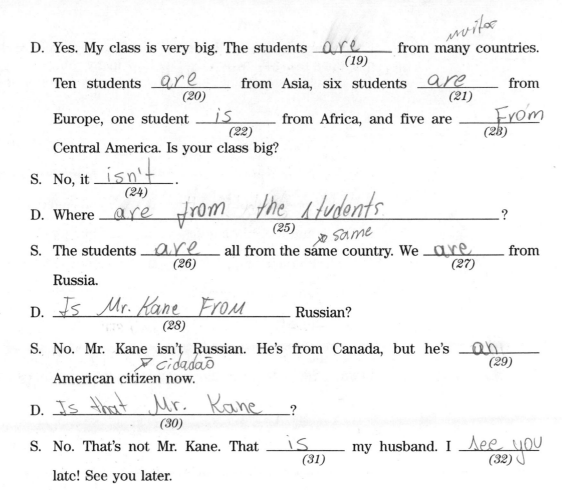

D. Yes. My class is very big. The students __are__ from many countries. *muito*
(19)

Ten students __are__ from Asia, six students __are__ from
(20)   (21)

Europe, one student __is__ from Africa, and five are __From__
(22)   (23)

Central America. Is your class big?

S. No, it __isn't__.
(24)

D. Where __are from the students__?
(25)

S. The students __are__ all from the same country. We __are__ from
(26)   *same*   (27)

Russia.

D. __Is Mr. Kane From__ Russian?
(28)

S. No. Mr. Kane isn't Russian. He's from Canada, but he's __an__
cidadão   (29)
American citizen now.

D. __Is that Mr. Kane__?
(30)

S. No. That's not Mr. Kane. That __is__ my husband. I __see you__
(31)   (32)

latc! See you later.

EXPANSION ACTIVITIES

CLASSROOM ACTIVITIES

1. Write a sentence about yourself. Give your height, a physical description, your nationality, your occupation, your age (optional), your gender (man or woman). Put the papers in a box. The teacher will read each paper. Guess who it is.

EXAMPLE:
I'm 5'8" tall.
I'm Mexican.
I'm thin.
I'm 21 years old.

2. Work with a partner. Describe a famous person (an actor, a singer, an athlete, a politician). Report your description to the class. Do not give the person's name. See if your classmates can guess who it is.

EXAMPLE:
He is a former basketball player.
He's tall.
He's famous.
He's an African American.

3. Check the words that describe you. Find a partner and ask each other questions using these words. See how many things you have in common. Tell the class something interesting you learned about your partner.

a. _____ happy

b. _____ from Africa

c. _____ from Asia

d. _____ from Europe

e. _____ interested in politics

f. _____ a grandparent

g. _____ under 20 years old

h. _____ in love

i. _____ afraid to speak English

j. _____ an only child[5]

k. _____ from the capital of my country

l. _____ an American citizen

m. _____ hungry

n. _____ married

o. _____ athletic

4. Fill in the blanks. Then find a partner and read your sentences to your partner. See how many times you match your partner's sentence.

a. Love is _____

b. This city is _____

c. Children are _____

d. The teacher is _____

e. Money is _____

f. The American president is _____

g. My friends are _____

h. I am _____

i. Public transportation in this city is _____

j. This book is _____

5. Work with a partner from the same country, if possible. Fill in a few items for each category. Report some information to the class.

[5] An *only child* has no sisters or brothers.

EXAMPLE: Typical of the U.S.

Common last names	Common cars	Popular tourist attractions	Popular sports	Language(s)	Capital city	Other big cities
Johnson Wilson	Ford Chevy Toyota	Disneyland the Grand Canyon	baseball basketball football	English	Washington, D.C.	New York Los Angeles Chicago

Your country _____

Common last names	Common cars	Popular tourist attractions	Popular sports	Language(s)	Capital city	Other big cities

WRITING

Write a paragraph using Exercise 23 as a model. For every negative statement that you write, add an affirmative statement. You may add other information, too.

EXAMPLE:

> My name is Mohammad. I'm not from an English-speaking country. I'm from Iran. I'm not a student at City College. I'm a student at Roosevelt University. I'm in an English class now. . . .

OUTSIDE ACTIVITIES

1. Interview an American (a neighbor, a co-worker, another student or a teacher at this college). Ask him or her the following questions. Report this person's answers to the class.

a. What city are you from?
b. Are your parents or grandparents from another country? Where are they from?
c. Is most of your family in this city?
d. Are you happy with this city? Why or why not?
e. What are your favorite places in this city?

2. Do you have a postcard from your hometown? Bring it to the class and tell about the picture.

3. Buy a postcard of this city. Write to a friend, giving some information about the picture or about this city. Read your postcard to the class.

Internet Activity

Using the Internet, find out more about the Statue of Liberty.

1. How tall is it?
2. Where is it?
3. Is it free for visitors?

Lesson Two

GRAMMAR
Simple Present Tense

CONTEXT
Washington, D.C.
Meet Sara Harris

LESSON FOCUS
A simple present tense verb has two forms:

eat—eats   run—runs   play—plays   have—has

We use the simple present tense for facts and regular activities.

Americans *speak* English.
The President *lives* in Washington, D.C.
Americans *elect* a president every four years.

Before You Read

1. What capital cities do you know?
2. What do you know about Washington, D.C.?

The Capitol

The Vietnam War Memorial

Read the following article. Pay special attention to the present tense verbs.

Homeworke
44.45-46-47-48.49.50

Washington, D.C.

Washington, D.C., is the capital of the United States. D.C. **means** District of Columbia. It is not a state; it is a special government district. More than half a million people **live** in Washington. Many residents **work** for the government.

Tourists from all over the United States and many other countries **visit** Washington. They **come** to see the Capitol, the building where Congress **meets.** Another popular tourist attraction is the White House, the President's home. Eight to ten thousand tourists **visit** the White House every day. Tour guides **show** visitors many rooms, but they **don't show** them the President's private family rooms or private offices.

además de

Besides government buildings, Washington also **has** many important monuments and museums. The Smithsonian Institution **has** 16 museums, galleries, and a zoo. The Smithsonian **includes** the Air and Space Museum. This very popular museum **shows** visitors real spaceships, such as the Apollo 11, which landed on the moon in 1969.

Many visitors **want** to see the Vietnam War Memorial. This wall of dark stone **has** all the names of American soldiers who died in the war in Vietnam.

Tourists **don't pay** to see government buildings and museums. However, tourists **need** tickets to see many places because these places are crowded.

A trip to Washington is an enjoyable and educational experience.

sobregarrego

Simple Present Tense—Forms

Subject	Base Form	Complement
I		
You		
We	**work**	in Washington.
They		
My friends		

Subject	-s Form	Complement
He		
She	**works**	in Washington.
It		
The President		

LANGUAGE NOTES

1. We use the base form when the subject is *I, you, we, they,* or a plural noun.
2. We use the -s form when the subject is *he, she, it,* or a singular noun.
3. Three verbs have an irregular -s form:

   have → has (pronunciation /hæz/)
   go   → goes
   do   → does (pronunciation /dʌz/)
4. After *family,* use a singular verb.

   My family *lives* in Korea.

EXERCISE 1 Fill in the blanks with the correct form of the verb.

EXAMPLE: Visitors ___*like*___ the museums.
(like/likes)

He - she - it, or singular noun use "s"

singular noun. use "s"

1. The President ___lives___ in the White House.
(live/lives)

Plural noun don't use "s"

2. Many people in Washington ___work___ for the government.
(work/works)

3. Washington ___has___ many beautiful museums. *singular noun use 's'*
(have/has)

Plural noun don't use "s"

4. Millions of tourists ___visit___ Washington every year.
(visit/visits)

5. Tour guides ___show___ visitors the White House. *Plural noun use "s"*
(show/shows)

6. The Vietnam War Memorial ___has___ the names of men and women
(have/has)
who died in the war. *use 's" when has "it"*

7. "D.C." ___means___ District of Columbia. *singular noun use "s"*
(mean/means)

2.2 Simple Present Tense—Uses

Examples	Uses
The President **lives** in the White House. Washington, D.C., **has** a good subway.	With general truths, to show that something is consistently true
Americans **eat** fries and hamburgers with their hands. Many Americans **have** a picnic on the Fourth of July.	With customs
We **take** a vacation every summer. We sometimes **go** to Washington.	To show regular activity (a habit) or repeated action
I **come** from Bosnia. He **comes** from Iraq.	To show a place of origin

EXERCISE 2 Write the correct form of the verb. Add more words to give facts.

EXAMPLE: I ___come from Colombia___.
(come)

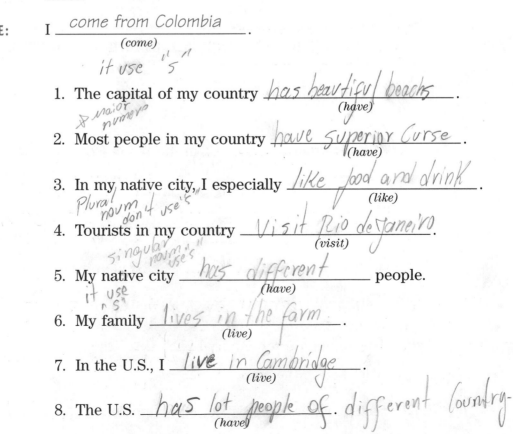

it use "s"

1. The capital of my country ___has beautiful beachs___.
(have)

2. Most people in my country ___have superior Curse___.
(have)

3. In my native city, I especially ___like food and drink___.
(like)

Plural noun don't use "s"

4. Tourists in my country ___visit Rio de Janeiro___.
(visit)

singular noun use "s"

5. My native city ___has different___ people.
(have)

it use "s"

6. My family ___lives in the farm___.
(live)

7. In the U.S., I ___live in Cambridge___.
(live)

8. The U.S. ___has lot people of___. different country-
(have)

9. I _attend 2 days for week_ College/School.
   (attend) frequentar

10. This school _has an excellent_ teachers.
    (have)

Spelling of the *-s* Form

Rule	Base Form	*-s* Form
Add **s** to most verbs to make the *-s* form.	hope eat	hopes eats
When the base form ends in *ss*, *sh*, *ch*, or *x*, add **es** and pronounce an extra syllable.	miss wash catch mix	misses washes catches mixes
When the base form ends in a consonant + *y*, change the *y* to *i* and add **es**.	carry worry	carries worries
When the base form ends in a vowel + *y*, add **s**. Do not change the *y*.	pay enjoy	pays enjoys

EXERCISE 3 Write the *-s* form of the following verbs.

EXAMPLES: eat _____ *eats* _____

study _____ *studies* _____

watch _____ *watches* _____

consonant + y

1. try _tries_
2. play _plays_ (vowel + y)
3. have _has_
4. go _goes_
5. worry _worries_ (cons + y)
6. finish _finishes_ (ends "sh")
7. do _does_
8. push _pushes_ (ends "sh")
9. enjoy _enjoys_ (vowel + y)
10. think _thinks_

use "es"
use "es"
use "es"
use "s"

11. say _says_ (vowel + y) use "s"
12. change _changes_
13. brush _brushes_ (ends "sh") use "es"
    obedecer
14. obey _obeys_ (vowel + y) use "s"
    Alcanzar
15. reach _reaches_ (ch use "es")
16. fix _fixes_
17. work _works_
18. raise _raises_ (levantar)
19. charge _charges_ (despezar)
20. see _sees_

use "s"

Simple Present Tense   **47**

Pronunciation of the -s Form

Pronounce /s/	Pronounce /z/	Pronounce /əz/
hope—hopes *esperança*	grab—grabs *granpo.*	miss—misses
eat—eats	read—reads	dance—dances
pick—picks	hug—hugs *abraço*	use—uses
laugh—laughs *Riso* *Risada*	live—lives	wash—washes
	hum—hums *zumbido*	watch—watches
	run—runs *corrida a pé*	change—changes
	borrow—borrows *pedir emprestado*	fix—fixes *Dilema*
	sing—sings	
	fall—falls	
	hear—hears *escutar*	
	see—sees	

LANGUAGE NOTES

1. We pronounce /s/ after voiceless sounds: /p, t, k, f/
2. We pronounce /z/ after voiced sounds: /b, d, g, v, m, n, ŋ, l, r/ and all vowels.
3. We pronounce /əz/ when the base form ends in *ss, ce, se, sh, ch, ge, x.*
4. The following verbs have a change in the vowel sound. Listen to your teacher pronounce these examples.
    do /du/—does /dʌz/
    say /sei/—says /sɛz/

EXERCISE 4 Go back to Exercise 3 and pronounce the base form and -s form of each verb.

EXERCISE 5 Fill in the blanks with the -s form of the verb in parentheses ( ). Pay attention to the spelling rules. Then pronounce each sentence.

EXAMPLE: A teacher _____ *tries* _____ to help students learn.
(*try*)

1. A pilot _____ *flies* _____ an airplane. *ends in consoant change y for "es" and "i"*
(*fly*)

2. A dishwasher _____ *washes* _____ dishes. *ends in "sh" put "es"*
(*wash*)

3. A babysitter _____ *watches* _____ children. *ends ch add "es"*
(*watch*)

4. A soldier _____Obeys_____ an officer. vowel + y add "s"
   (obey)

5. A citizen _____pays_____ taxes. vowel + y add "s"
   (pay)

6. A mechanic _____fixes_____ machines. vowel + y add "s"
   (fix)

7. A student _____studies_____. consonant + y ad "es" "an i"
   (study)

8. A student _____does_____ homework. " " use "s"
   Does a student *(do)* do homework.

9. A homemaker _____manages_____ a home. singular noun use "s"
   Does a home *(manage)* manage a home.

10. A secretary _____uses_____ administra a computer. " " use "s"
    (use)

11. A teacher _____teaches_____ students. ends in ch use "es"
    Does a teacher *(teach)* teach students.

EXERCISE **6** Write at least three sentences to tell about your profession (former, present, or future). Tell what someone in this profession does.

EXAMPLE: A car mechanic tries to find the problem in a car. Then he fixes the problem. A mechanic also changes parts, such as tires, oil, and brakes.

I'm a carpenter. I put doors, windows, xingles, pines, but I will want work with paint because is very interesting.

2.5 Comparing Affirmative Statements with *Be* and Other Verbs

I **am** a student. I **study** English.	You **are** right. You **know** the answer.	We **are** immigrants. We **come** from Guatemala.
They **are** kind. They **help** people.	The teacher **is** American. She **teaches** grammar.	He **is** busy. He **works** hard.

Dos she teach grammar.

EXERCISE **7** A student is comparing himself to his friend. Fill in the blanks with the correct form of the underlined verb.

EXAMPLES: My friend and I are very different.

I get up at 7 o'clock. He _____gets_____ up at 10.

I'm a good student. He's _____ a lazy student.
preguiçoso

1. I study every day. He _studies_ only before a test.
2. I always get A's on my tests. He _gets_ C's.
3. I have a scholarship. He _has_ a government loan.
4. I'm a good student. He_'s_ an average student.
5. He lives in a dormitory. I _live_ in an apartment.
6. He's from Japan. I_'m_ from the Philippines.
7. He studies with the radio on. I _study_ in a quiet room.
8. He watches a lot of TV. I _watch_ TV only when I have free time.
9. He eats a lot of meat. I _eat_ a lot of fish.
10. He uses a laptop computer. I _use_ a desktop computer.

Before You Read
1. Do you need a car in this city? Why or why not?
2. What are some interesting places to see in this city?

Read the following article. Pay special attention to the negative form of verbs.

Meet Sara Harris

Sara Harris is a single, thirty-year-old woman. She lives in Washington, D.C. She works just a few blocks from the White House. She has a job with the government.

Washington has a good subway, so Sara **doesn't need** a car. The subway is clean and the trains are quiet. The subway trains **run** until midnight. Sara uses the public transportation system, but if she is late or in a hurry, she takes a taxi. She **doesn't take** a taxi very often because it's too expensive.

Like many residents of Washington, Sara isn't a native of Washington. She comes from Chicago, Illinois. Her parents **don't live** in Washington. They live in Chicago.

Sara lives alone, but she has two cats. She also has a lot of friends. She **doesn't see** her friends during the week because she is so busy. She sees her friends on the weekends.

She works hard, so she **doesn't have** much time to visit the galleries and museums. When friends and relatives from out of town come to visit her, she gives them a tour of her city.

2.6   Negative Statements with the Simple Present Tense

Examples	Explanation
Sara **lives** in Washington. She **doesn't live** in Chicago.	We use *doesn't* + the base form with *he, she, it*, or a singular noun.
Her parents **live** in Chicago. They **don't live** in Washington.	We use *don't* + the base form with *I, you, we, they*, or a plural noun.

LANGUAGE NOTES

1. *Don't* is the contraction for *do not*. *Doesn't* is the contraction for *does not*.
2. Always use the base form after *don't* and *doesn't*.
3. American English and British English use different grammar to form the negative of *have*. Compare:
    AMERICAN: He *doesn't have* a dictionary.
    BRITISH: He *hasn't* a dictionary. OR He *hasn't got* a dictionary.

EXERCISE **8**   Fill in the blanks with the negative form of the underlined verb.

EXAMPLE: Sara <u>works</u> in Washington. She ___*doesn't work*___ in Chicago.

1. She <u>sees</u> her friends on the weekend. She __doesn't see__ her friends during the week.

2. Her friends <u>have</u> jobs. They __don't have__ much free time.

3. Her parents <u>live</u> in Chicago. They __don't live__ in Washington.

He, she, it or singular name use doesn't.

4. Her parents visit her in the spring. They _don't visit_ her in the winter.

5. Sara has time on the weekend. She _doesn't have_ time during the week.

6. Sara lives alone. She _doesn't live_ with her parents.

7. She works for the government. She _doesn't work_ in a private company.

8. She takes a taxi when she's in a hurry. She _doesn't take_ a taxi every day.

9. She has two cats. She _doesn't have_ a dog.

10. She visits museums and galleries when friends come to visit. She _doesn't visit_ museums and galleries every day.

EXERCISE 9 Tell if this school has or doesn't have the following items.

EXAMPLES:

ESL courses
This school has ESL courses.

classes for children
It doesn't have classes for children.

1. a library   5. a swimming pool   9. dormitories
2. a cafeteria   6. a gym   10. classes for children
3. copy machines   7. a student newspaper   11. a computer lab
4. a parking lot   8. a theater   12. e-mail for students

[Handwritten answers:]
1. This school has a library.
2. It doesn't a cafeteria.
3. This school has copy machines.
4. It doesn't have a parking lot.
5. It doesn't have a swimming pool.
6. This school has a gym.
7. This school has student newspaper.
8. This school has a theater.
9. This school has dormitories.
10. It don't have classes for children.
11. This school has a computer.
12. This school has e- for stude.

EXERCISE 10 Make an affirmative statement or a negative statement with the words given to state facts about the teacher. Use the correct form of the verb.

EXAMPLE:

speak Arabic
The teacher speaks Arabic.
OR
The teacher doesn't speak Arabic.

1. talk fast   6. pronounce my name correctly

2. speak English well   7. wear glasses *

3. speak my language   8. wear jeans to class

4. give a lot of homework   9. teach this class every day

5. give tests   10. watch the students during a test

---

52   Lesson Two

EXERCISE 11 Check (√) the items that describe you and what you do. Exchange your book with another student. Make statements about the other student.

EXAMPLES: _____ I have children.
Marta doesn't have children.

_√_ I like cold weather.
Marta likes cold weather.

1. _√_ I speak Chinese.
   He speaks Spanish.
2. _√_ I live alone.
   She lives alone.
3. _____ I live near school.
   He doesn't live near school.
4. _√_ I walk to school.
   We don't walk to school.
5. _√_ I speak Spanish.
   You don't speak Spanish.

6. _√_ I like summer.
   They like summers.
7. _√_ I like cold weather.
   He doesn't like cold. wea
8. _√_ I have a computer.
   Carlos has a computer.
9. _√_ I use the Internet.
   Carla uses the Internet.

EXERCISE 12 Fill in the blanks with the negative form of the underlined verb.

EXAMPLES: We <u>study</u> English grammar.

We ___*don't study*___ American history.

The teacher <u>speaks</u> English in class.

He/She ___*doesn't speak*___ another language in class.

1. The President <u>lives</u> in Washington, D.C.

   He _*doesn't live*_ in New York.

2. The President <u>serves</u> for four years.

   He _*doesn't serve*_ for six years.

3. The U.S. Congress <u>makes</u> the laws.

   The President _*doesn't make*_ the laws.

4. The President and his family <u>live</u> in the White House.

   The Vice President _*doesn't live*_ in the White House.

5. Tourists <u>see</u> many rooms in the White House.

   They _*don't see*_ the President's private living area.

6. The Washington subway <u>runs</u> all day.

   It _*doesn't run*_ after midnight.

7. People in Washington <u>pay</u> to ride the subway.

   They ___don't pay___ to enter most museums.

8. Some people <u>need</u> a car.

   Sara ___doesn't need___ a car.

9. Some workers <u>live</u> in Washington.

   Some workers ___don't live___ in Washington. They live near Washington.

10. We <u>study</u> American English.

    We ___don't study___ British English.

11. I <u>need</u> a grammar book in this course.

    I ___don't need___ a history book.

12. Sara <u>lives</u> in Washington.

    Her parents ___don't live___ in Washington.

13. Sara and her friends <u>go</u> out on the weekend.

    They ___don't go___ out on weekdays.

14. Washington, D.C., <u>has</u> a subway.

    Miami ___doesn't have___ a subway.

2.7 Comparing Negative Statements with *Be* and Other Verbs

I'm not from Mexico. I **don't speak** Spanish.	They**'re not** sure. *Convencido* They **don't know** the answer.
You **aren't** sick. You **don't need** a doctor.	We **aren't** lost. We **don't need** help.
She **isn't** hungry. She **doesn't want** dinner.	He**'s not** cold. He **doesn't want** a sweater.

EXERCISE 13 Check (√) the items that describe you and what you do. Exchange your book with another student. Make statements about the other student.

EXAMPLE: _____ I'm an immigrant.
Margarita isn't an immigrant. She comes from Puerto Rico.

EXAMPLE: _____✓_____ I have a computer.
Margarita has a computer.

(handwritten, left margin)
she has married
Carla has a child.
Carlos has a computer.

Mr. Jeff likes this city
ir has a Job.

(handwritten, top) Mama has a pet.

1. __✓__ I'm married.
Carla isn't married.
2. _____ I have children/a child.
They don't have a child.
3. _____ I have a computer.
Samuel doesn't have a computer.
4. _____ I'm an American citizen.
Odair doesn't an American Citizen.
5. _____ I like this city.
we don't like this city.
6. _____ I have a job.
she doesn't have a job.

7. _____ I'm a full-time student.
I'm not a full-time student.
8. _____ I have a pet.[1]
Odair doesn't have a pet.
9. _✗_ I'm an immmigrant.
she isn't an immmigrant.
10. _____ I'm happy in the U.S.
I'm not happy in the U.S.
11. _____ I like baseball.
Monh doesn't like baseball.
12. __✓__ I understand American TV.
I'm not understand American TV.

EXERCISE 14 Choose one of the items from the list below. Write sentences telling what this person does or is. Include negative statements. (You may work with a partner.) Read some of your sentences to the class.

(handwritten) He likes baseball

EXAMPLE: a good teacher

A good teacher explains the lesson.

A good teacher doesn't get angry at students.

A good teacher doesn't walk away after class when students have questions.

A good teacher is patient.

1. a good friend   3. a good doctor

2. a good mother or father 4. a good adult son or daughter

(handwritten)
✓ 1. A good friend has consideration children.
✓ 2. A good mother or father loves her/his son his patient.
3. A good doctor likes of the his patient.
4. A good adult son or daughter cares your parents his/her

EXERCISE 15 Read each statement. Then make a negative statement with the words in parentheses ( ).

EXAMPLE: Sara works in Washington. (Chicago)
She doesn't work in Chicago.

1. Colombians speak Spanish. (Brazilians)
They don't speak Brazilians.

[1]A *pet* is an animal that lives in someone's house. Dogs and cats are common pets.

2. I speak English in class. (my native language)

I don't speak my native language in class.

3. A, E, I, O, and U are vowels. (B, C, and D)

B, C, and D aren't vowels.

4. I'm from ____Brasil____. (the U.S.)
   (your country)

I'm not from the U.S.

5. Washington is a special government district. (a state)

It isn't a special state.

6. The subway in Washington is clean. (dirty)

The subway in Washington isn't dirty.

7. My brother works in Washington. (live in Washington)

He doesn't live in Washington.

8. Washington has an Air and Space Museum. (New York)

New York doesn't have an Air an Space Muse

9. Sara is busy during the week. (on the weekend)

She isn't busy on the weekend.

10. Sara is single. (married)

She isn't married.

11. A taxi ride is expensive. (a bus ride)

A bus ride isn't expensive.

2.8 *Yes/No* Questions and Short Answers with the Simple Present Tense

Examples	Explanation
Does Sara **live** in Washington? Yes, she **does**. **Do** her parents **live** in Washington? No, they **don't**.	We use *do* or *does* to form a *yes/no* question. We always use the base form after *do* or *does*. We can answer with a short answer.

Compare statements and questions:

Do/Does	Subject	Verb	Complement	Short Answer
	Tourists	**visit**	the White House.	
Do	they	**visit**	the President's private rooms?	No, they don't.
	The President	**lives**	in the White House.	
Does	the Vice President	**live**	in the White House?	No, he doesn't.

LANGUAGE NOTES

1. Use *does* with *he, she, it,* and singular subjects.
2. Use *do* with *I, you, we, they,* and plural subjects.
3. We usually answer a *yes/no* question with a short answer. The short answer uses a pronoun.
   Do Sara's parents live in Washington? No, *they* don't.
4. The short answer usually uses a contraction in the negative.
5. American English and British English use different grammar to form a question with *have.* Compare:
   AMERICAN: *Does* he *have* a car? Yes, he *does.*
   BRITISH: *Has* he a car? OR *Has* he *got* a car? Yes, he *has.*

EXERCISE 16 Ask your teacher a question with "Do you . . . ?" and the words given. Your teacher will respond with a short answer.

EXAMPLE: drive to school

A. Do you drive to school?

B. Yes, I do.   OR   No, I don't.

1. like your job *Do you like your job? Yes, I do.*
2. teach in the summer *Does he teach in the summer? Yes he does.*
3. have another job *Does he have another job? No, he doesn't.*
4. speak another language *Do you speak another language? Yes, I do.*
5. teach English to Americans *Does he teach English to Americans?*
   No, he doesn't.
6. know my language *Does he know my language? No, he doesn't.*
7. like to read students' homework *Does he like to read students' homework? Yes, he does.*
8. live far from the school *Does he live far from the school? Yes, he does.*
9. have a fax machine *Does he have a fax machine? Yes he does.*
10. have trouble with English spelling *Does he have trouble with English spelling? Yes, he does.*
11. have an e-mail address *Does he have an e-mail address? Yes, he does.*
12. like soccer *Does he like soccer? Yes, he does.*

EXERCISE 17 Two students are comparing teachers. Fill in the blanks to complete this conversation.

A. Do you ___*like*___ your English class?
   (Example: like)

B. Yes, I __do__ . I __have__ a very good teacher. Her name is
   (1)   (2 have)
   Ms. Lopez.

A. __Does she speak__ Spanish?
   (3)

B. No, she doesn't. She comes from the Philippines. She __speaks__
   (4 speak)
   English and Tagalog.

A. My teacher is very good too. But he __talks__ fast, and sometimes
   (5 talk)
   I __not understand__ him. He __gives__ a lot of homework.
   (6 not/understand)   (7 give)
   __Does she give__ a lot of homework?
   (8)

B. Yes, she does. And she __gives__ a test once a week. → una vez
   (9 give)

A. My teacher __wears__ jeans to class. He's very informal.
   (10 wear)
   __Does she wear__ jeans to class?
   (11)

B. No, she doesn't. She always wears a dress.

EXERCISE 18 Read each statement. Then write a *yes/no* question about the words in parentheses ( ). Write a short answer.

EXAMPLES: You know the present tense. (the past tense)
   Do you know the past tense? No, I don't.

   The school has computer classes. (gym classes)
   Does it have gym classes? Yes, it does.

1. The teacher uses the chalkboard. (a map)
   __Does teacher use a map? No he doesn't.__

2. You bring your textbook to class. (your dictionary)
   __Do you bring your dictionary to class? No I d__

3. We need practice with grammar. (with spelling)
   __Do we need practice with spelling? Yes, we d__

4. The teacher speaks English. (another language)

Does the teacher speak English? Yes, he does.

5. I understand the teacher. (you)

Do you understand the teacher. Yes I do.

6. The past tense has a lot of irregular verbs. (the present tense)

Does the present tense have a lot of irregular verbs? No, it do

7. The teacher speaks English fluently. (the students)

Do the students speak English fluently? No, they don't

8. Washington has a space museum. (a zoo) (*answer*: yes)

Does Washington have a zoo? Yes, it does.

9. People pay to use the subway in Washington. (to enter the White House) (*answer*: no)

Does people pay to enter the white house? No, she doesn't.

10. The subway trains run all day. (after midnight) (*answer*: no)

Does subway train run after midnight? No, it doesn't.

EXERCISE 19 Put a check next to customs from your native country. Then make an affirmative or negative statement about your country. Ask another student if this is a custom in his/her native country. (You may work with a partner.)

EXAMPLE: ✓ People take off their shoes before they enter a house.

A. Russians take off their shoes before they enter a house.
Do Mexicans take off their shoes before they enter a house?
B. No, we don't.

1. _F_ People take off their shoes before they enter a house.

2. _F_ People bow when they say hello.

3. _✓_ People shake hands when they say hello.

4. _✓_ People bring a gift when they visit a friend's house.

5. _F_ People eat with chopsticks.

bow

chopsticks

6. _Do_ On the bus, younger people stand up to let an older person sit down. ?

7. _Do_ Women cover their faces with a veil. ?

8. _Do_ People visit friends without calling first. ?

9. _Do_ Men open doors for women. ?

10. _Do_ Men give flowers to women for their birthdays. ?

11. _Do_ People celebrate children's day. ?

12. _Do_ High school students wear a uniform. ?

veil

2.9 Comparing *Yes/No* Questions with *Be* and Other Verbs

Are you lost?	No, I'm not.	**Am** I right?	Yes, you are.
Do you **need** help?	No, I don't.	**Do** I **have** the right answer?	Yes, you do.
Are they from Haiti?	Yes, they are.	**Is** the teacher British?	No, he isn't.
Do they **speak** French?	Yes, they do.	**Does** the teacher **have** an accent?	No, he doesn't.

EXERCISE 20 Read each statement. Then write a *yes/no* question about the words in parentheses ( ). Write a short answer.

EXAMPLES: Americans like baseball. (basketball) (yes)
Do Americans like basketball? Yes, they do.

Baseball is popular in the U.S. (rugby) (no)
Is rugby popular in the U.S.? No, it isn't.

1. Americans shake hands when they meet. (Mexicans) (yes)
   Do Mexicans shake hands when they meet? Yes, they do.

2. Children learn a language easily. (adults) (no)
   _____

3. Americans speak English. (Australians) (yes)
   Do Australians speak English? Yes they do.

4. Hot dogs are popular in the U.S. (tacos) (yes)
   Are tacos popular in the U.S? Yes, they are.

5. You understand American English. (British English)
   Do you understand British English? No I do

No, they don't.

6. Japanese people eat with chopsticks. (American people) (no)

   Eat American people with chopsticks?

7. English has a lot of irregular verbs. (Spanish) (yes)

   Does Spanish have

8. You are interested in the English language. (American history)

   Are you interrested in the American history?

9. The subway in Washington is clean. (quiet) (yes) *Yes I am.*

   Is the subway in Washington clean? Yes it is.

10. Sara works from Monday to Friday. (on the weekend) (no)

    Does Sara work on the weekend?
    No she doesn't.

2.10 Or Questions

Examples	Explanation

Do you study English **or** French?
  I study English.
Is Washington, D.C., on the east coast **or** the west coast?
  It's on the east coast.
	An *or* question gives a choice of answers. The first part of an *or* question has rising intonation; the second part has falling intonation. Listen to your teacher pronounce the examples to the left.

EXERCISE 21 Circle the words that are true for you, and make a statement about yourself. Then ask a question. Another student will answer.

EXAMPLE: I drink (coffee)/ *tea* in the morning.

A. I drink coffee in the morning.
   Do you drink coffee or tea in the morning?
B. I drink coffee too.

1. I speak *English* / *my native language* at home.

2. I prefer *classical music*/ *popular music*.

3. I'm *a resident of the U.S.* / *a visitor*.

4. I'm *married* / *single*.

5. I live in *a house* / *an apartment* / *a dormitory*.

6. I write with my *right hand* / *left hand*.

7. I'm from *a big city / a small town.*

8. I prefer *morning classes / evening classes.*

2.11 *Wh-* Questions with the Simple Present Tense

Wh- Word	*Do/Does Don't/Doesn't*	Subject	Verb	Complement	Short Answer
		My brother	**works**	in Washington.	
	Does	he	**work**	for the government?	No, he **doesn't**.
Where	**does**	he	**work?**		
Why	**doesn't**	he	**work**	for the government?	
		They	**have**	a car.	
	Do	they	**have**	an American car?	Yes, they **do**.
What kind of car	**do**	they	**have?**		

LANGUAGE NOTES

The correct word order for *wh-* questions is:
   Wh -word + *do/does/don't/doesn't* + Subject + Base Form of Verb (+ Complement)

EXERCISE 22 Fill in the blanks with the missing word.

EXAMPLE: Where ____*do*____ you live? I live in Detroit.

1. Where __does__ your brother live? He lives in New York.
2. How __many__ children do you have? I have two children.
3. __Were do you__ you study? I study in the library.
4. Why __don't__ you study at home? I don't study at home because it's too noisy.
5. How many languages __does__ your teacher __espeak__? He speaks two languages.
6. Where __does__ your sister __work__? She works downtown.

2.12 *Wh-* Questions with Prepositions

Wh- Word	*Do/Does*	Subject	Verb (Base Form)	Preposition
Where	does	your friend	come	from?
What floor	do	you	live	on?

LANGUAGE NOTES

1. In formal writing, we put the preposition before a question word. In conversation, we usually put the preposition at the end of the question.
   FORMAL: *On* what floor do you live?
   INFORMAL: What floor do you live *on*?
2. We use *whom* after a preposition. We often use *who* when the preposition is at the end.
   FORMAL: With *whom* do you live?
   INFORMAL: *Who* do you live with?
3. We can talk about a person's country of origin with *be* or *come*.
   Where *are* you from?
   Where *do* you *come* from?

EXERCISE 23 Ask and answer questions with the words given. First ask a *yes/no* question. Then use the words in parentheses ( ) to ask a *wh-* question, if possible.

EXAMPLE: live near school (where)
A. Do you live near school?
B. Yes, I do.
A. Where do you live?
B. I live on Green and Main.

1. speak Spanish (what language)
2. need English in your country (why)
3. have American friends (how many)
4. like this city (why)
5. live near the school (where)
6. plan to go back to your country (when) (why)
7. live alone (with whom OR who . . . with)
8. practice English outside of class (with whom OR who . . . with)
9. bring your dictionary to class (why)
10. have a cell phone (why)

EXERCISE 24 First ask the teacher a *yes/no* question. After you get the answer, use the words in parentheses ( ) to ask a *wh-* question, if possible. Your teacher will answer.

EXAMPLE: teach summer school (why)
A. Do you teach summer school?

B. No, I don't.
A. Why don't you teach summer school?
B. Because I like to travel in the summer.

[handwritten: Di Companhiro]

1. have an office mate (what/your office mate/teach)
   [handwritten: Do you have an office mate? What do you teach to your office mate?]
2. get paid on the first of the month (when)
   [handwritten: Do you get paid on the first of the month? When do you get paid?]
3. have a computer (what kind of computer)
   [handwritten: 3 - Do you have a computer? What kind of computer do you have?]
4. speak another language (what language)
   [handwritten: 4 - Do you speak another language? What language do you speak?]
5. teach summer school (why)
   [handwritten: 5 - Do you teach summer school? Why don't you teach summer school?]
6. work in another school (what other school . . . in)
   [handwritten: 6 - Do you work in another school? What other school do you work?]
7. correct the homework in school (where)
   [handwritten: 7 - Do you correct the homework in school? Where do you correct the homework?]
8. prefer evening classes (why)
   [handwritten: 8 - Do you prefer evening classes? Why don't you prefer evening classes?]
9. drive to school (how . . . get² to school)
   [handwritten: 9 - Do you drive to school? How long do you drive to school?]
10. like to teach English (why)
    [handwritten: 10 - Do you like to teach English? Why do you like teach english?]
11. come from this city (what city . . . from)
    [handwritten: 11. Do you come from this city? What city do you come from?]
12. have children (how many)
    [handwritten: 12. Do you have children? How many children do you have?]

EXERCISE 25 Ask and answer questions about another teacher with the words given. First ask a *yes/no* question. Then use the words in parentheses ( ) to ask a *wh-* question, if possible.

EXAMPLE: speak your language (what languages)
A. Does your teacher speak your language?
B. No, he doesn't
A. What languages does he speak?
B. He speaks English and French.

1. give a lot of homework (why)
   [handwritten: 1- yes, he does. why, does he give lot of homework? Does your teacher give a lot of homework? He gives a lot of homework for we train.]
2. write on the chalkboard (when)
   [handwritten: 2 - Does your teacher write on the chalkboard? Yes he does. When does he write on the chalkboard? When he want teachs new grammar]
3. use a tape recorder in class (why)
   [handwritten: Yes, he does. Why does he use a tape recorder in class? Does your teacher use a tape recorder? He uses a tape recorder in class for teach]
4. come to class late (what time)
   [handwritten: What time does he come to class? He comes to class at right time; seven thirty- Does your teacher come to class late. No he]
5. call you by your first name (why)
   [handwritten: 5- Does your teacher call you by your first name? Yes, he does.]
6. pronounce your name correctly (how)
   [handwritten: yes he does. How does he pronouce your name? Does your teacher pronouce correctly]
7. use a textbook (what textbook)
   [handwritten: Yes, he does. What textbook does he use? He uses Grammar in Context Themes for to. Does your teacher use a tex]
8. wear jeans to class (what)
   [handwritten: Yes he does. What does he wear to class. He wears pants blue, dress pants. Does your teacher wear Jeans to class:]

²*Get* means arrive.

[handwritten: P. 64. 69 -   themes p° today   26.27.28]

2.13 Questions about Meaning, Spelling, and Cost

Wh- Word	*Do/Does*	Subject	Verb Phrase	Answer
What	**does**	D.C.	**mean**?	It means District of Columbia.
How	**do**	you	**spell** "district"?	D-I-S-T-R-I-C-T
How	**do**	you	**say** "district" in Spanish?	"Distrito"
How much	**does**	your book	**cost**?	$20

LANGUAGE NOTES

Mean, *spell*, *say*, and *cost* are verbs and should be in the verb position of a question.

EXERCISE 26 Fill in the blanks in the conversation below with the missing words.

A. What ___'s___ your name?
   (example)

B. My name is Martha Gomez.

A. How __do you__ spell "Gomez"?
   (1)

B. G - O- M - E - Z. It's a Spanish name.

A. Are you __from__ Spain?
   (2)

B. No, I'm __not__.
   (3)

A. What country __do__ you come __from__?
   (4)   *(5)*

B. I come from Guatemala.

A. __Is__ your family here?
   (6)

B. No. My family is still in Guatemala. I call them once a week.

A. Isn't that expensive?

B. Yes, it __is__.
   (7)

A. How much __do you pay to call__ phone?
   (8)

B. A phone call to Guatemala costs about 25¢ a minute. But we don't talk for long. We just say hello.

A. How __do you say__ "hello" in Spanish?
   (9)

B. We say "hola." Please excuse me now. I'm late for my class. Hasta luego.

A. What ___does___ "hasta luego" _in English_ ?
   (10)   (11)

B. It means "see you later" in Spanish.

EXERCISE 27 Read each statement. Then ask a *wh-* question about the words in parentheses ( ). Answer with a complete sentence.

EXAMPLES: Mexico has thirty states. (the U.S.)

A. _How many states does the U.S. have?_

B. _It has 50 states._

Mexicans speak Spanish. (Americans)

A. _What language do Americans speak?_

B. _Americans speak English._

1. The Mexican president lives in Mexico City. (the American President)

   A. _Where does ~~live~~ the American President live?_

   B. _The American President lives in Whashington._

2. Mexicans speak Spanish. (Canadians)

   A. _What language do Candians speak?_

   B. _Canadians speak English an' little bit of French_

3. A college course costs a lot of money. (this course)

   A. _How much does this curse cost?_

   B. _This course costs $ 700._

4. "D.C." means District of Columbia. ("L.A.")

   A. _What does L.A mean?_

   B. _L.A means Los Angeles._

5. You spell "knife" K-N-I-F-E. ("enough")

   A. _How do you spell enough?_

   B. _You spell e-n-o-u-g-h._

6. China has more than 1 billion people. (the U.S.) (answer: about 275 million)

   A. _How many people does have in U.S?_

   B. _The U.S has about 275 million people._

---

7. Chinese people celebrate the New Year in February. (Americans)
   A. *When do the Americans people celebrate the New year*
   B. *Americans celebrate the New year in January.*

8. I don't know the word "large." ("large"/mean)
   A. *What does large mean?*
   B. *Large it means big.*

9. We say "book" in English. ("book" in Spanish) (answer: "libro")
   A. *How do you say book in Spanish?*
   B. *Book in Spanish we say libro.*

10. The teacher doesn't speak a foreign language in class. (why)
    A. *Why doesn't the teacher speak a foreign language in class.*
    B. *Because in class we learn just English.*

11. Australia has cold weather in July. (when/the U.S.)
    A. *When the U.S does have a cold weather?*
    B. *The U.S has a cold weather in october at March*

12. Mexicans celebrate Labor Day in May. (Americans) (answer: September)
    A. *When the Americans do celebrate Labor Day?*
    B. *Americans celebrate Labor Day in september.*

13. "Fall" means autumn. ("automobile")
    A. *What does automobile mean?*
    B. *Automobile means car.*

14. The school year starts in September. (when/end)
    A. *When does the school year end?*
    B. *Ends in June.*

2.14   Comparing *Wh-* Questions with *Be* and Other Verbs

Where **are** they from? What language **do** they **speak**?	How **are** you? How **do** you **feel**?
Where **am** I? What **do** I **need**?	Where **are** we? Where **do** we **go** now?
Who **is** she? Where **does** she **live**?	What **is** a stamp? What **does** "postage" **mean**?

Read this conversation between two new students, Ricardo (R) and Alexander (A). Fill in the blanks with the missing words.

R. Hi. My name _'s_ Ricardo. What _is your name_ ?
   (example)   (1)

A. Alexander.

R. Nice to meet you, Alexander. Where _you are from_ ?
                                           (2)

A. I _from_ from Ukraine.
       (3)

R. What languages _do you speak_ ?
                        (4)

A. I speak Ukrainian and Russian.

R. _Are you_ a new student?
       (5)

A. Yes, I am. What about you? Where _are you_ from?
                                        (6)

R. I _m_ from Peru.
      (7)

A. Where _is Peru_ ?
            (8)

R. It's in South America. We speak Spanish in Peru. I want to learn English and then go back to my country.

A. Why _do you want_ to go back to Peru?
            (9)

R. Because my father has an export business there, and I want to work with him.

A. What _does export mean_ ?
           (10)

R. "Export" means to sell your products in another country.

A. Why _do you want_ to know English?
           (11)

R. I need to know English because we have many American customers.

A. How many languages _does your father speak_ ?
                            (12)

R. My father speaks four languages: English, French, German, and Spanish, of course.

A. Tell me about your English class. _Do you like_ your English
                                          (13)
   teacher?

R. Oh, yes. I like her very much.

A. Who _is_ your English teacher?
          (14)

68   Lesson Two

why do you like.

R. Barbara Nowak.

When does he

A. How do you spell ?
   (15) *Whe do*

R. N-O-W-A-K. It's a Polish name.

A. How many students does your class have ?
   (16)

R. It has about 35 students. The classroom is very big.

A. What floor is it ?
   (17)

R. It's on the second floor.

A. When does your class begin ?
   (18)   (19)

R. It begins at 6 o'clock. I'm late. See you later.

A. What does mean "see you later" in Spanish?
   (20)

R. We say "hasta luego."

SUMMARY OF LESSON 2

1. The simple present has two forms: the base form and the **-s** form:

I You We They (Plural noun)	eat.	He She It (Singular noun)	eats.

2. Simple present tense patterns with the **-s** form:

AFFIRMATIVE:	The President **lives** in Washington, D.C.
NEGATIVE:	He **doesn't live** in New York.
YES/NO QUESTION:	**Does** he **live** in the White House?
SHORT ANSWER:	Yes, he **does**.
WH- QUESTION:	Where **does** the Vice President **live**?
NEGATIVE QUESTION:	Why **doesn't** the Vice President **live** in the White House?

3. Simple present tense patterns with the base form:

AFFIRMATIVE:	We **study** English in class.
NEGATIVE:	We **don't study** American history in class.
YES/NO QUESTION:	**Do** we **study** grammar?
SHORT ANSWER:	Yes, we **do**.
WH- QUESTION:	Why **do** we **study** grammar?
NEGATIVE QUESTION:	Why **don't** we **study** history?

4. Present tense patterns with the verb **be**:

AFFIRMATIVE:	The teacher **is** absent.
NEGATIVE:	She **isn't** here today.
YES/NO QUESTION:	**Is** she sick?
SHORT ANSWER:	No, she **isn't**.
WH- QUESTION:	Where **is** she?
NEGATIVE QUESTION:	Why **isn't** she here?

5. We use the simple present tense with:

General truths and facts	Washington, D.C., **has** over half a million people.
	Americans **speak** English.
Customs	Japanese people **take** off their shoes when they enter a house.
	Americans **don't visit** friends without an invitation.
Regular Activities	He **visits** his parents every summer.
	I **play** soccer once a week.

EDITING ADVICE

1. Don't forget to use the *-s* form when the subject is *he, she, it,* or a singular noun.

    He need^{s} more money.

    This school ~~have~~ *has* a big library.

2. Use the base form after *does* and *doesn't*.

    My father doesn't ~~has~~ *have* a car.

    Does your mother speak~~s~~ English well?

3. If you are living in the U.S., use the American form, not the British form, with *have*.

    He ~~hasn't~~ *doesn't have* a car.

    ~~Have you~~ *Do you have* a car?

4. Don't forget *do/does* in a question.

    Where *do* your parents live?

5. Use correct word order in a question.

your brother live
Where does ~~live your brother~~?

does your father have
What kind of car ~~has your father~~?

don't you
Why ~~you don't~~ like pizza?

6. Don't use *be* with another verb to form the simple present tense.

I
I'~~m~~ have 3 brothers.

She'~~s~~ lives in New York.

I don't
I'~~m not~~ have a car.

7. Don't use *be* in a simple present tense question that uses another verb.

Does
~~Is~~ your college have a computer lab?

Do
~~Are~~ you speak French?

8. Use correct spelling for the -*s* form.

studies
She ~~studys~~ in the library.

watches
He ~~watchs~~ TV every evening.

9. Use the correct negative form.

doesn't
He ~~not~~ know the answer.

don't
They ~~no~~ speak English.

10. Don't use an -*ing* form for simple present tense.

write
I ~~writing~~ a letter to my family once a week.

11. *Family* is a singular word. Use the -*s* form.

s
My family live in Germany.

12. Use the same verb in a short answer as in a *yes/no* question.

am
Are you hungry? Yes, I ~~do~~.

do
Do you like baseball? Yes, I ~~am~~.

13. Use the correct word order with questions about meaning, spelling, and cost.

                does "wonderful" mean
      What ~~means "wonderful"~~?

                  do bananas cost
      How much ~~cost bananas~~ this week?

          do you
      How spell "opportunity"?

          do you
      How say "opportunity" in your language?

LESSON 2 TEST / REVIEW

PART 1   Find the mistakes with the underlined words and correct them. Not every sentence has a mistake. If the sentence is correct, write **C**.

EXAMPLE: *I don't*
~~I'm not~~ speak English well.

What <u>does</u> the teacher <u>want</u>?   **C**

1. My mother <u>washes</u> my clothes every Sunday. C

2. I <u>haven't</u> a dictionary. *wrong*
I don't have a dictionary

3. <u>Where you live</u>? *wrong*
Where do you live?

4. He <u>no need</u> help from you.
He doesn't need help from you.

5. My sister <u>talks</u> a lot. C

6. You <u>aren't need</u> a dictionary for the test.
You don't need a dictionary for the test.

7. My brother <u>goes</u> to a state university. C

8. <u>Are</u> you want to buy a new computer?
Do you want to by a new computer?

9. Does your apartment <u>have</u> a dishwasher? Yes, it <u>is</u>. *does*

10. What kind of computers <u>has</u> this school?
What kind of computers does school ha

11. <u>How spell</u> "computer"?
How do you spell computer?

12. What <u>does</u> the teacher <u>want</u>? C

13. Why <u>you don't</u> want to practice English at home?
Why don't you want to practice English at home

14. How many children ~~do~~ _does_ your sister have? ℓ

15. How much costs a stamp? _a stamp cost?_
    How much does a stamp?
16. The teacher <u>doesn't speak</u> my language. ℓ

17. My mother <u>worries</u> a lot about me. ℓ

18. Miami <u>don't have</u> cold winters.
    Miami doesn't have cold winters.
19. <u>I'm not like</u> to use public transportation.
    I don't like to use public transportation.
20. <u>How say</u> "potato" in your language?
    How do you say potato in you language?
21. My friend <u>going</u> to Puerto Rico every winter.
    My friend goes to Puerto Rico every winter.
22. My family <u>has</u> a big house.
    My family have a big house.
23. <u>How many states does the U.S. have?</u> ℓ
    How many states does the U.S. have?
24. <u>What means</u> "adjective"?
    What does adjective mean?

PART 2   Write the -_s_ form of the following verbs. Use correct spelling.

EXAMPLE: take _____ _takes_ _____

1. go _____ _goes_ _____   5. play _____ _plays_ _____
2. carry ___ _carries_ ___   6. study ___ _studies_ ___
3. mix _____ _mixes_ _____   7. catch ___ _catches_ ___
4. drink ___ _drinks_ ___   8. say _____ _says_ _____

PART 3   Fill in the first blank with the affirmative form of the verb in parentheses ( ). Then write the negative form of this verb.

EXAMPLES: A monkey _____ _lives_ _____ in a warm climate.
               (live)

It _____ _doesn't live_ _____ in a cold climate.

Brazil _____ _is_ _____ a big country.
       (be)

Haiti _____ _isn't_ _____ a big country.

1. The English language _____ _uses_ _____ the Roman alphabet.
                       (use)

The Chinese language _doesn't use_ the Roman alphabet.

2. We _____speak_____ English in class.
   (speak)

   We _don't speak_ our native languages in class.

3. March _____has_____ 31 days.
   (have)

   February _doesn't have_ 31 days.

   Doesn't February have 31 days?

4. Mexico and Canada _____are_____ in North America.
   (be)

   Colombia and Ecuador _aren't_ in North America.

5. You _____pronouce_____ the "k" in "bank."
   (pronounce)

   You _don't pronouce_ the "k" in "knife."

6. The teacher _____teaches_____ the English language.
   (teach)

   Does the teacher teach English language.

   He/She _doesn't teach_ American history.

7. A green light _____means_____ "go."
   (mean)

   A yellow light _doesn't mean_ "go."

8. I _____come_____ from another country.
   (come)

   I _don't come_ from the U.S.

9. English _____is_____ hard for me.
   (be)

   My language _isn't_ hard for me.

PART 4
Write a *yes/no* question about the words in parentheses ( ).
Write a short answer.

EXAMPLES: January has 31 days. (February) (answer: no)
Does February have 31 days? No, it doesn't.

China is in Asia. (Korea) (answer: yes)
Is Korea in Asia? Yes, it is.

1. The U.S. has 50 states. (Mexico) (answer: no)

   Does Mexico have no states? No, it doesn't.

2. The post office sells stamps. (the bank) (answer: no)

   Does the bank sell stamps? No, it doesn't.

3. San Francisco is in California. (Los Angeles) (answer: yes)

   Is L.A in California? Yes, it is.

4. McDonald's sells hamburgers. (Burger King) (answer: yes)

Does Burger King sell hamburgers? Yes, it does.

5. January and March have 31 days. (April and June) (answer: no)

Does April and June have 31 days? No, they don't.

6. The President lives in the White House. (the Vice President) (answer: no)

Does the Vice President live in the Whitehouse. No, he doesn't.

7. Americans speak English. (Canadians) (answer: yes)

Do Canadians speak English? Yes, they do.

8. We come to class on time. (the teacher)

Does the teacher come to class on time? Yes, he does.

PART **5**

Read each statement. Then write a _wh-_ question about the words in parentheses ( ). You don't need to answer the question.

EXAMPLES: February has 28 days. (March)

How many days does March have?

Mexico is in North America. (Venezuela)

Where is Venezuela?

1. Mexicans speak Spanish. (Canadians)

What lenguague do Canadians speak?

2. The U.S. has 50 states. (Mexico)

How many states does Mexico have?

3. The President lives in the White House. (the Vice President)

Where does the Vice President live?

4. Thanksgiving is in November. (Christmas)

When christmas?

5. You spell "occasion" O-C-C-A-S-I-O-N. ("tomorrow")

How do you spell tomorrow?

6. "Occupation" means job or profession. ("occasion")

What does occasion mean?

7. The President doesn't make the laws. (why)

Why does the president make the laws.

8. Marek comes from Poland. (you)

Do you Marek come?

PART 6 Read this interview. Fill in the blanks with the missing word.

A. How old _____*are you*_____?
      (example)

B. I'm 30 years old.

A. _____*Are you*_____ married?
              (1)

B. No. I'm single.

A. _____*Do you live*_____ with your parents?
              (2)

B. No, I don't live with my parents.

A. Why _____*don't you live*_____ with your parents?
              (3)

B. I don't live with my parents because they live in another city.

A. Where _____*do they live*_____?
              (4)

B. They live in Chicago.

A. _____*Do*_____ you _____*live in*_____ Washington?
      (5)   *(6)*

B. Yes, I like it very much.

A. Why _____*do you like*_____ Washington?
              (7)

B. I like it because it has so many interesting museums and galleries. But I don't have time to visit these places very often. I work every day. When my parents visit, we go to galleries and museums.

A. When _____*do your parents visit you?*_____
              (8)

B. They visit me in the spring. They love Washington.

A. Why _____*do they love*_____ Washington?
              (9)

B. They love it because it's a beautiful, interesting city. And they love it because I'm here.

A. What kind of job _do you have_ ?
       (10)

B. I have a job with the government. I work in the Department of Commerce.

A. What _does Department_ of commerce mean?
       (11)

B. Commerce means business.

A. How _do you spell com?merce?_
       (12)

B. C-O-M-M-E-R-C-E.

A. _Do you liked_ your job?
       (13)

B. Yes. I like my job very much.

A. _Were do you live?_
       (14)

B. I live a few blocks from the White House.

A. _Do you have a_ have a car?
       (15)

B. No, I don't. I don't need a car.

A. How _do you go_ to work?
       (16)

B. I go to work by subway. If I'm late, I take a taxi.

A. How much _does a taxi ride cost?_
       (17)

B. A taxi ride from my house to work costs about $12.

A. _Is the subway_ clean?
       (18)

B. Oh, yes. The subway is very clean.

A. _Does the train run_ all night?
       (19)

B. No, the trains don't run all night. They run until midnight.

A. In my country, we don't say "subway." We use a different word.

B. How _do you say_ "subway" in your country?
       (20)

A. We say "metro."

EXPANSION ACTIVITIES

CLASSROOM ACTIVITIES

1. Check all the items below that tell about you. Find a partner and compare your list to your partner's list. Write three sentences telling about differences between you and your partner. (You may read your list to the class.)

a. ____ I have a cell phone.   i. ____ I play a musical instrument.

b. ____ I own a home.   j. ____ I sing well.

c. ____ I live in an apartment.   k. ____ I'm a good driver.

d. ____ I exercise regularly.   l. ____ I'm a member of a health club.

e. ____ I'm a vegetarian.   m. ____ I like pizza.

f. ____ I like classical music.   n. ____ I use a pager.

g. ____ I live with my parents.   o. ____ I write with my left hand.

h. ____ I have e-mail.

EXAMPLE: I have a cell phone. Sylvia doesn't have a cell phone.

2. Game: One student thinks of the name of a famous person and writes this person's initials on the chalkboard. Other students ask questions to try to guess the name of this person.
Sample Questions:
Is he an athlete?
Where does he come from?
Is he tall?
How old is he?

3. Game: One student comes to the front of the room. He or she thinks of an animal and writes the name of this animal on a piece of paper. The other students try to guess which animal it is by asking questions. The person who guesses the animal is the next to come to the front of the room.

EXAMPLE:
lion
Does this animal fly? No, it doesn't.
Does it live in water? No, it doesn't.
What does it eat? It eats meat.
Does this animal live in Africa? Yes, it does.
What color is this animal?

DISCUSSION

In a small group, discuss differences between classes and teachers in this school and another school you know.

EXAMPLES: In my college back home, students stand up when they speak. This class has some older people. In my native country, only young people study at college.

WRITING

Write about a tourist attraction in your country (or in another country you know something about).

INTERVIEW

Interview an American about his or her favorite tourist place in the U.S. Why does he/she like this place? What does this place have? What do tourists do there?

Internet Activities

1. Using the Internet, find information about one of the following places: Disneyland, the White House, the Holocaust Museum, Ellis Island, the Epcot Center, the Alamo, or any other American tourist attraction that interests you. Then answer these questions:

    What is it?
    Where is it?
    When is it open?
    What does it cost to enter?
    What does it have?

2. Using the Internet, find information about a museum or place of special interest in this city. Then answer these questions:

    What is it?
    Where is it?
    When is it open?
    What does it cost to enter?
    What does it have?

GRAMMAR

Singular and Plural
Articles and Quantity Words
There + *Be* + Noun

CONTEXT

Americans and Where They Live
Finding an Apartment
Calling about an Apartment

LESSON FOCUS

Nouns can be *singular* or *plural*[1].

I have one *brother*.   I have three *sisters*.

We can use *articles* and *quantity words* before nouns.

I have *an* aunt in New York.   I have *some* cousins in Boston.

We can introduce a noun with *there* + a form of *be*.

There's an apple in the refrigerator.

There are some peaches on the table.

[1] Some nouns have no plural form. These are noncount nouns. See Lesson 10 for information about noncount nouns.

1. Do you know anyone who lives alone?
2. Does your family own a house or rent an apartment?

Read the following information. Pay special attention to plural nouns.

Americans and Where They Live[2]

1. There are about 270 million **people** in the United States.
2. 56% of adult **Americans** are married.
3. Four million **children** (6%) under 18 live with **grandparents**.
4. 68% of **children** live with two **parents**.
5. 82% of single **parents** are **women**.
6. 25 million **Americans** (about 10%) live alone.
7. The average family has 3.19 **people**.
8. 65% of American **families** own their **homes**.
9. **People** pay 25% of their income on home **expenses**. **Renters** pay more than **owners**. (**Owners** pay 21% of their income. **Renters** pay 26%.)

Characteristics of Home Buyers, 1997	
Median purchase price	$159,700
First-time buyers	$135,400
Repeat buyers	$178,700
Average monthly mortgage payment	$ 1,114
As percent of income	32.8%
Average age (in years)	
First-time buyers	32.1
Repeat buyers	41.1

Living Arrangements of Children Under 18, 1997	
All children under 18	70,983
Living with:	
Two parents	48,386
One parent	19,799
Mother only	16,740
Father only	3,059
Other relatives	1,983
Nonrelatives only	815

[2] Statistics are from 1997 census estimates.

10. The average American moves 10 **times** in his or her lifetime. **Renters** move more than **owners**. Young **people** move more than older **people**.
11. The most expensive **homes** are in San Francisco and Boston. Other **cities** with expensive **homes** are San Diego, New York City, and Washington, D.C.
12. The average number of **rooms** in a house is 5.4.
13. 25% of **homeowners** are over 65 **years** old.

3.1   Regular Noun Plurals

Word Ending	Example Words	Plural Addition	Plural Form
Vowel	bee banana pie	+ s	bees bananas pies
Consonant	bed pin month	+ s	beds pins months
ss, sh, ch, x	class dish church box	+ es	classes dishes churches boxes
Vowel + y	boy day monkey	+ s	boys days monkeys
Consonant + y	lady story party	$\cancel{y}$ + ies	ladies stories parties
Vowel + o	patio stereo radio	+ s	patios stereos radios
Consonant + o	mosquito tomato potato	+ es	mosquitoes tomatoes potatoes
EXCEPTIONS: photos, pianos, solos, altos, sopranos, autos, avocados			
f or fe	knife leaf calf	$\cancel{f}$ + ves	knives leaves calves
EXCEPTIONS: beliefs, chiefs, roofs, chefs			

EXERCISE 1   Write the plural form of each noun.

EXAMPLES: leaf ___leaves___

toy ___toys___

1. dish ___dishs___
2. country ___Countries___
3. half ___halves___
4. book ___books___
5. boy ___boys___
6. girl ___girls___
7. bench ___benchies___
8. box ___boxes___
9. table ___tables___
10. stereo ___stereos___
11. knife ___Knives___
12. story ___Stories___
13. sofa ___Sofas___
14. key ___Keis___
15. movie ___movies___
16. bath ___baths___

17. mosquito ___mosquitoes___
18. lion ___lions___
19. fly ___flyies___
20. cow ___caws___
21. shark ___Sharks___
22. roach ___roaches___
23. fox ___foxes___
24. horse ___horses___
25. turkey ___turkeys___
26. chicken ___Chickens___
27. wolf ___wolves___
28. dog ___dogs___
29. squirrel ___squirrels (esquilo)___
30. pony ___ponyies___
31. duck ___ducks___
32. moth ___mothes___ (→ mariposa.)

3.2   Pronunciation of Plural Nouns

Pronounce /s/	Pronounce /z/		Pronounce /əz/
lip—lips	cab—cabs	can—cans	bus—buses
cat—cats	lid—lids	thing—things	cause—causes
rock—rocks	bag—bags	bill—bills	class—classes
cuff—cuffs	stove—stoves	car—cars	dish—dishes
month—months	sum—sums	bee—bees	beach—beaches
			garage—garages
			place—places
			tax—taxes

1. We pronounce /s/ after voiceless sounds: /p, t, k, f, Θ/
2. We pronounce /z/ after voiced sounds: /b, d, g, v, m, n, ŋ, l, r/ and all vowels.
3. We pronounce /əz/ after *s*, *se*, *ss*, *sh*, *ch*, *ge*, *ce*, *x*.

EXERCISE 2 Go back to Exercise 1 and pronounce the plural form of each word.

3.3 Irregular Noun Plurals

Singular	Plural	Examples	Explanation
man woman mouse tooth foot goose	men women mice teeth feet geese	One **man** is here. Two **men** are there. One **woman** is late. Five **women** are on time.	Vowel change
sheep fish deer	sheep fish deer	One **sheep** is here. Three **sheep** are there.	No change
child person	children people (OR persons)	One **person** is late. Five **people** are absent.	Different word form
	pajamas clothes pants/slacks (eye)glasses scissors	Your **clothes** are dirty. My **glasses** are broken.	No singular form

LANGUAGE NOTES

1. *People* is more common than *persons*.
   Five *people* in my class speak Spanish.
2. Number words (*hundred*, *thousand*, *million*) use the singular form.
   The U.S. has over 270 *million* people.
   Two *hundred* people live in my building.
3. Listen to your teacher's pronunciation of *woman* (singular) and *women* (plural). The difference is in the first syllable.

The following nouns have an irregular plural form. Write the plural.

EXAMPLE: man _____men_____

1. foot ___feet___   5. fish ___fish___
2. woman ___women___   6. mouse ___mice___
3. policeman ___policemen___   7. sheep ___sheep___
4. child ___children___   8. tooth ___teeth.___

EXERCISE **4** Use the plural of each noun to ask, "How many . . . do you have?" Another student will answer. For a zero answer, say, "I don't have any <plural form>."

EXAMPLE: sister
A. How many sisters do you have?
B. I have two sisters.   OR   I don't have any sisters.

How many children do you have?
I don't have any children

1. child   7. telephone

2. brother   8. watch

3. sister   9. television

4. niece   10. radio

5. nephew   11. cousin

6. aunt   12. computer

3.4 Making Generalizations

Examples	Explanation
A house is expensive. **Houses** are expensive.	We can make generalizations about the subject of the sentence two ways:
A child needs love. **Children** need love.	• By using the indefinite articles (*a* or *an*) with a singular noun. • By using the plural form of the noun with no article.
A family has responsibilities. **Families** have responsibilities.	We are saying that something is true of all members of a group.
I like American **houses**. I don't like big **buildings**.	After the verb, we usually use the plural form with no article to make a generalization.

EXERCISE 5 Change the subject from plural to singular. Make other necessary changes. (Both singular and plural give a generalization.)

EXAMPLE: Students have to learn grammar.

A student has to learn grammar.

1. Adults have a lot of responsibilities.

_____

2. Children like to play.

_____

3. Single parents have a hard job.

_____

4. Women live longer than men.

_____

5. Cars are expensive.

_____

6. Houses cost a lot of money.

_____

EXERCISE 6 Change the subject from singular to plural. Make other necessary changes. (Both singular and plural give a generalization.)

EXAMPLE: A student has many responsibilities.

Students have many responsibilities.

1. A child needs love.

_____

2. An egg has protein.

_____

3. A banana is yellow.

_____

4. A dog is intelligent.

_____

5. A dolphin doesn't live on land.

_____

6. A mouse is small.

_____

dolphin

EXERCISE 7   Use the plural form of the word in parentheses ( ) to make a generalization. Remember, don't use an article with the plural form to make a generalization. (You may work with a partner.)

EXAMPLES: (child)
Children like to watch cartoons.

_____

American (highway)
American highways are in good condition.

_____

1. (American)

American have good policemen.

2. American (child)

American children like play in the snow.

3. big (city) in the U.S.

Boston and New York are big cities in the U.S.

4. (teacher) at this college

Just 2 teachers are these college.
Teachers this college are very good

5. (student) at this college

Today has 120 students at these college.

6. American (doctor)

American doctors are the best in brest care

7. old (person) in the U.S.

50 percent of the people are old in the U.

8. American (woman)

American women like to watch moves.

EXERCISE 8 Use the noun in parentheses ( ) to give general information about your native country. Use the plural form with no article.

EXAMPLE: (woman)
Generally, women don't work outside the home in my native country.

my country thousand of people like to play soccer.
40% percent of people are old
ten women, one has diabetes.
ten men above 40 years old,
Prostate Cancer.

1. (person)
2. old (person)
3. (woman)
4. (man)

5. (house) *In Brasil house are different*
6. poor (person) *In Brasil has lot people poors*
7. (car) *Cars in Brasil are very expensive.*
8. (doctor) *Doctors in Brasil work hard.*

EXERCISE 9 Add a plural subject to these sentences to make a generalization.

EXAMPLE: _____Small children_____ need a lot of sleep.

Poor people have a hard life.

1. _____Dentist_____ make a lot of money.
2. _____Poor People_____ have a hard life.
3. _____Young Girls_____ talk on the phone a lot.
4. _____Lot people_____ are in good physical condition.
5. _____small children_____ believe in Santa Claus.
6. _____good parents_____ worry about children.

EXERCISE 10 Use the plural form of each noun to tell if you like or don't like the following:

EXAMPLE: apple
I like apples. OR I don't like apples.

consonant + o = es
vowel + o = s
ss, sh, ch x = es

√ do.

1. tomato
I like tomatoes.
2. orange
I love oranges.
3. strawberry
I enjoy strawberryies.
4. grape
I don't like grapes
5. banana
I like bananas

6. peach
I don't like peaches.
7. radish
I don't like radishes
8. pear
I like pears.
9. potato
I like potatoes.
10. cherry
I love cherryies
cereja

EXERCISE 11 Ask "Do you like" + the plural form of the noun. Another student will answer.

EXAMPLES: child
A. Do you like children?
B. Yes, I do.

dog
A. Do you like dogs?
B. No, I don't.

1. cat
Do you like cats?
2. dog
Do you like dogs?
3. American doctor
Do you like American doctors?
4. American car
Do you like American cars?
5. American movie
Do you like American movies?
6. fashion magazine
Do you like fashion magazines?
7. comic book
Do you like comic books?
8. computer
Do you like computers?
9. computer game
Do you like computer games?
10. strict teacher
Do you like strict teachers?
11. American supermarket
Do you like American supermarkets?
12. American textbook
Do you like American textbooks?

Before You Read 1. Do you live in a house, an apartment, or a dorm?[3] Do you live alone?
2. Do you like the place where you live? Why or why not?

APARTMENTS FOR RENT

5 rooms, 2 baths, fenced yard. Pets allowed. References required. Call 112-3345 after 6:00 p.m.

4 rooms, 1 bath, quiet dead end street. 2-car driveway. Call 122-3445 for appointment. → *Ask the teacher*

5 rooms, 1 bath, new kitchen and ...ting. Dish wash-

Read the following article. Pay special attention to *there* + *be* followed by singular and plural nouns.

---

[3] *Dorm* is short for *dormitory*, a building where students live.

Finding an Apartment

There are several ways to find an apartment. One way is to look in the newspaper. **There is** an "Apartments for Rent" section in the back of the newspaper. **There are** many ads for apartments. **There are** also ads for houses for rent and houses for sale.

Another way to find an apartment is by looking at the buildings in the neighborhood where you want to live. **There are** often "For Rent" signs on the front of the buildings. **There is** usually a phone number on the sign. You can call and ask for information about the apartment that you are interested in. You can ask:

How much is the rent?
Is heat included?
What floor is the apartment on?
Is there an elevator?
How many bedrooms **are there** in the apartment?
How many closets **are there** in the apartment?
Is the apartment available[4] now?

If an apartment interests you, you can make an appointment to see it. When you go to see the apartment, you should ask some more questions, such as the following:

Is there a lease?[5] How long is the lease?
Is there a janitor or manager?
Is there a parking space for each tenant? Is it free, or do I have to pay extra?
Are there smoke detectors? (In many places, the law says that the landlord must put a smoke detector in each apartment and in the halls.)
Is there a laundry room in the building? Where is it?

The landlord may ask you a few questions, such as:

Did you know...?

The most expensive apartments in the U.S. are in San Francisco.

How many people **are there** in your family?
Do you have any pets?

You should check over the apartment carefully before you sign the lease. If **there are** some problems, you should talk to the landlord to see if he will take care of them before you move in.

---

[4] *Available* means ready to use now.
[5] A *lease* is a contract between the owner (landlord or landlady) and the renter (tenant). It tells how much the rent is, how long the tenant can stay in the apartment, and other rules.

SINGULAR

There + Is (+ Not)	Singular Word	Singular Noun	Prepositional Phrase
There is	a	janitor	in my building.
There is	one	dryer	in the basement.
There isn't	a	back door	in my apartment.
There is	no	back door	in my apartment.

PLURAL

There + Are (+ Not)	Plural Word	Plural Noun	Prepositional Phrase
There are	—	numbers	on the doors of the apartments.
There are	several	windows	in the bedroom.
There are	many	Americans	in my building.
There are	some	children	in my building.
There are	two	closets	in the hall.
There aren't	any	shades	on the windows.
There are	no	shades	on the windows.

LANGUAGE NOTES

1. We use *there + is* to introduce a singular subject into a conversation. We use *there + are* to introduce a plural subject.[6]
2. We can make a contraction for *there is → there's*. We don't write a contraction for *there are*.
3. A sentence that begins with *there* often shows a place or a time.
    There's a good movie *at the Garden Theater.*
    There's a good movie *at 8 o'clock.*
4. If two nouns follow *there*, use a singular verb *(is)* if the first noun is singular. Use a plural verb *(are)* if the first noun is plural.
    There's *a* closet in the bedroom and two closets in the hall.
    There *are two* closets in the hall and one closet in the bedroom.
    There *is a* washer and a dryer in the basement.

---

[6] In conversation, you will sometimes hear *there's* with plural nouns.
    INFORMAL: There's a lot of empty apartments in my building.
    FORMAL: There are a lot of empty apartments in my building.

5. *There* never introduces a specific noun. Don't use a noun with a definite article (*the*) after *there*.

WRONG: There's the Eiffel Tower in Paris.

RIGHT: The Eiffel Tower is in Paris.

EXERCISE 12 Use the words given to make a statement about the place where you live (house or apartment). If you live in a dorm, use Exercise 13 instead.

EXAMPLES:
carpet/in the living room
There's a carpet in the living room.
OR
There isn't a carpet in the living room.

trees/in front of the building
There are two trees in front of the building.
OR
There are no trees in front of the building.

1. closet/in the living room
2. blinds/on the windows
3. door/in every room
4. window/in every room
5. lease
6. porch varanda
7. number/on the door of the apartment
8. overhead light/in every room
9. microwave oven/in the kitchen
10. back door
11. fireplace
12. smoke detector

blinds

porch

fireplace

EXERCISE 13 Make a statement about your dorm and dorm room with the words given. (If you live in an apartment or house, skip this exercise.)

EXAMPLES:
window/in the room
There's a window in the room.

curtains/on the window
There are no curtains on the window.
There are shades.

shade

---

1. closet/in the room
2. two beds/in the room
3. private bath/for every room
4. men and women/in the dorm
5. cafeteria/in the dorm
6. snack machines/in the dorm
7. noisy students/in the dorm
8. numbers/on the doors of the rooms
9. elevator(s)/in the dorm
10. laundry room/in the dorm

3.6   Questions with *There*

Is/Are + There	Noun Phrase	Prepositional Phrase	Short Answer
Is there	a laundry room	in your building?	No, there isn't.
Are there	any cabinets	in the kitchen?	Yes, there are.
Are there	any empty apartments	in your building?	Yes, there are.

How Many + Noun		Are There	Prepositional Phrase	Answer
How many closets		**are there**	in your apartment?	There are three.
How many apartments		**are there**	in your building?	There are ten.

LANGUAGE NOTES

1. We usually use *any* to introduce a plural noun in a *yes/no* question.
   Are there *any* empty apartments in your building?
2. Do not make a contraction for a short *yes* answer.
   Is there an elevator in your building?
   Yes, there is. NOT: Yes, there's.

EXERCISE 14   Ask and answer questions with *there* and the words given to find out about another student's apartment and building. (If you live in a dorm, use Exercise 15 instead.)

EXAMPLES: a microwave oven/in your apartment
A. Is there a microwave oven in your apartment?
B. No, there isn't.

closets/in the bedroom
A. Are there any closets in the bedroom?
B. Yes. There's one closet in the bedroom.

1. children/in your building   *Are there children in your building?*
   No there aren't.
2. a dishwasher/in the kitchen   *Is there dishwasher in the kit[c]*
   Yes there is.

3. a yard/in front of your building _Is there a yard in front your buiding? No there isn't._

4. trees/in front of your building _Are there trees in front of your buiding? Yes there are two trees._

5. a basement/in the building _Are there basement in the buiding. Yes there is._

6. a laundry room/in the basement _Is there a laundry room in the basement. Yes there is._

7. a janitor/in the building _Is there a janitor in the building. Yes there is._

8. noisy neighbors/in the building _Are there noise neighbors in the building? No there aren't._

9. nosy[7] neighbors/in the building _Are there nosy neighbors in the building? No there aren't._

10. an elevator/in the building _Is there an elevator in the building? No there isn't._

11. parking spaces/for the tenants _Are there parking spaces for the tenants? No there aren't._

12. a lot of closets/in the apartment _Are there a lot of closets in the apartment? Yes there are._

13. how many apartments/in your building _how many apartaments are in your building? In my building are 3 apartments._

14. how many parking spaces/in front of your building _how many parking spaces are in front of your building. There are 3 parking spaces._

EXERCISE 15 Ask and answer questions with *there* and the words given to find out about another student's dorm. (If you live in an apartment or house, skip this exercise.)

EXAMPLE:
a bicycle room/in your dorm
A. Is there a bicycle room in your dorm?
B. No, there isn't.

1. married students
2. private rooms
3. a bicycle room
4. a computer room
5. an elevator
6. a bulletin board

7. graduate students
8. a quiet place to study
9. an air conditioner/in your room
10. a parking lot/for your dorm
11. how many rooms/in your dorm
12. how many floors/in your dorm

EXERCISE 16 Use the words given to ask the teacher a question about his or her office. Your teacher will answer.

EXAMPLES:
pencil sharpener
A. Is there a pencil sharpener in your office?
B. No, there isn't.

---

[7] A *nosy* person is a person who wants to know everyone's business.

books
A. Are there any books in your office?
B. Yes. There are a lot of books in my office.

1. phone
2. answering machine
3. photos of your family
4. radio
5. copy machine

6. windows
7. calendar
8. bookshelves
9. plants
10. file cabinet

file cabinet

EXERCISE 17 A student is calling about an apartment for rent. Fill in the blanks with *there is, there are, is there, are there,* and other related words to complete this phone conversation between the student (S) and the landlady (L).

S.   I'm calling about an apartment for rent on Grover Street.

L.   We have two apartments available. ___There's___ a four-room
     (example)
     apartment on the first floor and a three-room apartment on the fourth
     floor. Which one are you interested in?

S.   I prefer the smaller apartment. ___Is there___ an elevator in the
     (1)
     building?

L.   Yes, there is. How many people ___are there___ in your family?
     (2)

S.   It's just for me. I live alone. I'm a student. I need a quiet apartment.
     Is this a quiet building?

L.   Oh, yes. ___there are___ no kids in the building.
     (3)

S.   I have a car. ___Are there___ parking spaces?
     (4)

L.   Yes. ___There are___ 20 spaces in back of the building.
     (5)

S.   How ___many___ apartments ___are there___ in the building?
     (6)   (7)

L.   ___There are___ 30 apartments.
     (8)

S.   Twenty parking spaces for 30 apartments? Then ___There are aren't___
     (9)
     enough spaces for all the tenants.

L.   Don't worry. Not everyone has a car. Parking is on a first-come, first-
     served basis.[8] And ___there are___ plenty of[9] spaces on the street.
     (10)

[8] A *first-come, first-served* basis means that people who arrive first will get something first (parking spaces, theater tickets, classes at registration).
[9] *Plenty of* means *a lot of.*

S. <u>Is there</u> a laundry room in the building?
(11)

L. Yes. There are washers and dryers in the basement.

S. How much is the rent?

L. It's $650 a month.

S. When can I see the apartment?

L. How about tomorrow at six o'clock?

S. That'll be fine. Thanks.

3.7 *There* vs. *They* and Other Pronouns

There	Other Pronouns
There's an empty apartment on the first floor.	**It's** available now.
There's a janitor in the building.	**He's** in the basement now.
There are a lot of parking spaces.	**They're** for the tenants.
There are two washing machines.	**They're** in the basement.

LANGUAGE NOTES

1. We use *there* + *be* to introduce a new noun. When we refer to the same noun again, we use *it, they,* or other pronouns.
2. We pronounce *there* and *they're* exactly the same. Listen to your teacher pronounce the sentences from the box above.

EXERCISE 18 Fill in the blanks with *there's, there are, it's* or *they're*.

EXAMPLE: <u>There's</u> a small apartment for rent in my building.

<u>It's</u> on the fourth floor.

1. <u>There are</u> two apartments for rent. <u>They are</u> not on the same floor.

2. <u>There's</u> a laundry room in the building. <u>It's</u> in the basement.

3. The parking spaces are in the back of the building. <u>They're</u> for the tenants with cars.

Singular and Plural; Articles and Quantity Words; *There* + *Be* + Noun **97**

4. The parking spaces don't cost extra. ~~It's~~ *[They are]* _____ free for the tenants.

5. The apartment is small. ~~There is~~ *It's* _____ on the fourth floor.

6. The building has 30 apartments. It's _____ a big building.

7. The student wants to see the apartment. It's _____ on Grover Street.

8. The building is quiet because *there are* no kids in the building.

9. How much is the rent? ~~There is~~ *It's* _____ $650 a month.

10. Is the rent high? No, *it isn't* _____ not high.

EXERCISE 19 Ask a question about this school using *there* and the words given. Another student will answer. If the answer is "yes," ask a question with *where*.

EXAMPLES: a cafeteria
A. Is there a cafeteria at this school?
B. Yes, there is.
A. Where is it?
B. It's on the first floor.

*No there are not
"   " aren't ⇒ Plural
"   " isn't ⇒ sing.*

lockers
A. Are there any lockers at this school?
B. Yes, there are.
A. Where are they?
B. They're near the gym.

*Is there a library at this school?
Yes, there is. Were is it.
It's on the 6th floor.*

1. a library   8. tennis courts

2. vending machines   9. dormitories

3. public telephones   10. a parking lot

4. a computer room   11. a bookstore

5. a cafeteria   12. copy machines

6. a gym   13. a student lounge *sala de espera*

7. a swimming pool   14. a fax machine

Before You Read 1. Does your neighborhood have more apartment buildings or houses?
2. Do you prefer to live alone, with a roommate, or with your family? Why?

Read the following phone conversation between a student (S) and the manager (M) of a building. Pay special attention to the definite article *(the)*, the indefinite articles *(a, an)*, and indefinite quantity words *(some, any)*?

Calling about an Apartment

S. Hello? I want to speak with **the** landlord.
M. I'm **the** manager of **the** building. Can I help you?
S. I need to find **a** new apartment.
M. Where do you live now?
S. I live in **a** big apartment on Wright Street. I have **a** roommate, but he's graduating, and I need **a** smaller apartment. Are there **any** small apartments for rent in your building?
M. There's one.
S. What floor is it on?
M. It's on **the** third floor.
S. Does it have **a** bedroom?
M. No. It's **a** studio apartment. It has **a** living room and **a** kitchen.
S. Is **the** living room big?
M. So-so.
S. Does **the** kitchen have **a** stove and **a** refrigerator?
M. Yes. **The** refrigerator is old, but it works well. **The** stove is pretty new.
S. When can I see **the** apartment?
M. **The** janitor can show it to you tomorrow at 9 a.m.

3.8 Articles and Quantity Words

SINGULAR:

Indefinite	Definite	Explanation
I live in **a** big building.	**The** building is near the college.	We introduce a singular noun with the indefinite articles (*a* or *an*). When we refer to this noun again, we use the definite article *the*.
There's **a** janitor in the building.	**The** janitor lives on the first floor.	
	May I speak to **the** landlord? He lives on **the** third floor. **The** basement is dirty.	We use *the* before a singular noun if this noun is the only one or if the speaker and listener share an experience and are referring to the same one. (In this case, they are talking about the same building.)

(continued)

Indefinite	Definite	Explanation
My building has **(some)** washing machines. Are there **(any)** dryers?	**The** washing machines are in the basement. Where are **the** dryers?	We introduce a plural noun with *some*, *any*, or no article. When we refer to this noun again, we use the definite article *the*.
	The tenants are angry. **The** washing machines don't work.	We use *the* before a plural noun if the speaker and the listener share the same experience. (In this case, they are talking about the same building.)

EXERCISE 20 These are conversations between two students. Fill in the blanks with *the, a, an, some,* or *any*.

Conversation 1

A. Is there _____*a*_____ copy machine in our library?
    (example)

B. Yes. There are several copy machines in ____*the*____ library.
    (1)

A. Are ~~were any~~ *the* copy machines free?
    (2)

B. No. You need to use ____*a*____ nickel[10] for ____*the*____ copy ma-
    (3)   *(4)*
    chines.

Conversation 2

A. Is there ____*a*____ cafeteria at this school?
    (1)

B. Yes, there is.

A. Where's ____*the*____ cafeteria?
    (2)

B. It's on ____*the*____ first floor.
    (3)

A. Are there ____*a*____ snack machines in ____*the*____ cafeteria?
    (4)   *(5)*

B. Yes, there are.

A. I want to buy ____*a*____ soft drink.
    (6)

B. ____*The*____ soft-drink machine is out of order today.
    (7)

[10] A *nickel* is a five-cent coin.

Conversation 3

A. Is there ___a___ bookstore for this college?
   (1)

B. Yes, there is.

A. Where is ___the___ bookstore?
   (2)

B. It's on Green Street.

A. I need to buy ___a___ dictionary.
   (3)

B. Today is ___a___ holiday. ___the___ bookstore is closed today.
   (4)   (5)

SUMMARY OF LESSON 3

1. Singular and Plural
   boy—boys
   box—boxes
   story—stories
   (Exceptions: men, women, people, children, feet, teeth)

2. *There + be*
   There's an empty apartment in my building.
   There are two washing machines in the basement.
   Are there any parking spaces?

3. Articles

   - To make a generalization:
     Singular   **A dog** has good hearing.
     Plural   **Dogs** have good hearing.
                I like **dogs**.

   - To introduce a new noun into the conversation:
     Singular   I have **a dog**.
     Plural   I have **(some) turtles**.
                 I don't have **(any) birds**.

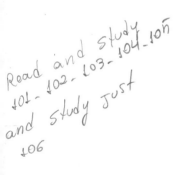

turtle

   - To talk about a previously mentioned noun:
     Singular   I have a dog. **The dog** barks when the letter carrier arrives.
     Plural   I have some turtles. I keep **the turtles** in the bathroom.

   - To talk about specific items or people from our experience:
     Singular   **The janitor** cleans the basement once a week.
     Plural   **The tenants** have to take out their own **garbage**.

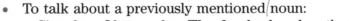

   - To talk about the only one:
     The President lives in Washington, D.C.
     The Statue of Liberty is in New York.

Singular and Plural; Articles and Quantity Words; *There + Be + Noun*

1. *People* is a plural noun. Use a plural verb form.

   People in my country ~~is~~ *are* very poor.

2. Don't use *the* with a generalization.

   ~~The~~ *D* dogs are friendly animals.

3. Don't confuse *there* with *they're*.

   I have two brothers. ~~There~~ *They're* in Florida.

4. Don't forget to use *there + is/are* to introduce a new subject.

   In my class *there are* ^ five students from Haiti.

5. Don't confuse *it's* and *there's*.

   ~~It's~~ *There's* a closet in my bedroom.

6. Don't confuse *have* and *there*.

   ~~Have~~ *There's* a closet in my bedroom.

7. Don't use *the + a* unique noun after *there*.

   ~~There's~~ *T* the Golden Gate Bridge *is* ^ in California.

8. Don't use *the* with the first mention of a noun when you and the listener do not share a common experience with this noun.

   I have ~~the~~ *a* new watch.

9. Don't use an apostrophe for a plural ending.

   She has three ~~brother's~~ *brothers*.

PART 1

A woman is showing her new apartment to her friend. Find the mistakes with the underlined words in this conversation and correct them. If the sentence is correct, write C.

A. Let me show you around my new apartment.

B. It's a big apartment.   **C**

A. It's big enough for my family. ~~They're~~ *There* are four bedrooms and two bathrooms. Has each bedroom a large closet. Let me show you my kitchen too.

X B. Oh. ~~It's a~~ *There is* (1) new dishwasher in your kitchen.

C A. It's wonderful. You know how I hate to wash dishes. (2)

C B. Is there a microwave oven? (3)

C A. No, there isn't, unfortunately. (4)

X B. ~~Are~~ *Are there any* (5) any washers and dryers for clothes? (5)

X A. Oh, yes. They're in the basement. In the laundry room ~~are~~ *there are* five washers and (6) (7) (8)
five dryers. I never have to wait.

X B. ~~There are~~ *Are there* a lot of people in your building? (9)

A. ~~In my building~~ thirty apartments. *In my buidiing there are thirty apartamentes.* (10)

B. *Is there* ~~Is~~ a janitor in your building? (11)

C A. Yes. There's a very good janitor. He keeps the building very clean. (12)

B. I suppose this apartment costs a lot.

C A. Well, yes. The rent is high. But I share the apartment with my cousins. (13)

PART 2

Write the plural form for each noun.

box ___boxes___   month ___months___   child ___children___

card ___cards___   match ___matches___   desk ___desks___

foot ___feet___   shelf ___shelves___   key ___keys___

potato ___potatoes___   radio ___radios___   story ___stories___

woman ___women___   mouse ___mice___   bus ___buses___

change f (next to month/shelf)

Fill in the blanks with *there, is, are, it,* or *they* or a combination of more than one of these words.

A. _Are there_ (example) any museums in Chicago?

B. Yes, _There are_ (1) a lot of museums in Chicago.

A. _Is there_ (2) a history museum in Chicago?

B. Yes, _there_ (3) is.

A. Where _is_ (4) the history museum?

B. _It's_ (5) near downtown.

A. _Are there_ (6) any mummies in this museum?

B. Yes, there are. _They are_ (7) from Egypt.

A. _Is there_ (8) a dinosaur in this museum?

B. Yes, there is. _It's_ (9) on the first floor.

A. How many floors _are there_ (10) in this museum?

B. _There are_ (11) two floors and a basement.

A. _Is there_ (12) a parking lot near this museum?

B. Yes, _there is_ (13), but _it's_ (14) not very big.

PART 4

Fill in the blanks with *the, a, an, some, any,* or *X* for no article.

A. Do you like your apartment?

B. No, I don't.

A. Why not?

B. There are many reasons. First, I don't like _the_ (example) janitor. He's impolite.

A. Anything else?

B. I want to get _a_ (1) dog.

A. So?

B. It's not permitted. _The_ (2) landlord says that _the_ (3) dogs make a lot of noise.

A. Can you get _a_ (4) cat?

B. Yes, but I don't like ~~every~~ ✗ cats.

(5)

A. Is your building quiet?

B. No. There are ___Some___ children in ___the___ building. When I try to

(6)   (7)

study, I can hear ___the___ children in the next apartment. They watch

(8)

TV all the time.

A. You need to find ___a___ new apartment.

(9)

B. I think you're right.

EXPANSION ACTIVITIES

CLASSROOM ACTIVITIES

1. Make a list of things you have, things you don't have but would like to have, and things you don't need. Choose from the list below and add any other items you can think of. Then find a partner and compare lists.

a computer	a house	a credit card
a VCR	a diamond ring	a speakerphone
a digital camera	a scale	a cell phone
an encyclopedia	an electric can opener	an orange juice squeezer
a pager	a microwave oven	a letter opener
an electric toothbrush	a waterbed	a blow dryer
a CD player		

I have:	I don't have, but would like to have:	I don't need:
a CD player a credit card a cell phone a computer	a digital camera a house a microwave oven learn good english lot money a Mercedes	a blow dryer an encyclopedia

a nice house
a nice girl.

Discuss your chart with a partner. Tell why you need or don't need some things. Tell why you want some things that you don't have.

2. People often use the newspaper to look for an apartment. The Sunday newspaper has the most ads. Bring in a copy of the Sunday newspaper. Look at the section of the newspaper that has apartments for rent. Ask the teacher to help you understand the abbreviations.

3. What other sections are there in the Sunday newspaper? Work with a partner and make a list of everything you can find in the Sunday paper.

There's a TV schedule for this week's programs.
There are a lot of ads and coupons.
There's a crossword puzzle.

4. Look at the information about two apartments for rent below. What are some of the advantages and disadvantages of each one? Discuss your answers with a partner or with the entire class.

Apartment 1	Apartment 2
a view of a park	on a busy street
rent = $750	rent = $650
fifth floor (an elevator in the building)	third floor walk-up
a new kitchen with a dishwasher	old appliances in the kitchen
pets not allowed	pets allowed
hardwood floors	a carpet in the living room
the janitor lives in the building	the owner lives in the building on the first floor
management controls the heat	the tenant controls the heat
no air conditioners	air conditioners in the bedroom and living room
faces north only	faces east, south, and west
a one-year lease	no lease
a large building—50 apartments	a small building—6 apartments
washers and dryers on each floor	a laundry room in the basement
parking spaces on first-come, first-served basis	a parking space for each tenant

5. Do you have a picture of your house, apartment, or apartment building? Bring it to class and tell about it.

6. Find a partner and pretend that one of you is looking for an apartment and the other person is the landlady, landlord, or manager. Ask and answer questions about the apartment, the building, parking, laundry, and rent. Write your conversation. Then read it to the class.

7. One student thinks of the name of a place (a zoo, a museum, downtown, the school cafeteria, a parking lot, a park, the public library, etc.) He or she writes the name of this place on a piece of paper. Other students try to guess this place by asking questions. You get ten guesses.

Sample Questions:

Are there a lot of people in this place?
Are there any pictures in this place?
Is it indoors or outdoors?

8. A student thinks of a word or phrase and writes blanks for each letter on the chalkboard. The other students try to guess the word by asking: "Is there a(n) _____ in this word?" If someone guesses a correct letter, the student at the chalkboard fills in the blank. The object of the game is to guess the word or phrase.

DISCUSSIONS

In a small group or with the entire class, discuss the following:

1. How do people rent apartments in your hometown? Is rent high? Is heat usually included in the rent? Does the landlord usually live in the building?

2. What are some differences between a typical apartment in this city and a typical apartment in your hometown?

WRITING

1. Write a description of a room or place that you like very much. (Review prepositions in Lesson One.)

EXAMPLE:

> My favorite place is my living room. There are many pictures on the walls. There's a picture of my grandparents behind the sofa. There are a lot of pictures of my children on the wall next to the sofa.
> There's a TV in the corner. Under the TV there is a VCR. There's a box of videocassettes next to the VCR. . . .

2. Write a comparison of your apartment in this city and your apartment or house in your hometown.

EXAMPLE:

> There are many differences between my apartment here and my apartment in Kiev, Ukraine. In my Kiev apartment, there is a door on every room. In my apartment here, only the bedrooms have doors. In my Kiev apartment, there is a small window inside each large window. In the winter, I can open this small window to get some fresh air. My apartment here doesn't have this small window. I have to open the whole window to get air. Sometimes the room becomes too cold. . . .

Internet Activity

Use the Internet to look for apartments for rent and houses for sale in this city (or nearby suburbs). What parts of this city or the suburbs have the highest rents and housing prices?

Lesson Four

GRAMMAR

Frequency Words with the Simple Present Tense
Prepositions of Time

CONTEXT

Three Special Days

LESSON FOCUS

Frequency words, such as *always, usually, never*, tell
how often we repeat an activity.

I *usually* drink coffee with breakfast.
I *never* drink coffee at night.

Prepositions of time, such as *in, on, at*, tell when an
activity takes place.

I work *on* Saturday.
My birthday is *in* June.

Before You Read

1. What is your favorite holiday? When is it?
2. Do you celebrate Mother's Day? When?
3. Do you send cards for special occasions?

Read the following article. Pay special attention to the frequency words.

Three Special Days

Valentine's Day is a day of love. It is **always** on February 14. On this day, men **often** give flowers or candy to their wives or girlfriends. Candy manufacturers make candy or candy boxes in the shape of a heart. Sweethearts **often** give each other gifts. People **sometimes** send cards, called valentines, to close friends and relatives. A valentine **usually** has a red heart and a message of love. It **often** has a picture of Cupid, a symbol of romantic love. Young children **usually** have a party at school and exchange cards.

Another special day is Saint Patrick's Day. It is **always** on March 17. It is really an Irish holiday, but many Americans like St. Patrick's Day even if they are not Irish. We **sometimes** say that on St. Patrick's Day everybody is Irish. In New York City, there is **always** a parade on St. Patrick's Day. People **often** wear green clothes on this day. One symbol of St. Patrick's Day is the shamrock.

Businesses are **never** closed for Valentine's Day or St. Patrick's Day. People **never** take a day off from work for these days. Schools and government offices are **always** open (except if these days fall on a Sunday).

Another special day is Mother's Day. It is **always** in May, but it isn't **always** on the same date. It is **always** on the second Sunday in May. People **usually** buy presents for their mothers and grandmothers or send special cards. Families **often** have dinner in a restaurant.

People enjoy these holidays. Greeting card companies also enjoy these holidays. They **always** sell a lot of cards and make a lot of money at these times.

Did you know...?

Valentine's Day began in ancient Rome to honor Juno, the Roman goddess of women and marriage.

4.1 Frequency Words with the Simple Present Tense

Frequency Word	Frequency	Examples
Always ~sempre~	100%	Mother's Day is **always** in May.
Usually ~usualmete~		I **usually** take my mother out to dinner.
Often ~frequéntemente~		People **often** wear green on St. Patrick's Day.
Sometimes ~de vez em quanto~		I **sometimes** watch the parade.
Rarely/Seldom ~raramente~		We **rarely** give flowers to children.
Never ~nunca~	0%	Businesses are **never** closed for Valentine's Day.

mothers burtday

EXERCISE 1   Choose the correct word to fill in the blanks.

EXAMPLE: Husbands ___*often*___ give flowers or candy to their wives on Valen-
                    (never, seldom, often)
tine's Day.

1. Valentine's Day is ___*always*___ on February 14.
   (always, sometimes, never)

2. People ___*often*___ send valentine cards to their sweethearts.
   (rarely, often, never)

3. A valentine card ___*usually*___ has a red heart and a message of
   (never, rarely, usually)
   love.

4. Young children ___*never*___ have a Valentine's Day party at *partido*
   (usually, always, never)
   school.

5. Saint Patrick's Day is ___*always*___ on March 17.
   (always, sometimes, never)

6. A St. Patrick's Day card ___*never*___ has a red heart.
   (always, usually, never)

7. In New York City, there is ~seldom~ *always* a parade on Saint
   (always, seldom, never)
   Patrick's Day.

8. Card companies ___*always*___ do a lot of business before holidays.
   (never, always, seldom)

9. Businesses are ___*never*___ closed for St. Patrick's Day and
   (always, usually, never)
   Valentine's Day.

Is mother's day always in May?

10. Mother's Day is __always__ in May.
    (always, usually, never)

11. Mother's Day is __never__ on a Saturday in the U.S.
    (always, never, sometimes)

4.2 Position of Frequency Words

Subject	Frequency Word	Verb	Complement
I	**usually**	buy	a card for my mother.
People	**never**	take	the day off for St. Patrick's Day.

Subject	*Be*	Frequency Word	Complement
Businesses	are	**never**	closed for St. Patrick's Day.
Mother's Day	is	**always**	in May.

LANGUAGE NOTES

1. Frequency words come after the verb *be* but before other main verbs.
2. The following words can also come at the beginning of a sentence: *usually, often, sometimes.*
   Stores are *usually* open on Mother's Day.
   Usually stores are open on Mother's Day.
   A valentine *often* has a red heart.
   Often a valentine has a red heart.

EXERCISE 2 Add a frequency word to each sentence to make a **true** statement about yourself.

EXAMPLE: I eat fish.
I usually eat fish on Fridays.

1. I cook the meals in my house.
   Refeição
   I always cook the meals in my house. I usually the meals in my house.
2. I stay home on Sundays.
   I never stay home on sundays.
+ 3. I buy the Sunday newspaper.
   I always buy the sunday newspaper.
4. I read the newspaper in English.
   I always read the newspaper in English.
5. I use public transportation.
   I never use public transportation.
6. I'm tired in class.
   I never tired in class.

7. I use my dictionary to check my spelling.

I never use my dictionary to check my spelling.

8. I buy greeting cards.

I always by greeting cards.

EXERCISE 3 Add a verb (phrase) to make a **true** statement about people from your country or cultural group.

EXAMPLE: people/often

Russian people often go to the forest on the weekends to pick mushrooms.

1. people/often

   frequent.

   Brazilian people often read newspaper.

2. people/seldom

   Brazilian people seldom are unpolite.

3. women/usually

   Brazilian women usually like go to the beach.

4. women/rarely

   American women rarely eat Brazilian food.

5. men/usually

   Brazilian men usually play soccer.

6. men/rarely

   Brazilian men rarely like play golf.

EXERCISE 4 Add a verb phrase to make a **true** statement about yourself.

EXAMPLE: I/never

I never go to bed after 11 o'clock.

OR

I'm never in a good mood in the morning.

1. I/never

   I never forget 9-11-2001.

2. I/always/in the morning

   I always eat my breakfast in the morning.

3. I/usually/on Sunday

I usually wak up later on sunday.

4. I/often/on the weekend

I often go in the church on the weekend.

5. I/seldom

I seldom clean my car.

6. I/sometimes/in class

I sometimes can't be in class.

EXERCISE 5 Use the words given below to write a sentence about your impressions of Americans. Discuss your answers in a small group or with the entire class.

1. Americans/rarely

Americans rarely like to play soccer.

2. Americans/often

Americans often drink protein.

4.3 Yes/No Questions with *Ever*

Do/Does	Subject	Ever	Main Verb	Complement	Short Answer
Do	you	**ever**	celebrate	Mother's Day?	Yes, I always do.
Does	your father	**ever**	cook	the meals?	No, he never does.

Be	Subject	Ever		Complement	Short Answer
Is	Mother's Day	**ever**		on a Sunday?	Yes, it always is.
Are	you	**ever**		bored in class?	No, I never am.

LANGUAGE NOTES

1. We use *ever* in a *yes/no* question when we want an answer that has a frequency word.
2. In a short answer, the frequency word comes between the subject and the verb.
3. The verb after *never* is affirmative. We do not put two negatives together.
   Is Mother's Day ever on a Saturday?
   No, it never *is*.

4. We can give a short *yes* or *no* answer with just the frequency word.
    Do you *ever* buy your mother a present for Mother's Day?
    Yes, *always*.
    Is St. Patrick's Day *ever* on a Sunday?
    Yes, *sometimes*.

EXERCISE 6 Add *ever* to ask these questions. Another student will answer.

EXAMPLES: Do you eat in a restaurant?
    A. Do you ever eat in a restaurant?
    B. Yes, I often do. OR Yes, often.

    Do you ever ask for directions on the street?
    Yes, sometimes

    Are you bored in class?
    A. Are you ever bored in class?
    B No, I never am. OR No, never.

    Are you ever late to class?

1. Do you use public transportation?   *ou ever use public transportation? No, I never do.*
2. Do you drink coffee at night?   *ever drink coffe at night? No, I never do.*
3. Do you drink tea in the morning?   *ever drink tea in the morning? Yes, I always do*
4. Do you speak English at home?   *u ever speak English at home? Yes sometimes.*
5. Do you watch TV at night?   *u ever watch tv at night? Yes, I usually.*
6. Do you rent videos?   *you ever rent videos? Yes, sometimes.*

7. Are you late to class?   *No, I never am.*
8. Do you ask for directions on the street?
9. Are you homesick?   *Are you ever homesick? No I never am.*
10. Are you lazy on Saturdays?   *Are you lazy on saturdays. Yes sometimes*
11. Does it snow in March?   *Does it ever snow in March. Yes, it sometimes does.*

EXERCISE 7 Add *ever* to these questions to ask about Americans. Another student will answer.

EXAMPLES: Do Americans eat fast food?
    A. Do Americans ever eat fast food?
    B. Yes, they sometimes do.

    Are Americans friendly to you?
    A. Are Americans ever friendly to you?
    B. Yes, they usually are.

1. Do Americans eat with chopsticks?

2. Do Americans carry radios?

3. Do Americans say "Have a nice day"?

4. Do Americans kiss when they meet?

5. Do Americans shake hands when they meet?

6. Are Americans impolite to you?

---

7. Do Americans pronounce your name incorrectly?

8. Do Americans ask you what country you're from?

9. Are Americans curious about your country?

EXERCISE **8**   Fill in the blanks with a frequency word to make a statement about yourself. Then ask a question with *ever*. Another student will answer.

EXAMPLE: I _____never_____ jog in the morning.
A. Do you ever jog in the morning?
B. No, I never do.

1. I _always_ ride a bike in the summer.
   Do you ever ride a bike in the summer? Yes, I always do.
2. I _always_ visit relatives on Sunday.
   Do you ever visit relatives on sunday? Yes, I always do.
3. I _never_ go to sleep before 9 p.m.
   Do you ever go to sleep before 9 p.m.? No, I never do.
4. (Women: Do A. Men: Do B.)

   A. I _usually_ wear high heels. *Do you ever wear high heels*

   B. I _usually_ wear a suit and tie. *Do you ever wear suit and t*

5. I _always_ do exercises. *Do you ever do exercises?*

6. I _always_ eat meat. *Do you ever eat meat?*

7. I _sometime_ drink colas. *Do you ever drink colas.?*

8. I _usually_ buy the Sunday newspaper. *Do you ever buy the sunday newspaper*

9. I _never_ put sugar in my coffee. *Do you ever put sugar in yo coffee.*

10. I _always_ take a nap in the afternoon.
    Do you ever take a nap in the afternoon.

11. I _sometimes_ eat in a restaurant.
    Do you ever eat in a restaurant?

12. I _sometimes_ use a fax machine.
    Do you ever use a fax machine?

13. I _never_ bake bread. *Do you ever bake bread.?*

14. I _always_ use cologne or perfume.
    Do you ever use cologne or perfume.

15. I _sometimes_ take a bubble bath.
    Do you ever take a bubble bath?

bubble bath

4.4 Frequency Expressions and Questions with *How Often*

How Often	Do/Does	Subject	Verb	Complement	Answer
How often	do	you	visit	your mother?	Once a week.
How often	does	the mail	come?		Every day.

LANGUAGE NOTES

1. We ask a question with *how often* when we want to know the frequency of an activity.
2. Expressions that show frequency are these:
    every day (week, month, year)
    every other day (week, month, year)
    from time to time
    once in a while
3. Frequency expressions can come at the beginning of a sentence or at the end of a sentence.
    I learn more about Americans *every day.*
    Every day I learn more about Americans.
    From time to time, I look up words in my dictionary.
    I look up words in my dictionary *from time to time.*

EXERCISE 9 Ask a question with "How often do you . . . ?" and the words given. Another student will answer.

EXAMPLE: get a haircut
A. How often do you get a haircut?
B. I get a haircut every other month.

1. come to class
2. shop for groceries
3. wash your clothes
4. call long distance to your country
5. go out to dinner

6. use public transportation
7. renew your driver's license
8. buy the newspaper
9. go to the movies

EXERCISE 10 Linda has a list to remind her of the things she has to do on a regular basis. Write questions and answers about her activities.

- drive daughter to ballet lessons - Tu, Th
- pick up son at baseball practice - Mon, Wed
- shop for groceries - Sat
- take the dog for a haircut - 3rd day of every month
- go to the beauty salon - 5th day of every month
- visit Mom - Fri
- go to the gym - Mon, Wed, Fri morning
- prepare the kids' lunches - Mon to Fri
- change oil in car - Jan, April, July, Oct

EXAMPLE:

How often does she drive her daughter to ballet practice?

She drives her daughter to ballet practice twice a week.

1. How often does she pick up her son at baseball pract
   She picks up her son at baseball pratice twice a

2. How often does she shop for groceries?
   She shops for groceries at Saturday.

3. How often does she take the dog for a haircut?
   She takes the dog for haircut on the 3rd day of every m

4. How often does she go to the beauty salon?
   She goes to the beauty salon on the fifth day of every mo

5. How often does

6. How often does she go to the gym?
   She goes to the gym tree times at week.

7. How often does she prepare the kids' lunches
   She prepares the kids' lunches five times a

8. How often does she chenge oil in car?
   She changes oil in car the first 4th 7th 10th
   months of the year for times a year.

EXERCISE 11 Write a few sentences about a member of your family or another person you know. Use frequency words.

EXAMPLE: My sister never helps with the housework.

She always gets good grades.

She sometimes leaves dirty dishes in the sink.

My brother never cleans his car.

He goes shopping for groceries every Mon.

He goes to the church every

saturday morning.

EXERCISE 12 Use the words in parentheses ( ) to complete this conversation. Put the words in the correct order. Use the correct form of the verb.

A. Let's go to a movie tonight.

B. I can't. My mother _____*always makes*_____ dinner for me on Fridays.
 (example: make/always)

If I don't visit her, she _____usually complains_____. And if I don't call her,
 (1 complain/usually)

she worries.

A. _____How often do you call_____ her?
 (2 how/often/you/call)

B. _____I every day call to her_____ .
 (3 I/every day/call her)

A. Why do you call her so often?

B. She's old now, and she _____often be_____ lonely.
 (4 often/be)

A. Well, invite your mother to go to the movies.

B. Thanks, but she has a favorite TV show on Friday nights.

She _____always watchs_____ it.
 (5 watch/always)

A. _____Does she ever_____ go out?
 (6 ever/she)

B. She _____raraly does_____. She prefers to stay home.
 (7 rarely/do)
She likes to cook, knit, and watch TV.

A. Is she a good cook?   knit

B. Not really. She _usually cooks_ the same thing every week:
(8 usually/cook)
chicken on Friday, fish on Saturday, meatloaf on Sunday. . . . Her
routine _never changes_. Only Mother's Day is different.
(9 change/never)

A. What _do you usually do_ on Mother's Day?
(10 you/do/usually)

B. My sister and I _usually buy_ her flowers and take her to
(11 usually/buy)
a restaurant.

A. Does she like that?

B. Not really. She _usually says_, "Don't waste your money.
(12 usually/say)
Flowers _always dies_ in a day or two. And my cooking is
(13 die/always)
better than restaurant food."

A. _Is she always_ hard to please?
(14 be/she/always)

B. Yes, she is.

A. _Is she ever_ satisfied?
(15 be/she/ever)

B. Not usually. She _always says_, "I don't want Mother's Day
(16 always/say)
once a year. I want it every day."

EXERCISE 13 Read this student's composition about his teacher. Find the mistakes with the underlined words and correct them. Add the verb *be* where necessary. If the underlined words are correct, write C.

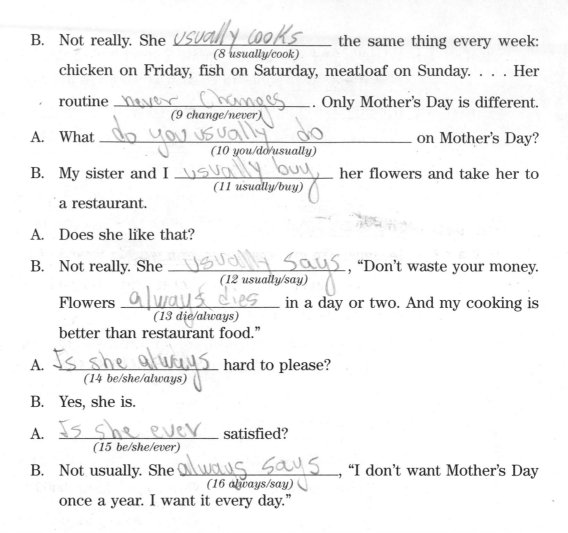

My English teacher ~~is~~ Barbara Nowak. She ~~teach~~ *teaches* grammar and composition at City College. She ^is very nice, but she's very strict. She ~~give~~ *gives* a lot of homework, and we take a lot of tests. If I pass the test, I *am* very happy. English's *is* hard for me.

Every day, at the beginning of the class, she takes attendance and we hand in our homework. Then she explains the grammar. We do exercises in the book. The book have *has* a lot of exercises. Most exercises is *are* easy, but some are hard. Sometimes we say the answers out loud, but sometimes we write the answers. Sometimes the teacher asks a student to write the answers on the chalkboard.

He or she

The students like Barbara because she ~~make~~ *makes* the class interesting.
She ~~brings often~~ *She often brings* songs to class, and we learn the words. Sometimes we
watch a movie in class. ~~Always I~~ *I always.* enjoy her lessons.

After class I sometimes ~~going~~ to her office if I want more help. She *is*
very kind and always ~~try~~ *tries* to help me.

Barbara dresses very informally. Sometimes she wears a skirt, but
~~she wears usually~~ *She usually wears.* jeans. She about 35 years old, but ~~she's~~ looks like a
teenager. (In my country, ~~never a teacher wear~~ *a teacher never* jeans.)

I very happy with my teacher. She understand the problems of a
foreigner because she's also a foreigner. ~~She's~~ comes from Poland, but
she speaks English very well. She know it's hard to learn another language.

4.5 Prepositions of Time

Preposition	Example

On: days and dates	When do you go to church?
	   On Sundays.
	When do Americans celebrate Independence Day?
	   On July 4.

In: months	When do Americans celebrate Mother's Day? **In** May.
In: years	When do Americans vote for President? **In** 2000, 2004, 2008, and so on.

At: specific time of day	What time do you eat lunch?
	   At noon.
	What time does the class start?
	   At 8 o'clock.
	What time do you go to bed?
	   At midnight.

In the morning
In the afternoon
In the evening
	When do you work?
	   In the morning.
	When do you go to school?
	   In the evening.

At night	When do you call your family? **At** night.

(continued)

Preposition	Example
In: seasons	When do we have vacation? **In** the summer.
From . . . to: a beginning and ending time	What hours do they work? **From** nine **to** five.

EXERCISE 14 Answer these questions. Use the correct preposition.

1. When do you get up in the morning?
   At 5:7 ~~o'clock~~ am.

2. What time does your English class begin?
   ~~From~~ It begin 7.30 at 9.30

3. What days does your English class meet?
   On thusday an thurday.

4. When is your birthday?
   It's May

5. What time do you go to bed?
   At 10:30 PM.

6. When do Americans celebrate Labor Day?
   They celebrate it in sepentember.

7. When do students in your country have vacation?
   They have vacation in december.

8. When is Valentine's Day?
   It's in febuary.

9. When is Mother's Day in the U.S.?
   The Mother's Day it's in may.

10. When is Mother's Day in your country?
    The Mother's Day in my country is in may-

SUMMARY OF LESSON 4

1. Frequency Words:

Most Frequent	always	100%
↑	usually	↑
	often	
	sometimes	
↓	rarely/seldom	↓
Least Frequent	never	0%

2. The Position of Frequency Words:

AFTER THE VERB *BE*: He is **always** late.

BEFORE A MAIN VERB: I **usually** walk to work.

3. The Position of Frequency Expressions:
    Every day I watch TV.
    I watch TV **every day**.

4. Frequency Questions and Answers:
    Do you **ever** wear a suit and tie? I seldom do.
    Are you **ever** bored in class? Yes, sometimes.
    How often do you go to the library? About once a month.

5. Review prepositions of time on pages 121–122. Review the simple present tense in Lessons 1 and 2.

EDITING ADVICE

1. Put the frequency word in the correct place.

    am never
    I ~~never am~~ bored in class.

    I always
    ~~Always I~~ drink coffee in the morning.

Do you
ever go

2. Don't separate the subject and the verb with a frequency phrase.

    once in a while
    She ~~once in a while~~ visits her grandmother.

    Every other day we
    ~~We every other day~~ write a composition.

3. Don't use a negative verb with *never*.

    do
    Do you ever take the bus to school? No, I never ~~don't~~.

    We never ~~don't~~ eat in class.

4. Use *ever* in questions. Answer the question with a frequency word.

    sometimes
    Do you ever listen to the radio in the morning? Yes, I ~~ever~~ do.

LESSON 4 TEST / REVIEW

PART 1

Find the mistakes with the underlined words, and correct them (including mistakes with word order). Not every sentence has a mistake. If the sentence is correct, write **C**.

EXAMPLES: Do you ever drink coffee? No, I never ~~don't~~. *(do)*

I never eat spaghetti.   **C**

---

1. Always I give my mother a present for Mother's Day.
   I always give my mother a presente for Mother's Day

c 2. I rarely go downtown.

c 3. They never are on time.

4. It snows seldom in April.
   It seldom snows in April.

5. Do you ever take the bus? ~~Yes, I never do.~~ *Yes, I always do.*

6. Are you ever late to class? ~~Yes, always I am.~~ *Yes, I always do.*

7. Do you ever use chopsticks? ~~Yes, I ever do.~~ *Yes, I always do.*

8. What often do you go to the library? I go to the library twice a month.
   How often do you go to the library? I go to the library

9. I once in a while eat in a restaurant.
   I eat in a restaurant once in a while.

10. Every other day she cooks chicken.
    She cooks chicken every other day.

PART 2

This is a conversation between two students. Fill in the blanks to complete the conversation.

A. Who _____*is*_____ your English teacher?
   (example)

B. His name _____*is*_____ David.
   (1)

A. _____*Do you like*_____ David?
   (2)

B. Yes. I like him very much.

A. _____*Does*_____ he wear a suit to class?
   (3)

B. No, he _____*doesn't*_____. He always _____*wears*_____ jeans
   (4)   *(5)*
   and running shoes.

✱ A. *How ~~are is him~~ old is he?* _____?
   (6)

B. He _____*is*_____ about 60 years old.
   (7)

A. _____*Does he speak*_____ your language?
   (8)

B. No, he doesn't speak Spanish, but he _____*speaks*_____ Polish and
   (9)
   Russian. And English, of course.

A. _____*How often*_____ does your class meet?
   (10)

B. It meets three days a week: Monday, Wednesday, and Friday.

A. My class _____*don't meet*_____ two days a week: Tuesday and Thursday.
   (11)

B. Tell me about your English teacher.

A. Her name _____is_____ (12) Dr. Misko. She never _____wears_____ (13) jeans to class. She _____always_____ (14) wears a dress or suit. She _____doesn't espeak_____ (15) my language. She only _____speaks_____ (16) English.

B. Do you like her?

A. Yes, but she _____gives_____ (17) a lot of homework and tests.

B. _____How often_____ (18) does she give a test?

A. Once a week. She gives a test every Friday. I _____don't_____ (19) like tests.

B. My teacher sometimes teaches us American songs. _____Does_____ (20) your teacher _____sometimes_____ (21) _____teache_____ (22) you American songs?

A. No, she never _____does_____ (23).

B. What book _____your class uses_____ (24)?

A. My class uses *Grammar in Context*.

B. What _____does context meas_____ (25)?

A. "Context" means the words that help you understand a new word or idea.

B. How _____do you spell context?_____ (26)

A. C-O-N-T-E-X-T.

PART 3   Fill in the blanks with the correct preposition.

EXAMPLE: Many people go to church _____on_____ Sundays.

1. We have classes _____in_____ the evening.

2. Valentine's Day is _____in_____ February.

3. Valentine's Day is _____on_____ February 14.

4. A news program begins _____at_____ 6 o'clock.

5. I watch TV _____at_____ night.

6. We have vacation ___in___ the summer.

7. Many Americans work ___from___ 9 ___to___ 5 o'clock.

8. I drink coffee ___in___ the morning.

9. I study ___in___ the afternoon.

EXPANSION ACTIVITIES

CLASSROOM ACTIVITIES

1. Find a partner. Interview your partner about one of his or her teachers, friends, or relatives. Ask about this person's usual activities.

EXAMPLE:
A. What's your math teacher's name?
B. Her name is Kathy Carlson.
A. Does she give a lot of homework?
B. No, she doesn't.
A. What does she usually wear to class?
B. She usually wears a skirt and blouse.
A. Does she ever wear jeans to class?
B. No, she never does.

2. In a small group or with the entire class, use frequency words to talk about the activities of a famous person (the President, a singer, an actor, etc.).

EXAMPLE:
The President of the U.S. often meets with leaders of other countries.

3. Find a partner. Talk about a special holiday that you and your family celebrate. Ask your partner questions about the date of the holiday, food, clothing, preparations, activities, and so on.

EXAMPLE:
A. We celebrate the Lunar New Year.
B. Do you wear special clothes?
A. Yes, we do.
B. What kind of clothes do you wear?

4. Look at the list of Linda's activities on page 118. Write a list to remind yourself of things you do on a regular basis. Find a partner. Compare your list to your partner's list.

5. In the left column on the next page is a list of popular customs in the U.S. Do people in your native country or cultural group have similar customs? If so, put a check (✓) in Column A. If not, put a check in Column B. Discuss your answers in a group.

American Customs	A Similar custom in my native country or cultural group	B Completely different custom in my native country or cultural group
1. Americans often say, "Have a nice day."		
2. When someone sneezes, Americans usually say, "God bless you."		
3. Americans often ask, "How are you?" People usually reply, "I'm fine, thanks. How are you?"		
4. Americans rarely visit their friends without calling first.		
5. Americans are often in a hurry. They rarely have free time.		
6. Americans often eat popcorn in a movie theater.		
7. Americans often eat in fast-food restaurants.		
8. Americans often say "OK."		
9. Americans often wear shorts and sandals in the summer.		
10. Americans often listen to a personal stereo.		
11. When eating, Americans usually hold a fork in the right hand and a knife in the left hand.		
12. Banks in the U.S. often have a time/temperature sign.		
13. American restaurants usually have salt and pepper shakers on the table.		
14. When a radio or TV breaks down, Americans often buy a new one. They rarely try to repair it.		
15. Americans often send greeting cards to close friends and relatives for birthdays, anniversaries, holidays, and illnesses.		
16. The Sunday newspaper often has store coupons.		
17. There is a special day for sweethearts, like Valentine's Day.		

WRITING

1. Write about one of your teachers. Describe your teacher and tell about his or her classroom behavior and activities.

2. Write about a holiday that you celebrate. Tell how you celebrate this holiday, or write about how you celebrate your birthday or another special day.

OUTSIDE ACTIVITY

1. Ask an American to do Exercise 5. See how your answers compare to an American's answers. Report the American's answers to the class.

2. Go to a drug store, supermarket, or card store. Is there a special holiday at this time (for example, Father's Day, Thanksgiving, Christmas, Chanukah)? Read the messages in a few cards. Make a card for someone you know. Write your own message.

Internet Activities

1. Find a greeting card site on the Internet. Send an electronic greeting card to someone you know.

2. Using the Internet, find the answers to these questions:

    a. When is Father's Day in the U.S.?

    b. What is the origin of Mother's Day?

    c. When is Thanksgiving?

Lesson Five

GRAMMAR
Possession
Object Pronouns

CONTEXT
Names
William Madison's Name

LESSON FOCUS

Nouns have a *possessive* form.
> *Marilyn's* house is beautiful.
> *My parents'* car is new.

We can also use *possessive adjectives* to show possession or relationship.
> *Her* house is beautiful.
> *Their* car is new.

We can use *object pronouns* to substitute for object nouns.
> Do you live near your *parents*?
> Yes, I live near *them*.

129

1. What is your complete name? What do your friends call you?
2. Do you like your name?

Read the following article. Pay special attention to possessive forms.

Names

Americans usually have three names: a first name, a middle name, and a last name (or surname). For example: Marilyn Sue Ellis or Edward David Orleans. Some people use an initial when they sign **their** names: Marilyn S. Ellis, Edward D. Orleans. Not everyone has a middle name.

American women often change **their** last names when they get married. For example, if Marilyn Ellis marries Edward Orleans, her name becomes Marilyn Orleans. Not all women follow this custom. Sometimes a woman keeps **her** maiden name[1] and adds **her husband's** name, with or without a hyphen (-): For example, Marilyn Ellis-Orleans or Marilyn Ellis Orleans. Sometimes a woman does not use **her husband's** name at all. In this case, if the couple has children, they have to decide if **their** children will use **their father's** name, **their mother's** name, or both. A man does not usually change **his** name when he gets married.

Some people have **their mother's** last name as a middle name: John Fitzgerald Kennedy, Franklin Delano Roosevelt.[2]

Did you know...?

The five most common last names in the U.S. are Smith, Johnson, Williams, Jones, and Brown.

5.1 Possessive Form of Nouns

Noun	Ending	Examples
Singular noun: father mother	Add apostrophe + *s*	I use my **father's** last name. I don't use my **mother's** last name.
Plural noun ending in -*s*: parents boys	Add apostrophe only	My **parents'** names are Ethel and Herman. Ted and Mike are **boys'** names.

(continued)

[1] A *maiden name* is a woman's family name before she gets married.
[2] These are the names of two American presidents.

Noun	Ending	Examples
Irregular plural noun: children women	Add apostrophe + s	What are your **children's** names? Marilyn and Sandra are **women's** names.
Names that end in s: Mr. Harris Charles	Add apostrophe only OR Add apostrophe + s	Do you know **Charles'** wife? OR Do you know **Charles's** wife?

LANGUAGE NOTES

1. We use the possessive form for people and other living things.
   My *brother's* name is Joe.
   My *dog's* name is PeeWee.
2. For inanimate objects, we usually use "the _____ of _____."
   The door of the classroom is closed.
   Washington College is *the name of my school*.

EXERCISE 1 Fill in the blanks with the possessive form of a noun to make a **true** statement.

EXAMPLE I use my _____*father's*_____ last name.

1. I use my ___*father's*___ last name.

2. I don't use my ___*mother's*___ last name.

3. An American married woman often uses her ___*husband's*___ last name.

4. A married woman in my native culture uses her ___*husband's*___ last name.

5. An American single woman usually uses her ___*parents'*___ last name.

6. An American man rarely uses his ___*Mother's*___ last name.

7. John Kennedy had his ___*mother's*___ maiden name as a middle name.

Some of the following sentences can show possession with '*s* or '. Rewrite these sentences. Write "no change" for the others.

EXAMPLES: The teacher knows the names of the students.
The teacher knows the students' names.

The door of the classroom is usually closed.
No change.

1. The teacher always corrects the homework of the students.
   The teacher always corrects the students home~~~

2. The name of the textbook is *Grammar in Context*.
   No change :

3. The job of the teacher is to explain the grammar.
   The teacher's job is explain the grammar.

4. What are the names of your parents?
   What are your parent's names?

5. The color of the book is blue.
   No change

6. Do you use the last name of your father?
   Do you use your father's last name?

7. What is the name of your dog?
   What is your dog's name?

8. The names of my children are Jason and Jessica.
   My children's name are Jason and Jess~~~

5.2 Possessive Adjectives

Subject Pronouns	Possessive Adjectives	Examples
I	my	*I* like **my** name.
you	your	*You're* a new student. What's **your** name?
he	his	*He* likes **his** name.
she	her	*She* doesn't like **her** name.
it	its	Is this your dog? Is *it* friendly? What's **its** name?
we	our	*We* use **our** nicknames.
they	their	*They* are my friends. **Their** last name is Jackson.

LANGUAGE NOTES

1. Be careful not to confuse *his* and *her*.

   My mother lives in Chicago. *Her* brother lives in Las Vegas.

   My uncle speaks English well. *His* wife is American.

2. We can use a possessive adjective and a possessive noun together. We can use two (or more) possessive nouns together.

   My sister's name is Marilyn.

   My *sister's husband's* name is Edward.

EXERCISE 3 Fill in the blanks with the possessive adjective that relates to the subject.

EXAMPLE: I like _____my_____ teacher.

1. He loves _____his_____ mother.

2. She loves _____her_____ father.

3. A dog loves __~~his~~ its__ master.

4. Many American women change _____their_____ names when they get married.

5. Sometimes a woman keeps _____her_____ maiden name and adds _____her_____ husband's name.

6. American men don't usually change __~~his~~ their__ names when they get married.

7. Do you use _____your_____ father's last name?

8. I bring _____my_____ book to class.

9. We use _____our_____ books in class.

10. The teacher brings _____his_____ book to class.

11. Some students do _____their_____ homework in the library.

5.3 Questions with *Whose*

Whose + Noun	Auxiliary Verb	Subject	Verb	Answer
Whose name	do	you	use?	I use my **father's** last name.
Whose pen	does	she	need?	She needs **your** pen.
Whose book	is	that?		It's **Bob's** book.
Whose glasses	are	those?		They're **my** glasses.

132-136 -

Write a question with *whose* and the words given. Answer with the words in parentheses ( ).

EXAMPLES:

wife/that (Robert)

Whose wife is that? That's Robert's wife.

children/these (Robert)

Whose children are these? These are Robert's children.

1. office/this (the dean)

    Whose office is this? This is the dean's office.

2. offices/those (the teachers)

    Whose offices are those? Those are the teacher's offic[e]

3. dictionary/that (the teacher)

    Whose dictionary is that? That's the teacher's dictionar[y]

4. books/those (the students)

    Whose books are those? Those are the student's book[s]

5. car/that (my parents)

    Whose car is that? That's is my parents' car.

6. house/this (my cousin)

    Whose house is this? This is my cousin's house

7. papers/those (Mr. Ross)

    Whose papers are those? Those are Mr Ross' papa[rs]

8. diskettes/these (the programmer)

    Whose diskettes are these? These are the progra[mmer's] diskettes.

5.4 Possessive Pronouns

Examples	Explanation
You don't know my name. I know **yours**.	*Yours = your name*
Your name is easy for Americans. **Mine** is hard.	*Mine = my name*

LANGUAGE NOTES

1. When we use a possessive pronoun, we omit the noun. COMPARE:
    Her children have American names.
    My children have Spanish names. OR *Mine* have Spanish names.

2. Compare these three forms:

Subject Pronouns	Possessive Adjectives	Possessive Pronouns
I	my	mine
you	your	yours
he	his	his
she	her	hers
it	its	—
we	our	ours
they	their	theirs
who	whose	whose

3. After a possessive noun, we can omit the noun.
    Robert's wife speaks English, but *Peter's* doesn't.
    (*Peter's* = Peter's wife)

EXERCISE 5   In each sentence below, replace the underlined words with a possessive pronoun.

EXAMPLE: Your book is new. My book is old.
    Your book is new. Mine is old.

1. His name is Charles. Her name is Paula. Hers is Paula.

2. My car is old. Your car is new. Yours is new.

3. I like my English teacher. Does your brother like his English teacher?
    Does your brother like his?

4. I have my dictionary today. Do you have your dictionary?
    Do you have yours?

5. Please let me use your book. I don't have my book today.
    I don't have mine today.

6. Whose sweater is this? Whose sweater is that?
    Whose is that?

7. My parents' apartment is big. Our apartment is small.
    Ours is small.

8. My teacher comes from Houston. Paula's teacher comes from El Paso.
    Hers comes from El Paso.

Possession; Object Pronouns   **135**

5.5 The Subject and the Object

Examples	Explanation
S V O Bob likes Mary. We like movies.	The **subject** (S) comes before the verb (V). The **object** (O) comes after the verb. The object is a person or a thing.
S V O S V O Bob likes Mary because **she** helps **him**. SV O S V O I like movies because **they** entertain **me**.	We can use pronouns for the **subject** and the **object**.

Before You Read
1. What are common American names?
2. What is a very common first name in your country or native culture? *Maria*
   What is a very common last name? Is your name common in your *Santos,*
   country or native culture?

Read the following conversation. Pay special attention to object pronouns.

William Madison's Name

A. I have many questions about American names. Can you answer **them** for me?

B. Of course.

A. Tell **me** about your name.

B. My name is William, but my friends call **me** Bill.

A. Why do they call **you** Bill?

B. Bill is a common nickname for William.

A. Is William your first name?

B. Yes.

A. What's your full name?

B. William Michael Madison.

A. Do you ever use your middle name?

B. I only use **it** for very formal occasions. I sign my name William M. Madison, Jr. (junior).

A. What does "junior" mean?

B. It means that I have the same name as my father. His name is William Madison, Sr. (senior).

A. What's your wife's name?

B. Anna Marie Simms-Madison. I call **her** Annie.

A. Why does she have two last names?

B. Simms is her father's last name, and Madison is mine. She uses both names with a hyphen (-) between **them**.

A. Do you have any children?

B. Yes. We have a son and a daughter. Our son's name is Richard, but we call **him** Dick. Our daughter's name is Elizabeth, but everybody calls **her** Lizzy.

A. What do your children call **you**?

B. They call **us** Mommy and Daddy, of course.

5.6 Object Pronouns

Subject	Object	Examples: Subject	Verb	Object
I	me	You	love	me.
you	you	I	love	you.
he	him	She	loves	him.
she	her	He	loves	her.
it	it	We	love	it.
we	us	They	love	us.
they	them	We	love	them.

LANGUAGE NOTES

1. We can use an object pronoun to substitute for an object noun.
   I have *a middle name*. I use *it* when I sign my name.
   Richard is my son's name. We call *him* Dick.
   I have some *questions*. Can you answer *them* for me?
   My mother lives near me. I visit *her* once a week.

2. We use *them* for plural people and things.
   I have two brothers. You know *them*.
   I need my books. I use *them* in class.

3. An object pronoun can follow a preposition.
   I have two last names. I use both *of them*.
   My sister has a son. She always talks *about him*.

EXERCISE 6   Fill in the blanks. Substitute the underlined words with an object pronoun.

EXAMPLE: I look like <u>my father</u>, but my brother doesn't look like _____*him.*_____

1. <u>My brother's</u> name is William, but we call ___him___ Bill.

2. <u>I</u> understand the teacher, and the teacher understands ___me___ .

3. I use <u>my dictionary</u> when I write, but I don't use ___it___ when I speak.

4. I like <u>this city</u>. Do you like ___it___ too?

5. I talk to <u>Americans</u>, but I don't always understand ___them___ .

6. We listen to <u>the teacher</u>, and we talk to ___him___ .

7. When <u>we</u> make a mistake, the teacher corrects ___us___ .

8. <u>The President</u> has advisors. They help ___him___ make decisions.

9. <u>You</u> understand me, and I understand ___you___ .

10. <u>My friends</u> sometimes visit me, and I sometimes visit ___them___ .

EXERCISE 7   Two students are talking. Fill in the blanks with an appropriate object pronoun.

A.   How do you like Ms. Miller, your new English teacher?

B.   I like ___*her*___ , but she gives a lot of homework. This week we
        (example)

have to write a composition, and she says we have to type ___it___ .
                                                                          (1)

May I borrow your typewriter?

A.   I never use ___it___ any more. I have a computer. You can come
              (2)

to my house and use ___it___ , if you like.
                              (3)

B.   But I don't know how.

A.   I'll teach ___you___ .
              (4)

B.   It's going to be hard. I don't know anything about computers.

A.   Don't worry. You just need to know a few basic commands. You can

learn ___them___ in less than an hour.
          (5)

B.   I don't want to bother __you__ .
             (6)

A.   You're not bothering __me__ . I'm glad to help __you__ . Come
                      (7)   (8)
    to my house tomorrow.

B.   Can I bring my brother too? You can teach both of __us__ at the
                                              (9)
    same time.

A.   Do I know your brother?

B.   Of course. You sit next to __him__ in math class.
                        (10)

A.   Do you mean Roberto?

B.   Yes. He's my brother.

A.   Of course! He looks just like __you__ . Sure. Bring __him__ .
                                (11)   (12)
    I'll be happy to teach both of __you__ at the same time.
                                    (13)

B.   Thanks a lot. I'll see __you__ tomorrow.
                    (14)

EXERCISE 8   Fill in the blanks with *I, I'm, my, mine,* or *me*.

EXAMPLE: __I'm__ a foreign student. __I__ come from Japan.

__My__ roommate's parents live in the U.S., but __mine__ live in

Japan. __My__ parents write to __me__ twice a month.

1.   __I'm__ 20 years old.

2.   __My__ parents don't live in the U.S.

3.   __I__ study at the University of Wisconsin.

4.   __My__ major is engineering.

5.   __I__ have a roommate.

6.   __My__ roommate's name is Kelly. __Mine__ is Yuki.

7.   __My__ roommate helps __me__ with my English.

EXERCISE 9   Fill in the blanks with *he, he's, his,* or *him*.

EXAMPLE: I have a good friend. __His__ name is Paul. __He's__ Puerto

Rican. __He__ lives in New York. I like __him__ .

1.   __He's__ married.

---

2. __He__ works in an office.

3. __He's__ an accountant. ~~of finances.~~

4. __His__ son helps __him__ in __his__ business.

5. __He's__ 37 years old. __He's__ wife is 35.

6. My wife and __his__ wife are friends.

7. My wife is a doctor. __He's__ is a computer programmer.

EXERCISE 10 Fill in the blanks with *she, she's, her,* or *hers*.

EXAMPLE: I have a friend. _____Her_____ name's Diane. _____She's_____ American. _____She_____ lives in Boston. My native language is Korean. _____Hers_____ is English.

1. __she's__ an interesting person.

2. I like __her__ very much.

3. __She's__ married.

4. __She__ has two children.

5. My children go to Dewey School. __Her's__ go to King School.

6. __She's__ a nurse. __She__ likes __her's__ job.

7. __Her__ husband is a teacher.
    Is her husband a teacher?

EXERCISE 11 Fill in the blanks with *they, they're, their, theirs,* or *them*.

EXAMPLE: Diane and Richard are my friends. _____They_____ live in Boston. _____Their_____ house is beautiful. _____They're_____ happy. I see _____them_____ on the weekends.

1. __They're__ Americans.

2. __They__ both work.

3. __They__ have two children.

4. __Their__ children go to public school.

5. My apartment is small. __Theirs__ is big.

6. __They're__ interested in art.

7. I talk to __them__ once a week.

EXERCISE 12 Fill in the blanks about a cat. Use *it*, *it's*, or *its*.

EXAMPLE: _____It's_____ an independent animal. _____It_____ always lands on _____its_____ feet.

1. _____ likes to eat fish.

2. _____ a small animal.

3. _____ fur is soft.

4. _____ catches mice.

5. _____ claws are sharp.

6. _____ a clean animal.

7. Do you see that cat? Yes, I see _____ .

claws

EXERCISE 13 Fill in the blanks with *we*, *we're*, *our*, *ours*, or *us*.

EXAMPLE: _____We_____ study English. _____We're_____ foreign students. _____Our_____ teacher is American. He helps _____us_____ .

1. _____ come from different countries.

2. _____ in class now.

3. _____ classroom is comfortable.

4. The teacher asks _____ a lot of questions.

5. The teacher's textbook has the answers. _____ don't have the answers.

6. _____ interested in English.

EXERCISE 14 Fill in the blanks with *you*, *you're*, *your*, or *yours*.

EXAMPLE: _____You're_____ a good teacher. Students like _____you_____ . My other teacher's name is hard to pronounce. _____Yours_____ is easy to pronounce.

1. _____You_____ explain the grammar well.

2. We all understand _____you_____ .

3. Our pronunciation is sometimes hard to understand. _____Yours_____ is clear.

4. _____You're_____ a kind teacher.

5. _____You're_____ class is very interesting.

6. _____You_____ have a lot of experience with foreign students.

5.7   Questions about the Subject or about the Complement

Compare these statements and related questions about the complement:

Wh- Word	*Do/Does*	Subject	Verb	Complement
What	does	Susan she She	needs need? needs	something. a new TV.
Where	do	My parents your parents They	live live? live	in Peru. in Colombia.
Who(m)	does	Your sister she She	likes like? likes	someone. her boyfriend.

Compare these statements and related questions about the subject:

Subject	Verb	Complement	Short Answer
Someone	has	my book.	
Who	has	my book?	Tom does.
Someone	needs	help.	
Who	needs	help?	I do.

LANGUAGE NOTES

1. Most *wh-* questions in the present tense use *do* or *does*. These questions ask about the complement.

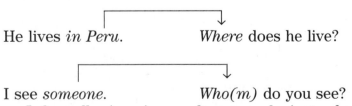

He lives *in Peru.*   *Where* does he live?

I see *someone.*   *Who(m)* do you see?
NOTE: Informally, Americans often say *who* instead of *whom*.

2. Some *wh-* questions ask about the subject.

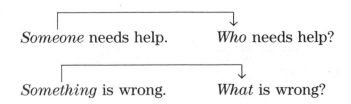

Someone needs help.   *Who* needs help?

Something is wrong.   *What* is wrong?

3. Notice that we use the *-s* form of the verb to ask a present tense question about the subject. The answer can be singular or plural.

Who *has* a new car?
Jake *has* a new car.
Bill and Ann *have* a new car.

EXERCISE 15 Talk about some jobs in your house. Ask another student, "Who _____s in your house?" The other student will answer.

EXAMPLES: take out the garbage
A. Who takes out the garbage in your house?
B. My brother does.

vacuum the carpet
A. Who vacuums the carpet in your house?
B. Nobody does. We don't have carpets.

1. cook the meals
2. make your bed
3. pay the bills
4. wash the dishes
5. shop for groceries
6. wash the clothes
7. vacuum the carpet
8. dust the furniture
9. sweep the floor

vacuum

dust

sweep

EXERCISE 16 Fill in the blanks with *who, whom, who's,* or *whose*.

EXAMPLE: ___Who___ speaks Japanese? Yoko does.

1. ___Who___ has the textbook? The teacher does.
2. ___Who's___ your English teacher? Bob Marks is.
3. There's a dictionary on the floor. ___Whose___ dictionary is it?
4. ___Whom___ do you see on the weekends? I see my friends.

EXERCISE 17 Circle the correct word to complete this conversation between two students.

EXAMPLE: A. (Who, (Who's,) Whose, Whom) your English teacher?
B. ((My,) Mine, Me) teacher's name is Charles Flynn.

A. (My, Mine, Me) is Marianne Peters. She's Mr. Flynn's wife.

B. Oh, really? His last name is different from (she, her, hers).

A. Yes. She uses (her, hers, his, he's) father's last name, not her (husband's, husbands', husbands, husband).

B. Do they have children?

A. Yes.

B. (Whose, Who's, Who, Whom) name do the children use?

A. (They, They're, Their, Theirs) children use both last names.

B. How do you know so much about (you, you're, your, yours) teacher and (she, she's, her, hers) children?

A. We talk about (we, us, our, ours) names in class. We also talk about American customs. She explains her customs, and we explain (our, ours, us).

B. Mr. Flynn doesn't talk about (her, his, he's, hers) family in class.

A. Do you call (her, his, him, he) "mister"?

B. Of course. (He, He's, His) the teacher. We show respect.

A.   But we call Marianne by (her, hers, she) first name. (She, She's, Her) prefers that.

B. I prefer to call (our, us, ours) teachers by (they, they're, their, theirs) last names. That's the way we do it in my country.

A. And in (me, my, mine) too. But (we, we're, us) in the U.S. now. There's an expression: When in Rome, do as the Romans do.[3]

SUMMARY OF LESSON 5

1.   Pronouns and Possessive Forms

Subject Pronoun	Object Pronoun	Possessive Adjective	Possessive Pronoun
I	me	my	mine
you	you	your	yours
he	him	his	his
she	her	her	hers
it	it	its	—
we	us	our	ours
they	them	their	theirs
who	whom	whose	whose

[3] This expression means that you should follow the customs of the country you are in.

Subject	**I** come from Cuba.	**They** come from Korea.
Object	The teachers helps **me**.	The teacher helps **them**.
Possessive Adjective	**My** name is Rosa.	**Their** names are Kim and Park.
Possessive Pronoun	Your country is big. **Mine** is small.	Your country is big. **Theirs** is small.

Subject	**Who** has a new car?
Object	With **whom** do you live? (FORMAL) **Who** do you live with? (INFORMAL)
Possessive Adjective	I have my book. **Whose** book is that?
Possessive Pronoun	This is my dictionary. **Whose** is that?

2. Possessive Forms of Nouns
    Jack*'s* car is old.
    His parent*s'* car is new.
    The children*'s* toys are on the floor.
    What's the name *of our textbook*?

EDITING ADVICE

1. Don't confuse *you're* (you are) and *your* (possessive form).

   You're
   ~~Your~~ a good person.

   your
   Where's ~~you're~~ book?

2. Don't confuse *he's* (he is) and *his* (possessive form).

   His
   ~~He's~~ name is Paul.

   He's
   ~~His~~ a good student.

3. Don't confuse *it's* (it is) and *its* (possessive form).

   It's
   ~~Its~~ a beautiful day today.

   its
   A monkey uses ~~it's~~ tail to climb trees.

4. Don't confuse *his* (masculine) and *her* (feminine).

My brother loves ~~her~~ *his* daughter.

My sister loves ~~his~~ *her* son.

5. Don't confuse *my* and *mine*.

I don't have ~~mine~~ *my* book today.

6. Don't confuse *they're* and *their*.

I have two American friends. ~~They're~~ *Their* names are Bob and Sue.

7. Use the correct pronoun (subject or object).

I have a daughter. I love ~~she~~ *her* very much.

My father and ~~me~~ *I* like to go fishing.

8. Don't use *the* with a possessive form.

~~The~~ *M*y daughter's boyfriend is very tall.

I need ~~the~~ your dictionary.

9. Don't use *do* or *does* in a *who* question about the subject.

Who ~~does have~~ *has* a Spanish dictionary?

10. Don't separate *whose* from the noun.

Whose *book* is this ~~book~~?

11. Don't confuse *whose* and *who's*.

~~Who's~~ *Whose* coat is that?

12. Use the correct word order for possession.

~~Dog my neighbor~~ *My neighbor's dog* makes a lot of noise.

13. Put the apostrophe in the right place.

My ~~parent's~~ *parents'* car is new.

14. Don't use the possessive form for non-living objects.

Grammar in Context is the ~~book's name~~ *name of the book*.

PART 1   Find the mistakes with the underlined words and correct them. Not every sentence has a mistake. If the sentence is correct, write **C.**

EXAMPLES: *Whose*
~~Who's~~ book is that?

Who's your best friend?   **C**

1. Where does ~~you're~~ *your* brother live?

2. Paul is in my English class but ~~his~~ *he's* not in my math class.

3. *It's* Its important to know a second language.

4. Whose name do you use, your father's or your mother's?   *C*

5. Who wants to leave early today? We all do.

6. Maria's son goes to a bilingual school. Her son's teacher comes from Cuba.   *C*

7. I visit my girlfriend once a week. ~~His~~ *Her* son likes to play with mine.

8. The door of the classroom is open.   *C*

9. Do you know the first name the teacher?
Do you know the teacher's first name?

10. I have two married brothers. My brother's wives are wonderful women.   *C*

11. ~~Your~~ *You* always late to class.

12. My the brother's car is new.   *My brother's car is new.*

13. Whose is this umbrella?   *Whose umbrella is this?*

14. She likes her mother-in-law because ~~mother her husband~~ always helps her. *her husband's mother*

15. Do they visit their parents often?

16. A dog wags (moves) its tail when it's happy.   *C*

17. Susan and Linda are women's names.   *C*

18. Who does have a red pen?
Who has a red pen?

19. My friend and ~~me~~ eat dinner together once a week.
My friend and I

20. Whose pen is this?   *C*
Whose pen is this?

PART **2**   Choose the correct word to complete these sentences.

EXAMPLE: Most American women change _____ *c* _____ names when they get married, but not all do.

  a. her   b. hers   c. their   d. theirs

1. I have two _sisters_ .
    a. sisters   b. sister's   c. sisters'   d. sister

2. _Their_ names are Marilyn and Charlotte.
    a. Their   b. Theirs   c. They're   d. They   e. Hers

3. _They're_ both married.
    a. Their   b. They're   c. They   d. Them   e. There

4. Marilyn uses _____.
    a. the last name her husband
    b. the last name of his husband
    c. her husband's last name
    d. his husband's last name

5. Charlotte uses _our_ father's last name.
    a. we   b. our   c. ours   d. us

6. I have one brother. _He's_ married.
    a. He's   b. His   c. He   d. Him

7. _His_ wife is very nice.
    a. Him   b. Her   c. His   d. He's

8. _My_ first name is Sandra.
    a. My   b. Mine   c. I'm   d. Me

9. My friends call _me_ "Sandy."
    a. me   b. my   c. mine

10. My sister often uses her middle name, but I rarely use _mine_ .
    a. my   b. mine   c. me   d. I'm

11. You have a dog, but I don't know _its_ name.
    a. it   b. it's   c. its

12. _Who's_ your teacher?
    a. Whom   b. Who   c. Whose   d. Who's

13. The teacher's name is on _____.
    a. the door of her office
    b. her office's door
    c. the door her office
    d. her the office's door

148   Lesson Five

14. __d__
    a. Who's is that office?
    b. Whose is that office?
    c. Who's office is that?
    ✗d. Whose office is that?

15. Her ___child's___ names are Ricky and Eddie.
    ✗a. childs'   ✗b. children's   c. childrens   d. childrens'

16. ___Who___ has the newspaper?
    a. Whom   b. Whose   ✓c. Who   d. Who's

17. Who ___needs___ more time with the test?
    a. need   b. does need   ✗c. needs   d. does needs

PART 3

Two women are talking about names. Fill in the blanks with possessive forms, subject pronouns, or object pronouns. Some blanks need an apostrophe or an apostrophe +s.

A. What's your last name?

B. It's Woods.

A. Woods sounds like an American name. But ___you're___ Polish, aren't you?
    (example)

B. Yes, but Americans have trouble pronouncing ___my___ name, so I use
    (1)
    the name "Woods."

A. What's ___your___ real last name?
    (2)

B. Wodzianicki.

A. My name is hard for Americans too, but ___they___ like my name, and I
    (3)
    don't want to change ___mine___. I'm proud of it.
    (4)

B. What's ___your___ last name?
    (5)

A. Lopez Hernandez.

B. Why do ___you___ have two last names?
    (6)

A. I come from Mexico. Mexicans have two last names. Mexicans use both
    parents ___parent's___ names.
    (7)

B. What happens when a woman gets married? Does she use ___her___
    (8)
    parents ___s___ names and ___her___ husband's ___s___ name
    (9)   *(10)*   *(11)*
    too?

A. No. When a woman gets married, she usually drops ___her___ (12)

mother_'s_ (13) name. She adds "of" (in Spanish, "de") and ___hers___ (14)

husband_'s_ (15) name. My sister is married. ___Her___ (16) name is

Maria Lopez de Castillo. Lopez is ___her___ (17) father_'s_ ___last___ (18) name

and Castillo is her husband_'s_ (19) name. ___Her___ (20) kids_'___ (21)

last name is Castillo Lopez.

B. That's confusing. Everybody in the family has a different last name.

A. It's not confusing for us. You understand your customs, and we under-

stand ___ours___ (22).

B. Do your sister_'s_ (23) kids have American first names?

A. My sister gave ___them___ (24) Spanish names, but ___their___ (25) friends gave

them American names. Her daughter_'s_ ___first___ (26) name is Rosa, but

___her's___ (27) friends call her Rose. ___Her___ (28) son_'s_ (29) name is

Eduardo, but ___his___ (30) friends call ___him___ (31) Eddie. Ricardo

is the youngest one. ___He's___ (32) still a baby, but when he goes to

school, ___his___ (33) friends will probably call ___him___ (34) Rick.

EXPANSION ACTIVITIES

CLASSROOM ACTIVITIES

1. Find a partner. Compare yourself to your partner. Compare physical characteristics, clothes, family, home, job, car, etc. Report some interesting facts to the class.

EXAMPLE:

My hair is straight. Mark's is curly.
His eyes are blue. Mine are brown.
My family lives in this city. Mark's family lives in Romania.

2. One student will ask these *who* questions. Raise your hand if this is a fact about you. The first student will answer the question after he or she sees raised hands.

EXAMPLE:

Who has kids?
Ben, Maria, and Lidia have kids.
Who has a cell phone?
No one has a cell phone.

1. Who has kids? *No body has kids.*
2. Who likes cartoons? *Every body like.*
3. Who plays soccer? *Every body play soccer.*
4. Who has a computer? *Elizabeth, odair, Luciadna*
5. Who has an e-mail address? *Just Elizabethe doesn't has.*
6. Who likes to swim? *Mirian, Elizabeth, odair likes swim.*
7. Who is a vegetarian? *Just Mirian is vegetarian.*
8. Who wants a grammar test? *Odair, Mirian want but Elizabeth doesn't.*
9. Who has American friends? *Every body has friends.*
10. Who has a pet? *Mirian and Elizabeth dont have, but odair*
11. Who lives in a house?
12. Who is over 6 feet tall? *Any body does.*
13. Who watches TV in the morning? *Odair, Elizabeth do, and odair have/does*
14. Who is a sports fan? *Every body like.*
15. Who gets a lot of junk mail? *No body gets junk mail?*
16. Who exercises every day?
17. Who has a motorcycle?
18. Who has a middle name?
19. Who wants to become an American citizen?
20. Who plays a musical instrument?

3. Think of something unusual that you do or are. Write a sentence telling what you do or are. Then ask a question to find out who else does or is this.

EXAMPLE:

I have a pet snake. Who else has a pet snake?
I play volleyball. Who else plays volleyball?
I am a Buddhist. Who else is a Buddhist?

(Variation: On a piece of paper, write something unusual that you do or are. Give the papers to the teacher. The teacher reads a statement. Other students—and the teacher—try to guess who wrote the paper. Example: Someone has a pet snake. Who has a pet snake?)

JOKE

A woman is outside of her house. A dog is near her. A man walks by and is interested in the dog. He wants to pet the dog. He asks the woman, "Does your dog bite?" The woman answers no. The man pets the dog and the dog bites him. He says, "You told me that your dog doesn't bite." The woman answers, "This is not my dog. Mine is in the house."

DISCUSSION   Discuss naming customs in your native culture. Do people have a middle name? Do fathers and sons ever have the same name? Tell about your name. Does it mean something?

OUTSIDE ACTIVITY   Ask an American to tell you about his or her name. Tell the class something interesting you learned from this American.

Internet Activity

 Find a phone directory on the Internet. Look up your last name in a major American city, such as New York City, or in the city where you live. How many people in this city have your last name?

GRAMMAR
Present Continuous Tense[1]

CONTEXT
Student Life
In the School Cafeteria

LESSON FOCUS
We use the present continuous tense to talk about an action in progress now.

We're *studying* Lesson Six now.

The teacher *is explaining* the grammar now.

[1] The present continuous tense is sometimes called the present progressive tense.

1. What are you studying this semester?
2. How many credit hours are you taking?
3. Besides English, are you learning something new?

Read the following letter. Pay special attention to the present continuous verbs.

Student Life

Dear Family,

I'm writing you this letter to tell you about my life at college in the U.S. Many new things **are happening**, and I want to tell you all about my life here.

First of all, **I'm living** in a dormitory with an American roommate. His name is Ben Kaplan, and he's from California. **He's majoring** in chemistry. You know, of course, **I'm majoring** in music. Ben and I are very different, but we get along[2] very well. We speak English all the time, and because of him, my English **is improving**. He's not here right now because he**'s studying** for a big test with some friends.

This semester **I'm taking** five courses (18 credit hours). It's hard, but **I'm getting** good grades. **I'm learning** a new instrument—the guitar. It's a lot of fun for me and not very difficult. **I'm meeting** a lot of new people in my classes, students from all over the world.

There's one thing I'm not happy about. The food here in the dorm cafeteria is not very good. It's greasy, and **I'm gaining** weight. Ben and I **are thinking** about getting an apartment for next semester. We want to cook for ourselves and have more freedom.

Thank you for the sweater you sent me. **I'm wearing** it now. It's so cold this week. In fact, it**'s snowing** now. It's so strange to see snow. **I'm looking** out my window. Children **are playing** in the snow. They**'re making** a snowman and **throwing** snowballs.

I have to finish this letter now. **I'm writing** a term paper[3] for my music theory class. Please write soon and tell me what **is happening** with all of you.

I hope you are all well.

Love,
Dan

Sincerely or Best.

Did you know...?

Forty-one percent of college students in the U.S. are over 25 years old. (This includes part-time students.)

---

[2] When people *get along well*, they have a good relationship.
[3] A *term paper* is a paper that students write for class. The student researches a topic. It often takes a student a full semester (or term) to produce this paper.

6.1 The Present Continuous Tense—Forms

Subject	Be	Verb + *-ing*
I	am	studying.
You We They Jim and Sue	are	reading. learning. practicing. writing.
He She It Jim	is	eating. sitting. sleeping. standing.

LANGUAGE NOTES

1. We can make a contraction with the subject pronoun and a form of *be*. Most nouns can also contract with *is*.[4]
   Dan's writing a letter.   *We're* studying verb tenses.
   He's wearing a sweater.   *It's* snowing.
2. To form the negative, put *not* after the verb *am/is/are*.
   Dan *isn't* writing a composition. He's writing a letter.
   The children *aren't* playing inside. They're playing in the snow.

EXERCISE 1   Fill in the missing part of each sentence.

EXAMPLES: I __'m__ writing a letter.

I'm look __ing__ out my window.

1. My roommate and his friend __are__ studying.

2. I'm learn __ing__ to play the guitar.

3. New things __are__ happening.

4. I'm meet __ing__ a lot of new people.

5. I __'m__ major __ing__ in music.

6. My roommate is __major__ ing in chemistry.

[4] See Lesson 1, page 9 for exceptions.

7. I'm _wearing_ a sweater now.

8. Children are _throw_ ing snowballs.

The Present Continuous Tense—Uses

Examples	Use
Dan **is writing** a letter to his family now. It**'s snowing** now.	To show that an action is in progress now, at this moment.
Dan and his roommate **are gaining** weight. Dan **is writing** a term paper this semester. He **is majoring** in music.	To show a long-term action that is in progress. It may not be happening at this exact moment.
He **is wearing** a sweater. He **is sitting** near the window.	To describe a state or condition, using the following verbs: _sit, stand, wear, sleep._

LANGUAGE NOTES

When the subject is doing two or more things, we don't repeat the verb _be_ after _and._

Children are making a snowman _and throwing_ snowballs.

EXERCISE 2   Answer the following questions with a complete sentence.

EXAMPLE: What's Dan majoring in?
He's majoring in music.

1.   Why's Dan's English improving?
Because he speaking English all the time.

2.   What instrument is he learning to play?
He's learning a new instrument — the guitar.

3.   How many courses is he taking this semester?
He's taking five courses.

4.   Why's Dan unhappy about the food?
He's gaining weight.

5.   What are Dan and his roommate thinking about doing?
They are tinking about getting an apartament next se

6.   What's Dan wearing now?
He's wearing a sweater.

7.   What are you majoring in?
I'm majoring in English.

8.   How many credit hours are you taking?
I'm don't taking any credits hours.

Spelling of the *-ing* Form

Rule	Verbs	*-ing* Form
Add *-ing* to most verbs. (Note: Do not drop the *y* of the base form.)	eat go study	eat**ing** go**ing** study**ing**
For a one-syllable verb that ends in a consonant + vowel + consonant (CVC), double the final consonant and add *-ing*.	p l a n ↓ ↓ ↓ C V C s t o p ↓ ↓ ↓ C V C s i t ↓ ↓ ↓ C V C	plan**ning** stop**ping** sit**ting**
Do not double a final *w*, *x*, or *y*.	show mix stay	show**ing** mix**ing** stay**ing**
For a two-syllable verb that ends in CVC, double the final consonant only if the last syllable is stressed.	refér admít begín	refer**ring** admit**ting** begin**ning**
When the last syllable of a two-syllable verb is not stressed, do not double the final consonant.	lísten ópen óffer	listen**ing** open**ing** offer**ing**
If the verb ends in a consonant + *e*, drop the *e* before adding *-ing*.	live take write	liv**ing** tak**ing** writ**ing**

EXERCISE 3 Write the *-ing* form of the verb. (Two-syllable verbs that end in CVC have accent marks to show which syllable is stressed.)

EXAMPLES: play _____ *playing* _____

make _____ *making* _____

1. plan ___ *planning* ___
2. ópen ___ *o'peninnig* ___
3. sit ___ *sitting* ___
4. begín ___ *begining* ___
5. hurry ___ *hurrying* ___

6. háppen ___ *happenig* ___
7. stay ___ *staying* ___
8. grow ___ *growing* ___
9. marry ___ *marrying* ___
10. grab ___ *grabbing* ___

11. write _writing_   16. drive _driving_
12. fix _fixing_   17. wait _waiting_
13. wipe _wiping_   18. serve _serving_
14. carry _carrying_   19. visit _visiting_
15. drink _drinking_   20. prefér _preferring_

EXERCISE 4   Fill in the blanks with the present continuous tense of the verb in parentheses ( ). Use correct spelling.

EXAMPLE: Dan ____is writing____ a letter. What is Dan writing.
                     (write)

1. He ___is living___ in a dorm.
        (live)

2. Dan and his roommate _are gaining_ weight.
   What are Dan and his (gain) roommate gaining.

3. Dan _isn't majoring_ in chemistry.
        (not/major)

what ×4. Children outside _is making_ a snowman and _throwing_ snowballs.
                           (make) What are children (throw) making
yes/no 5. Dan's _writing_ a term paper on music theory.
                  (write)

what D ×6. I'm _filling_ in the blanks with the correct verb form.
              (fill)   Are you filling in the blanks?

What   ×7. My teacher _is making_ corrections. What is My teacher
                     (make)   making?

8. We've _using_ the textbook.
         (use)

yes/no → 9. We _aren't studying_ reading now.
                (not/study) Are we studying reading now?

10. We're _finishing_ Exercise 4.
           (finish)
   What are we finishing?

EXERCISE 5   Make a **true** affirmative statement or negative statement about your activities now with the words given.

EXAMPLES: wear a watch
             I'm wearing a watch (now).

             drink coffee
             I'm not drinking coffee (now).

1. sit in the back of the room   I'm sitting in the back of the room
2. speak my native language   I don't speaking my native la
3. pay attention I'm paying attention.
4. ask questions I don't asking questions.
5. learn the present continuous tense
   I'm learnig the present continuous tense.

6. look out the window
   I don't looking out the wind
7. look at the chalkboard
   I'm looking at the chalk
8. write a composition
   I'm writing a composi
9. use my textbook
   I'm use my textbook
10. wear jeans
    I'm wearing jeans.

EXERCISE 6 Make a **true** affirmative statement or negative statement about yourself with the words given. Talk about a long-term action.

EXAMPLES: look for a job
I'm looking for a job.

live in a hotel
I'm not living in a hotel.

1. look for a new apartment
2. learn a lot of English
3. gain weight
4. lose weight
5. spend a lot of money
6. save my money *

Are you writing a term paper?
7. write a term paper
8. try to understand American customs
9. meet Americans
10. learn how to drive
11. live in a dorm
12. plan to return to my hometown

6.4 Questions with the Present Continuous Tense

Wh- Word	Be + Not	Subject	Be	Verb-ing	Complement	Short Answer
		Dan	is	wearing	a sweater.	
	Is	Dan		wearing	a hat?	No, he isn't.
What	is	Dan		wearing?		
Why	isn't	Dan		wearing	a hat?	
		Who	is	wearing	a hat?	
		Children	are	playing.		
	Are	they		playing	inside?	No, they aren't.
Where	are	they		playing?		
Why	aren't	they		playing	inside?	

LANGUAGE NOTES

When the question is "What . . . doing?" we usually answer with a different verb. Compare these questions and answers.

What's he *doing*? He's *writing* a letter.
What *are* the children *doing*? They're *playing* in the snow.
What *are* you *doing*? I'm *studying* verbs.

the children are playing
Ask?

EXERCISE 7 Use the words given to ask a question about what this class is doing now. Another student will answer.

EXAMPLE: we/use the textbook now
A. Are we using the textbook now?
B. Yes, we are.

1. the teacher/wear a sweater
   Is the teacher wearing a sweater?
   No he isn't.
2. the teacher/write on the chalkboard
3. the teacher/erase the chalkboard
4. the teacher/sit at the desk
5. the teacher/take attendance
6. the teacher/explain the grammar
7. the teacher/help the students
8. we/practice the present continuous tense
   Are we practicing the present continuous tense?
   Yes, we are.

9. we/practice the past tense *Are we practicing past tense?*
10. we/review Lesson 5 *Are we reviewing Lesson 5*
11. we/make mistakes *Are we making mistakes?*
12. what/the teacher/wear *What is the teacher wear*
13. where/the teacher/stand or sit *where is the teacher standing or sitting?*
14. what exercise/we/do *What exercise are we doing*
15. what/you/think about *what are you thinking about?*

EXERCISE 8 Ask a question about a long-term action with the words given. Another student will answer.

EXAMPLE: you/study math this semester
A. Are you studying math this semester?
B. Yes, I am.

1. you/plan to buy a car *Are you planning to buy a car?*
2. you/study biology this semester *Are you studying biology this semester?*
3. you/take other courses this semester *Are you taking other courses this semester?*
4. you/look for a new apartment *Are you looking for a new apartament?*
5. you/look for a job *Are you looking for a job?*

6. your English/improve *Is your English improving?*
7. your vocabulary/grow *Is your vocabulary growing.*
8. the teacher/help you *Is the teacher helping you?*
9. the students/make progress *Are the students making progress*
10. you/learn about other students' countries *Are you learning about other students countries?*

EXERCISE 9 Ask and answer questions about Dan's letter.

EXAMPLE: Dan/lose weight
A. Is Dan losing weight?
B. No, he isn't. He's gaining weight.

1. Dan/live in an apartment *Is Dan living in an apartament? No he isn't. He's living in an house.*
2. he/major in art *Is he majoring in art?*
3. he/study the guitar
4. his roommate/major in chemistry *Is his roommate majoring in Chemistry?*

5. Dan/wear a new sweater
6. he/take/18 credit hours
7. what/Dan/major in *What is Dan major in?*
8. how many courses/Dan/take *How many courses is Dan taking? He's taking 5 courses.*

No, he isn't. He's majoring in Chemistry.
(D Quimica.

160 Lesson Six

EXERCISE 10 Read each sentence. Then ask a *wh-* question about the words in parentheses ( ). Another student will answer.

EXAMPLE: We're doing an exercise. (What exercise)
             A. What exercise are we doing?
             B. We're doing Exercise 10.

1. We're practicing a tense. (What tense)
   What tense are we practicing?
2. We're using a textbook. (What kind of book)
   What kind of book are we using?
3. You're listening to the teacher. (Why)
   Why aren't you listening to the teacher?
4. The teacher's helping the students. (Why)
   Why isn't the teacher helping the students?
5. I'm answering a question. (Which question)
   Wich question am I answering?
6. We're practicing questions. (What kind of questions)
   What kind of questions are we practicing?
7. Your English ability is improving. (Why)
   Why isn't your English ability improving?
8. Your life is changing. (How)
   How is your life changing?
9. You're taking courses. (How many courses)
   How many courses are you taking.

EXERCISE 11 Read each statement. Then write a question about the words in parentheses ( ). Write an answer. Refer to Dan's letter on page 154.

EXAMPLE: Dan is writing a letter. (to whom)   OR   (who . . . to)
             A. Who is he writing to?   OR   To whom is he writing?
             B. He's writing to his family.

1. He's learning a new instrument. (what instrument)
   A. _What instrument is he learning?_
   B. _He's learning the guitar._

2. He's gaining weight. (why)
   A. _Why is he gaining weight?_
   B. _He's gaining weight because the food is greasy._

3. His roommate is studying. (who . . . with) OR (with whom)
   A. _With whom is he studying?_
   B. _He's studying with his roommate?_

4. He's wearing something new. (what)

A. _What is he wearing?_

B. _He's wearing a sweater._

5. His English is improving. (why)

A. _Why is his English improving?_

B. _He's living with American roommate._

6. He's taking courses. (how many courses)

A. _How many courses is he taking?_

B. _He's taking five courses._

7. He's meeting new students. (what kind)

A. _What kind is he meeting?_

B. _He's meeting students of different countries_

EXERCISE 12 Fill in the blanks with *I'm* or *I'm not* + the *-ing* form of the verb in parentheses ( ) to tell if you are doing these things now or at this general point in time. Then ask another student if he or she is doing this activity now. The other student will answer. (You may work with a partner.)

EXAMPLES: (plan) _I'm planning_ to buy a computer.
A. Are you planning to buy a computer?
B. Yes, I am.

(learn) _I'm not learning_ to drive a car.
A. Are you learning to drive a car?
B. No, I'm not.

1. (wear) _Are you wearing_ jeans.

2. (hold) _Are you holding_ a pencil.

3. (chew) _Are you chewing_ gum.

4. (think) _Are you tinking_ about the weekend.

5. (live) _Are you living_ in a dorm.

6. (plan) _Are you planning_ to take a vacation.

7. (look) _Are you looking_ for a job.

8. (plan) _Are you planning_ to buy a computer.

9. (take) _Are you taking_ a computer class this semester.

10. (get) _Are you getting_ tired.

11. (gain) _Are you gaining_ weight?

12. (learn) _Are you learnig_ about the history of the U.S.?

13. (learn) _Are you learning_ how to drive?

EXERCISE 13 A woman is calling her husband from a cell phone in her car. Fill in the blanks to complete the conversation.

A. Hello?

B. Hi. It's Betty.

A. Oh, hi, Betty. This connection is so noisy. Where _are you calling_ from?
    (example)

B. I'm _calling_ from the car. I'm _using_ the cell phone.
    (1)   (2)

A. _Are you driving_ home now?
    (3)

B. No, I'm not. I'm driving to the airport.

A. Why _is you driving_ to the airport?
        (4)

B. I'm going to pick up a client of mine.

A. I can't hear you. There's so much noise.

B. Airplanes _are flying_ overhead. They're very low.
                (5)

A. I can't hear you. Talk louder please.

B. I'm _speaking_ as loud as I can. I'm _going_ to
        (6)   (7)
    the airport to pick up a client of mine. I'm late. Her plane
    is coming (arriving) now and I'm stuck⁵ in traffic. I'm getting
        (8)
    nervous. Cars aren't moving.

A. Why _aren't they_ moving?
        (9)

B. There's an accident on the highway.

A. I worry about you. _Are you wearing seat belt._?
                        (10)

B. Of course, I'm wearing my seat belt.

A. That's good.

B. What _are you doing_ now?
        (11)

⁵ When you are stuck in traffic, you can't move because other cars aren't moving.

A. I ___checking___ the computer. I'm ___looking___ for
   (12)   (13)
information about cars on the Internet.

B. What ___are the kids___ doing?
        (14)

A. The kids? I can't hear you.

B. Yes, the kids.

A. Meg ___is watching___ TV. Pam ___is doing___ her
   (15)   (16)
homework.

B. Why ___isn't___ Meg doing her homework?
        (17)

A. She doesn't have any homework today.

B. ___Are you preparing___ dinner for the kids?
        (18)

A. No, I'm not preparing dinner. I'm ___waiting___ for you to come
                                    (19)
home and prepare the dinner.

B. Please don't wait for me. Oh. Traffic is finally moving. Talk to you
later.

Before You Read
1. What American behaviors are strange to you?
2. Is your behavior in the U.S. different from your behavior in your country?

Read the following letter. Pay special attention to verbs—simple present and present continuous.

In the School Cafeteria

Dear Family,

I'm **sitting** in the school cafeteria now. I'm **writing** this letter between classes. I **see** many strange behaviors and customs around me. You always **ask** me about American customs, so I **think** you probably **want** to know about life in the U.S.

I'm **looking** at a young couple at the next table. The young man and woman **are touching, holding** hands, and even **kissing**. It looks strange because people never **kiss** in public in our country. At another table, a young man and woman **are sitting** with a baby. The man **is feeding** the baby. Men never **feed** the baby in our country. Why **isn't** the woman **feeding** the baby?

Two women **are putting** on make-up. I **think** this is bad public behavior. These women **are wearing** shorts. In our country, women never **wear** shorts.

A group of students **is listening** to the radio. The music is very loud. Their music **is bothering** other people, but they **don't care**. I'm **sitting** far from them, but I **hear** their music.

A young man **is resting** his feet on another chair. His friend **is eating** a hamburger with his hands. Why **isn't** he **using** a fork and knife?

These kinds of behaviors **look** bad to me. I'm **trying** to understand them, but I'm **having** a hard time. I still **think** many of these actions are rude.[6]

Your son,
Ali

6.5 Contrast of Present Continuous and Simple Present

FORM

Simple Present	Present Continuous
He sometimes **wears** a suit.	He **is wearing** jeans now.
He **doesn't** usually **wear** shorts.	He **isn't wearing** a belt.
Does he ever **wear** a hat?	**Is** he **wearing** a T-shirt?
Yes, he **does**.	No, he **isn't**.
When **does** he **wear** a hat?	What **is** he **wearing**?
Who **wears** a hat?	Who **is wearing** a T-shirt?

(continued)

---

[6] *Rude* means impolite.

Example	Explanation
The President **lives** in the White House. We usually **learn** about American life. Americans **eat** hamburgers with their hands.	Use the simple present tense to talk about a general truth, a habitual activity, or a custom.
Ali **is writing** to his family now. He **is looking** at Americans in the cafeteria. He **is trying** to understand American customs. He **is learning** more and more about Americans all the time.	Use the present continuous for an action that is in progress at this moment. Use the present continuous for a longer action that is in progress at this general time.

LANGUAGE NOTES

1. When we use *live* in the simple present, we mean that this is a person's home. In the present continuous, it shows a temporary, short-term residence.
    Ali *is living* in a dorm this semester.
    His family *lives* in Jordan.
2. "What do you do (for a living)?" asks about your job. "What are you doing?" asks about your activity at this moment.
    What *does* she *do* for a living? She's a nurse.
    What *is* she *doing*? She's *waiting* for the bus.

EXERCISE **14** Two students meet in the cafeteria and discuss American customs and customs of their native country. Fill in the blanks with the correct form of the verb in parentheses ( ). Practice the simple present and the present continuous.

A. Hi. What ___are you doing___ here?
(example: you/do)

B. I'm ___eating___ lunch. I always ___eat___ lunch at this
  (1 eat)   *(2 eat)*

  time. But I'm ___observing___ American behavior and customs.
  (3 also/observe)

A. What do you mean?

B. Well, look at that man over there. He's ___wearing___ an earring.
  (4 wear)

  It looks so strange. Only women ___wear___ earrings in my
  (5 wear)

  country.

A. It *is* strange. And look at that woman. She's _wearing_ three
(6 wear)
earrings in one ear!

B. And she's _wearing_ running shoes with a dress. In my country, _vestido_
(7 wear)
people only _use_ running shoes for sports activities.
(8 use)

A. Look at that student over there. He's _using_ a colored pen
(9 use)
to mark his textbook. In my country, we never _write_ in
(10 write)
our textbooks because they _belong_ to the college, not to
(11 belong)
the students. _(>pertence._

B. Many college activities are different here. For example, my English
teacher usually _sits_ at the desk in class. In my country,
(12 sit)
the teacher always _stands_ in class. And the students al-
(13 stand)
ways _stand up_ when the teacher _enters_ the
(14 stand up) (15 enter)
room.

A. And college students always _study_ English or another
(16 study)
foreign language. Here, nobody knows another language. My American roommate _is taking_ five courses this semester, but no
(17 take)
foreign language.

B. By the way, how many classes _are you taking_ this semester?
(18 you/take)

A. Four. In my country, I usually _take_ eight courses a
(19 take)
semester, but my adviser here says I can only take four. _(>Consellero_

B. I have to go now. My girlfriend _is waiting_ for me at the library.
(20 wait)

6.6 Action vs. Nonaction Verbs

Action	Nonaction
Ali **is learning** about American customs.	He **knows** American customs are different.
Ali **is wearing** a heavy coat. _pesada_	He **hates** winter. _odeia_
Ali **is buying** his textbooks.	The books **cost** $85.

LANGUAGE NOTES

1. We do not usually use the present continuous tense with certain verbs, called nonaction verbs. These verbs describe a state or condition, not an action. We use the simple present tense, even when we talk about now. Nonaction action verbs are: *~ parecer*

believe	know	own	seem ~ *parecer*
cost	like	prefer	understand
hate	love	remember	want
hear	need	see	

2. *Hear* and *see* are nonaction verbs. *Listen* and *look* are action verbs.
   Some students **are listening** to the radio. Ali **hears** the music.
   Ali **is looking** at students in the cafeteria. He **sees** some strange behaviors.

EXERCISE 15 Fill in the blanks with the simple present or the present continuous tense of the verb in parentheses ( ).

EXAMPLES: I ___understand___ the explanation now.
              (understand)

   I ___am writing___ now.
        (write)

1. I ___studying___ English this semester.
     (study)

2. We're ___using___ the textbook now.
         (use)

3. We ___need___ a lot of practice with verb tenses.
        (need)

4. We're ___comparing___ action and nonaction verbs.
          (compare)

5. I ___don't remember___ every grammar rule. ~ *regra*
     (not/remember)

6. I ___see___ the chalkboard.
      (see)

7. I'm ___don't looking___ at the clock now. I'm ___looking___ at
        (not/look)   (look)
   my book.

8. I ___don't need___ my dictionary now.
      (not/need)

9. We ___aren't writing___ a composition now.
        (not/write)

10. We ___don't hear___ the students in the next room.
         (not/hear)

11. We're ___learning___ about nonaction verbs.
      (learn)

12. We ___know___ a lot of grammar.
      (know)

6.7   *Think, Have,* and the Sense Perception Verbs

Action	Nonaction
He **is thinking** about his family.	He **thinks** that touching in public is bad.
He **is having** lunch in the cafeteria.	He **has** free time now.
He **is having** new experiences in the U.S.	He **has** new American friends.
	His friend **has** the flu now.
He **is looking** at a woman in shorts.	This behavior **looks** bad to him.
He **is smelling** the coffee.	The coffee **smells** delicious.

LANGUAGE NOTES

1. *Think* can be an action or a nonaction verb.
   • When we think <u>about</u> something, *think* is an action verb.
   • When *think* means to have an opinion about something, *think* is a nonaction verb.
2. *Have* can be an action or a nonaction verb.
   • When *have* shows possession, relationship, or illness, it is a nonaction verb.
   • When *have* means to experience something or to eat or drink something, it is an action verb.
3. The sense perception verbs (*look, taste, feel, smell*) can be action or nonaction verbs.
   • When the sense perception verbs describe a state, they are nonaction verbs.
   • When they describe an action, they are action verbs.

EXERCISE 16 Fill in the blanks with the simple present or the present continuous tense of the verb in parentheses ( ).

EXAMPLES: I ___am thinking___ about my family.
                        (think)

  I ___think___ that life in the U.S. is not perfect.
            (think)

1. She's _smelling_ the flowers.
   (smell)

2. The flowers _smell_ beautiful.
   (smell)

3. They _are thinking_ about their children.
   (think)

4. They _think_ that their children are wonderful.
   (think)

5. I'm _having_ a good time in the U.S.
   (have)

6. I _have_ a lot of new friends.
   (have)

7. I _don't have_ a lot of free time.
   (not/have)

8. My friend _has_ a cold now and he can't go out
   (have)

   today, so I _having_ lunch alone now.
   (have)

9. He's _looking_ at a car now.
   (look)

10. The car _looks_ new.
    (look)

EXERCISE 17 Fill in the blanks with the simple present or the present continuous of the verb in parentheses ( ). Use the simple present for regular activity and with nonaction verbs.

EXAMPLES: Ali _wants_ to understand American behavior.
(want)

He _is looking_ at some Americans in the cafeteria now.
(look)

1. Ali _is writing_ a letter now.
   (write)

2. He's _sitting_ in the school cafeteria now.
   (sit)

3. He _sees_ a couple with a baby.
   (see)

4. He often _goes_ to the cafeteria between classes.
   (go)

5. He _writes_ to his family once a week.
   (write)

6. He _thinks_ that his family _want_ to
   (think)   (want)
   know about American customs.

7. He's _looking_ at a young man and woman.
   (look)

   They _are holding_ hands.
   (hold)

170   Lesson Six

8. This behavior ___looks___ bad in his country.
   (look)

9. He's ___thinking___ about American customs now.
   (think)

10. Some women ___are wearing___ shorts now.
    (wear)

11. Women in Ali's country never ___wear___ shorts.
    (wear)

12. American customs ___seem___ strange to him.
    (seem)

EXERCISE 18 Read each sentence. Write the negative form of the underlined word, using the word(s) in parentheses ( ).

EXAMPLES: Ali is <u>looking</u> at Americans. (people from his country)
            He isn't looking at people from his country.

            He <u>knows</u> about Arab customs. (American customs)
            He doesn't know about American customs.

1. The father <u>is feeding</u> the baby. (the mother)
   She isn't feeding the baby.

2. Ali's <u>sitting</u> in the cafeteria. (in class)
   He isn't in class.

3. He <u>understands</u> Arab customs. (American customs)
   He doesn't understand American customs.

4. American men and women sometimes <u>kiss</u> in public. (Arab men and women)
   They don't kiss in public.

5. Americans <u>use</u> their hands to eat a hamburger. (to eat spaghetti)
   They don't use the hands to eat espaghetti

6. A man <u>is wearing</u> an earring in one ear. (in both ears)
   He isn't wearing an earring in both ears.

7. Americans <u>seem</u> strange to him. (Arabs)
   Arabs don't seen strange to Americas.

8. American men <u>like</u> to take care of a baby. (Ali)
   Ali doesn't like to take care of a baby.

9. American women often <u>wear</u> shorts in the summer. (Moslem women/ never)

Moslem women never wear shorts in the summe

EXERCISE 19 Read each sentence. Then write a *yes/no* question about the words in parentheses ( ). Write a short answer.

EXAMPLES: American women sometimes wear earrings. (American men/ever)
Do American men ever wear an earring? Yes, they do.

The women are wearing shorts. (the men)
Are the men wearing shorts? No, they aren't.

1. Ali is writing. (his homework)
   Is Ali writing his homework. Yes, he is.

2. He's watching people. (American people)
   Is he watching American People. Yes, he

3. He understands Arab customs. (American customs)
   Does he understand American customs. Yes, h

4. American men wear shorts in the summer. (American women)
   Do American women wear shorts in the su
   yes, they do.

5. The man is eating. (a hot dog)
   Is the man eating a hot dog. Yes, he

EXERCISE 20 Read each statement. Then write a *wh-* question about the words in parentheses ( ). An answer is not necessary.

EXAMPLES: A young man is resting his feet on a chair. (why)
Why is he resting his feet on a chair?

Ali lives in the U.S. (where/his family)
Where does his family live?

1. Ali is writing a letter. (to whom)   OR   (who . . . to)

2. Ali wants to know about American customs. (why)

---

3. Two women are putting on make-up. (where)

   _____

4. American men and women touch and hold hands in public. (why)

   _____

5. Ali writes to his family. (how often)

   _____

6. The man isn't using a fork. (why/not)

   _____

7. Women don't wear shorts in some countries. (why)

   _____

8. Americans often wear blue jeans. (why)

   _____

9. "Custom" means tradition or habit. (what/"behavior")

   _____

SUMMARY OF LESSON 6

Uses of Tenses

Simple Present Tense	
General truths	Americans **speak** English. Oranges **grow** in Florida.
Regular activity, habit	I always **speak** English in class. I sometimes **eat** in the cafeteria. I **visit** my parents every Friday.
Customs	Americans **shake** hands. Japanese people **bow**.
Place of origin	Miguel **comes** from El Salvador. Marek **comes** from Poland.
With nonaction verbs	She **has** a new car. I **like** the U.S. You **look** great today.

Present Continuous (with action verbs only)	
Now	We **are reviewing** now.
	I **am looking** at page 174 now.
A long action in progress at this general time	Dan **is learning** how to play the guitar.
	He **is gaining** weight.
A descriptive state	She **is wearing** shorts.
	He **is sitting** near the door.
	The teacher **is standing**.

EDITING ADVICE ✐

1. Include *be* with a continuous tense.

          is
   He ‸working now.

2. Use the correct word order in a question.

          are you
   Where ~~you're~~ going?

          don't you
   Why ~~you don't~~ like New York?

3. Don't use the present continuous with a nonaction verb.

          has
   She ~~is having~~ her own computer.

4. Use the *-s* form when the subject is *he, she,* or *it.*

          has   *s*
   He ~~have~~ a new car. He like‸ to drive.

5. Don't use *be* with a simple present tense verb.
   I̶'̶m̶ need a new computer.

6. Use *do* or *does* in a simple present tense question.

          does   *live*
   Where ~~lives~~ your mother‸?

7. Don't use the -s form after *does*.

  Where does he takes the bus?

Review the Editing Advice for the simple present tense on pages 70–72.

LESSON 6 TEST / REVIEW

PART 1

Find the mistakes with the underlined words and correct them. Not every sentence has a mistake. If the sentence is correct, write **C**.

EXAMPLES: She's owning a new bike now.
owns

I'm not studying math this semester.   **C**

1. Why you aren't listening to me?
   Why aren't you listening to me?
2. Usually I'm go home after class.
   I usually go home after class.
3. I think that he's having trouble with this lesson. *c*

4. She's thinking about her family now. *c*

5. Does she needs help with her homework?
   Does she need help with her homework?
6. What kind of car do you have? *c*

7. What he's studying now?
   What is he studying now?
8. Does he has any children?
   Does he have any children?
9. He's wearing jeans now. *c*

10. My teacher speak English well.
    My teacher speaks English well.
11. I'm speak my native language at home.
    I speak my native language at home.
12. The baby sleeping now.
    The baby is sleeping now.
13. When begins summer?
    When does summer begin?
14. Where does your family lives?
    Where does your family live?

Present Continuous Tense   **175**

This is a conversation between two students, Alicia (A) and Teresa (T), who meet in the school library. Fill in the blanks with the simple present or the present continuous of the verb in parentheses ( ).

T.   Hi, Alicia.

A.   Hi, Teresa. What _____are you doing_____ here?
(example: you/do)

T.   I'm looking _____ for a book on American geography. What about you?
(1 look)

A.   I'm returning _____ a book. Do you want to go for a cup of coffee?
(2 return)   *(3 you/want)*

T.   I can't. I'm waiting _____ for my friend. We're working _____
(4 wait)   *(5 work)*

on a geography project together, and we _____need_____ to finish
(6 need)

it by next week.

A.   _____Do you like_____ your geography class?
(7 you/like)

T.   Yes. I especially _____like_____ the teacher, Bob. He's a handsome
(8 like)

young man. He's very casual. He always _____wears_____ jeans and
(9 wear)

a T-shirt to class. He _____has_____ an earring in one ear.
(10 have)

A.   That's _____seems_____ very strange to me. I _____tink_____
(11 seem)   *(12 think)*

that teachers in the U.S. are very informal. How _____does Bob teach_____
(13 Bob/teach)

the class? By lecturing?

T.   No. We _____usually work_____ in small groups, and he
(14 usually/work)

_____helps_____ us by walking around the classroom.
(15 help)

A.   _____Does he give_____ hard tests?
(16 he/give)

T.   No. He _____doesn't believe_____ in tests.
(17 not/believe)

A.   Why _____doesn't he believe_____ in tests?
(18 he/not/believe)

T.   He _____thinks_____ that students get too nervous during a test.
(19 think)

He _____says_____ it's better to work on projects. This week
(20 say)

we're working _____ on city maps.
(21 work)

A.   That's _____sounds_____ interesting.
(22 sound)

T.   Why _____do you ask_____ me so many questions about my teacher?
(23 you/ask)

A. I'm ___thinking___ about taking a geography course next semester.
       (24 think)

T. Bob's very popular. Be sure to register early because his classes always ___fill___ quickly. Oh. I ___see___ my
       (25 fill)   (26 see)

   friend now. She's ___walking___ toward us. I have to go now.
              (27 walk)   to my direction.

A. Good luck on your project.

T. Thanks. Bye.

PART 3 Fill in the blanks with the negative form of the underlined word.

EXAMPLE: Teresa is in the library. She ___isn't___ at home.

1. Alicia wants to go for a cup of coffee. Teresa ___doesn't want___ to go for a cup of coffee.

2. Teresa is looking for a book. Alicia ___isn't look___ for a book.

3. They are talking about school. They ___don't talking___ about the news.

4. They have time to talk now. They ___don't have___ time for a cup of coffee.

5. Students in the geography class work in small groups. They ___don't work___ alone.

6. Alicia's teacher gives tests. Teresa's teacher ___doesn't give___ tests.

7. Teresa is waiting for a friend. Alicia ___doesn't waiting___ for a friend.

8. The teacher seems strange to Alicia. He ___doesn't seem___ strange to Teresa.

9. Alicia is returning a book. Teresa ___isn't returning___ a book.

PART 4 Read each sentence. Then write a *yes/no* question about the words in parentheses ( ). Write a short answer.

EXAMPLE: Teresa is looking for a book. (a geography book)
   Is she looking for a geography book? Yes, she is.

1. Bob likes projects. (tests)
   Does he like tests? Yes, he does.

Does she have time now?

2. Alicia has time now. (Teresa)

Ask B *Is she having time now? Yes, she*

3. They are talking about their classes. (their teachers)

Yes they are.

Are their teachers talking about their classes?

4. Bob wears jeans to class. (ever/a suit)

Bob ever

Does he ever wear a suit to class. Yes, he always

5. Alicia wants to go for coffee. (Teresa)

Does she want to go for coffee? Yes, she does

6. American teachers seem strange to Alicia. (to Teresa) *Yes they do.*

Do American teachers seem strange to Alicia?

7. Teresa is working on a geography project. (Alicia) *Yes, she is.*

Is Alicia working on a geography project.

PART 5   Read each sentence. Then write a question with the words in parentheses ( ). An answer is not necessary.

EXAMPLE: Bob is popular. (Why)
Why is he popular?

1. Bob sounds interesting. (Why)

Why does he sound interesting?

2. Bob doesn't like tests. (Why)

Why doesn't he like tests?

3. Teresa and her friend are working on a project. (What kind of project)

What kind of project are they working on?

4. Teresa studies in the library. (How often)

How often does she study in the library.

What kind of book is she looking for?

5. Teresa is looking for a book. (What kind)

What kind is she looking for a book.

6. Teresa is waiting for her friend. (Why)

Why is she waiting for her friend

7. Her classmates aren't writing a term paper. (Why)

Why aren't her classmates writing a term paper?

CLASSROOM ACTIVITIES

1. Think of a place (cafeteria, airport, train station, bus, playground, church, opera, movie theater, laundromat, office at this school, kindergarten class-room, restaurant, department store, etc.) Pretend you are at this place. Write three or four sentences to tell what people in this place are doing. Other students will guess where you are.

EXAMPLE:
People are walking fast.
People are carrying suitcases.
People are standing in long lines.
They're buying tickets.
Guess: Are you at the airport?

2. Pretend you are calling from your cell phone. You are telling your family where you are. Fill in the blanks to tell what you and other people are doing. Then find a partner and see how many of your sentences match your partner's sentences.

a. I'm at the supermarket. I'm _____. Do you need any-thing while I'm here?

b. I'm in my car. I'm _____.

c. I'm in the school library. I'm _____. People _____ me to be quiet because I'm _____ to you on my cell phone.

d. I'm in a taxi. I'm on my way home. I'm _____ you to let you know that _____.

e. I'm at the bus stop. I _____ for the bus, but it's late. I don't want you to worry.

f. I'm at a shoe store. I _____.

g. I'm at the playground with the kids. The kids _____.

h. I'm at church. The pastor is _____ but nobody is listening. Some people _____.

i. I'm at the movies. I can't talk now because the movie _____.

j. I'm in the bedroom. I have to talk softly because my husband _____.

k. I'm in class now. I can't talk. The teacher _____.

In a small group or with the entire class, discuss behaviors that are strange to you. What American behaviors are not polite in your native culture?

Go to the school cafeteria, student union, or other crowded place. Sit there for a while and look for unusual behaviors. Write down some of the unusual things you see. Report back to the class.

Internet Activity

Find the web site of a college in this city. Answer the following questions:

1. Where is it?

2. What's the tuition?

3. Does this college have evening classes?

4. Does this college have more than one location?

5. Does it have a graduate program?

6. Does it have dormitories?

7. Does it have ESL classes?

8. When is the next registration?

GRAMMAR

Future Tenses—*Will* and *Be Going To*
Comparison of Tenses.

CONTEXT

Registering for Wedding Gifts
Jason and Katie—Starting a Married Life

LESSON FOCUS

We have two ways of talking about the future. We
can either use *will* or *be going to* plus a base form to
talk about the future.

We *will study* the future tense.
The teacher *is going to explain* the grammar.

1. When you go to a wedding, what kind of gift do you buy?
2. Do you ever give money as a gift?

Read the following conversation. Pay special attention to future tense verbs.

Registering for Gifts

Convite *do you want go out with me?*

A. I have an invitation to my cousin's wedding.

B. **Are you going to go**?

A. Of course. It**'s going to be** in a beautiful hotel. Two hundred fifty people **will be** there.

B. What is the tradition about buying gifts in the U.S.?

A. Some people give money.

B. Money? Is that a good gift?

A. Yes. They're a young couple. They**'ll need** a lot of money to start their new home. But I**'m not going to give** money. I**'m going to buy** something for their new home.

B. What **are you going to buy**?

A. I don't know yet. I**'m going to go** to the department store and check the "bridal registry."

B. What's that?

A. When a couple is planning a wedding, they often register for gifts at a store. That means they choose gifts that they want to receive. When I go to the store, I**'ll look** at the list and see what they want.

B. Is this an American custom?

A. Yes. I think it's a good idea. This way, my cousin and his new wife **will get** exactly what they need. They **won't have** five toasters and six food processors.

Did you know...?

In the U.S., the average wedding for 250 guests costs $15,000.

B. I'm really shocked. In my country, we give the gifts that we want to give. The newlyweds[1] appreciate the gift even if they receive five of the same thing.

A. Well, our customs are different.

B. **Are** your cousin and his bride **going to open** the gifts at the wedding?

A. Probably not. They**'ll open** them at home. Then they**'re going to send** thank-you cards to the guests a few weeks later.

B. **Aren't** they **going to thank** the guests at the wedding?

A. They **will** if they can. But many guests **will leave** before the bride and groom have a chance to thank them.

B. **I'll** never **understand** American customs.

A. Of course, you **will**. Maybe you **won't like** them, but I'm sure you**'ll understand** them.

7.1 Future with *Will*

Subject	Will	(Not)	Verb	Complement
I	will		buy	a gift.
I	will	not	give	money.
There	will		be	250 people at the wedding.

LANGUAGE NOTES

1. We use *will* with all persons to form the future tense. *Will* doesn't have an -s form.
   I *will leave*.   She *will leave*.
2. We can make a contraction with the subject pronoun and *will*.
   I will = I'll   It will = It'll
   You will = You'll   We will = We'll
   He will = He'll   They will = They'll
   She will = She'll
3. Put *not* after *will* to form the negative. The contraction for *will not* is *won't*.
   They *won't open* the gifts at the wedding.
4. You can put a frequency word between *will* and the main verb.
   She will *never* understand American customs.

[1] *Newlyweds* are the bride and groom soon after they get married.

Fill in the blanks with an appropriate verb in the future tense. Use *will*.

EXAMPLE: The wedding ___*will be*___ in a church.

Will the wedding in a church?

1. Two hundred guests ___*will be*___ at the wedding.

2. Some people ___*will give*___ money as a gift.

3. Other people ___*won't buy*___ a present at a store.

Will other people buy a present at a store?

4. Some people ___*won't be*___ the list in the store to see what the bride and groom want.

5. The newlyweds ___*will open*___ their presents at home.

7.2 Future with *Be Going To*

Subject	Be	(Not)	Going To + Verb	Complement
I	am		going to send	a gift.
We	are	not	going to take	a gift to the wedding.
There	are		going to be	musicians at the wedding.

LANGUAGE NOTES

1. In informal speech, *going to* before another verb often sounds like "gonna." We don't write "gonna." Listen to your teacher's pronunciation of *going to* in the following sentences:
    He's going to buy dishes.
    They're going to get married in a month.
    NOTE: We often use the preposition *in* with the future to mean *after*.

2. We often shorten *going to go* to *going*.
    He *is going to go* to the wedding. = He *is going* to the wedding.

3. We don't pronounce "gonna" before a noun.
    He's going to the wedding. (Pronounce: going to)

= abbreviation

EXERCISE 2 Fill in the blanks with an appropriate verb in the future tense. Use *be going to*.

EXAMPLE: They ___*are going to thank*___ the guests at the wedding.

1. The newlyweds ___*are going to send*___ thank-you cards to all the guests.

2. They ___*are going to open*___ the gifts at home.

3. I'm going to buy _____ something useful for their new home.

4. After the wedding in the church, the guests are going to go to a restaurant for dinner.

5. There are going to be a lot of people at the wedding.

7.3 Will and Be Going To—Uses

Use	Will	Be Going To
Prediction	The newlyweds **will** be very happy together.	The newlyweds **are going to** be very happy together.
Fact	Some people **will** give money.	Some people **are going to** give money.
Plan		They **are going to** get married on March 6. I **am going to** buy a gift.
Promise	I **will** always love you.	
Offer to help	A. This gift box is heavy. B. I**'ll** carry it for you.	

LANGUAGE NOTES

1. Use either *will* or *be going to* for facts about the future and for predictions.
2. When we have a plan to do something, we usually use *be going to*.
3. When we make a promise or offer to help, we usually use *will*.

EXERCISE 3 Tell if you have plans to do these things or not. Use *be going to*.

EXAMPLE: meet a friend after class
I'm (not) going to meet a friend after class.

1. get something to eat after class
2. watch TV tonight
3. eat dinner at home tonight
4. go to the library this week
5. go shopping for groceries this week
6. stay home this weekend

7. take a vacation this year

8. move (to a different apartment) this year

9. buy a car this year

EXERCISE 4   Tell if you predict that these things are going to happen or not in this class. Use *be going to.*

EXAMPLE: we/finish this lesson today
We are going to finish this lesson today.

1. the teacher/give a test soon
2. the test/be hard
3. most students/pass the test
4. I/pass the test
5. the teacher/give everyone an A
6. my English/improve

7. we/finish this book by the end of the semester
8. the next test /cover the future tense
9. we/have a party at the end of the semester

EXERCISE 5   Fill in the blanks to complete these statements. Use *be going to.*

EXAMPLE: I don't understand the meaning of a word. I *'m going to look it up in* my dictionary.

1. It's hot in here. I _____ a window.

2. It's too noisy in this house. I can't study. I _____ in the library.

3. She's hungry. She _____ dinner now.

4. My mother in Poland always worries about me. I _____ to tell her that I'm fine.

5. We don't have any milk in the house. When I go out shopping, I _____ some milk.

6. She plans to be a doctor. She _____ medical school next year.

7. I'm not happy with my job. I _____ and look for another one.

8. I _____ next week. Here's my new address.

9. My parents miss me very much. They _____ next month to visit for three weeks.

10. There's a great new movie at the Garden Theater. My friends and I _are going to watch_ tomorrow night. Do you want to go with us?

EXERCISE 6   Tell if you predict that these things will happen or not in the next 50 years. Use *will*. You may work with a partner or in a small group.

EXAMPLE: people/have more free time
I think people won't have more free time. They will spend more time at their jobs and less time with their families.

1. there/another world war

2. the economy of the U.S./get worse

3. people in the U.S./have fewer children

4. Americans/live longer
   I think the Americas will live longer, because, theyr will have a good lifestyle.

5. health care/improve
   I hope health care will improve.

6. cars/use solar energy²

7. divorce/increase

8. crime/get worse

9. people/get tired of computers
   I think people won't get tired of computers.

10. technology/continue to grow
    I think technology will continue to grow.

EXERCISE 7   Some friends of yours are going to have a birthday soon, and you want to buy them a present or do something special for them. What will you buy or do for these people?

EXAMPLE: Maria's birthday is in the winter.
I'll buy her a sweater.   OR   I'll take her skiing.

1. Bill loves to go fishing. I'll buy fishing staff. ~~go pick up Bill to go fishing~~

2. Tina loves to eat in restaurants.
   I'll invite Tina to go dinner out in her birthday.

3. Carl needs a new radio.
   I'll buy a new radio for my friend Carl.

4. Jim has a new CD player.
   I'll buy a new CDs for Jim players in his CD player.

5. Lisa loves the beach in the summer.
   I'll go invite Lisa to go in the Copacabana beach with me.

6. Tom loves movies.
   I'll take tom to watch the new move. It name is The Passion of Crist.

² *Solar energy* comes from the sun.

EXERCISE 8 A man is proposing marriage to a woman. He is making promises. Fill in the blanks to complete these statements.

EXAMPLE: I _____*will be*_____ a good husband to you.

1. I love you very much. I (always) _*I'll always love*_ you.

2. I want to make you happy. I'll _*promise*_ everything I can to make you happy.

3. I don't have a lot of money, but I'll _*work hard*_ and try to make money.

4. We'll _*have*_ children, and I'll _*be*_ a good father to them.

5. We'll _*get fat*_ old together.

6. We'll _*be*_ best friends and take care of each other.

7. You are the only woman for me. I (not) _*I won't look*_ at another woman.

EXERCISE 9 Offer to help in these situations using *will* + an appropriate verb.

EXAMPLE: A. I have to move next Sunday. It's so much work.

B. _Don't worry. I'll help you pack._

1. A. My hands are full. I need to open the door.

   B. _Don't worry. I'll open it for you._

2. I need stamps, but I have no time to go to the post office.

   B. I'm going to the post office. _Don't worry. I'll buy them for you_

3. A. I cook every night. I'm tired of cooking.

   B. Take a break. I'll _take care of dinner_ tonight.

4. A. I don't have experience with computers. I have to write my composition on the computer.

   B. Come to my house after class. _I'll help you do it._

5. A. I always drive when we go to the country. I'm tired.

   B. No problem. I'll _drive_ this time.

6. A. Let's go out to dinner tonight.

B. I can't. I don't have any money.

A. No problem. _I'll pay this time and you pay me back tomorrow._

7. A. I can't pay my phone bill. I'm not working now and don't have much money.

B. Don't worry. _I'll lend you money_. You can pay me back next month.

8. A. The phone's ringing and I'm eating a sandwich. My mouth is full.

B. Finish your lunch. _I'll ~~ask~~ the phone for you._
↳ answer

7.4 Questions with *Be Going To* and *Will*

Compare statements and questions with *be going to*.

Wh- Word	Be (+ *Not*)	Subject	Be	Going to + Base Form	Complement	Short Answer
		They	**are**	**going to** leave	soon.	
	Are	they		**going to** leave	tomorrow?	No, they **aren't**.
When	**are**	they		**going to** leave?		
Why	**aren't**	they		**going to** leave	tomorrow?	
		Who	**is**	**going to** leave?		

Compare statements and questions with *will*:

Wh- Word	Will/ Won't	Subject	Will +	Base Form	Complement	Short Answer
		She	**will**	eat	lunch.	
	Will	she		eat	a sandwich?	Yes, she **will**.
What	**will**	she		eat	for lunch?	
Why	**won't**	she		eat	a salad?	
		Who	**will**	eat	lunch?	

EXERCISE 10 Ask another student a *yes/no* question with *are you going to* about a later time today. Then ask a *wh-* question with the words in parentheses ( ) whenever possible.

EXAMPLE: listen to the radio (when)
A. Are you going to listen to the radio tonight?
B. Yes, I am.
A. When are you going to listen to the radio?
B. After dinner.

1. watch TV (what show) *Are you going watch t.v? yes, I am*
What show are you going watch in the t.v? *I am*
2. listen to the radio (when)
Are you going listen to the radio? When are you going
3. read the newspaper (what newspaper)

Ask about ← 4. eat dinner (with whom) OR (who . . . with)
Are you going eat dinner? Who are you going eat dinner
5. take a shower (when)

6. go shopping (why)
Are you going to ̶t̶o̶ shopping? Why are you going to go s
7. call someone (whom)
Are you going to call someone? When are you going
8. use a computer (why)
why aren't you going to use a computer?
9. do your homework (when)

EXERCISE 11 Ask another student a *yes/no* question with *be going to* and the words given. Then ask a *wh-* question with the words in parentheses ( ) whenever possible.

EXAMPLE:
study another English course after this one (which course)
A. Are you going to study another English course after this one?
B. Yes, I am.
A. Which course are you going to study?
B. I'm going to study level 4.

1. go back to your country (when) (why) *Are you going to your Cou*
Yes, I am. When are you going to go?
2. study something new (what)
Are you going to study something new? What new are
— 3. look for a job (when) *going to study?* *Yes, I am.*
Are you going to look for a job?
4. get an A in this course (what grade) *when are*
you
5. transfer to another school (why) (which school)

6. visit other American cities (which cities) *Are you going to visit*
American cities? Which cities are you going to
7. buy a computer (why) (what kind) *I am going to visit N.Y.*

EXERCISE 12 A 13-year-old girl is thinking about her grown sister and her own future. She is asking herself these questions. Fill in the blanks to complete the questions.

EXAMPLE: My sister is married. Will ___*I get*___ married?

1. My sister has a wonderful husband. Will ___*I have*___ a wonderful husband?

2. My sister has two children. How many children ___*will I have*___ ?

radio.

3. My sister is serious now that she has children. I'm not serious. _Will I be_ serious someday?

4. My sister has a college education. College is so expensive now. Who _will pay for_ my education?

5. My sister is a computer programmer. What _will I be_ when I grow up?

6. I'm short now. _Will_ I always _be_ short or _will_ I _be_ tall like my sister?

7. My sister lives in Boston now. Where _will I live_?

8. There are a lot of job opportunities in Boston now. _Will I have_ a lot of job opportunities there when I grow up?

7.5 Future Tense + Time/*If* Clause[3]

Time or *If* Clause (Simple Present)	Main Clause (Future)
When I **go** to the store,	I **will look** at the list of gifts.
If the newlyweds **need** dishes,	I **will buy** dishes for them.

Main Clause (Future)	Time or *If* Clause (Simple Present)
I **will go** to the wedding	if I **get** an invitation.
She **will thank** the guests	before they **leave**.

LANGUAGE NOTES

1. The sentences in the chart have two clauses. We use the future tense only in the main clause; we use the simple present tense in the time clause/*if* clause.
2. If the time or *if* clause comes first, we separate the two clauses with a comma.

[3] A *clause* is a group of words that has a subject and a verb. Some sentences have more than one clause.

EXERCISE **13** This is an old fable.[4] It's the story of a young lady. She is carrying a pail of milk to the market. As she walks there, she thinks about what she will do with the money that the milk will bring. Fill in the blanks with the correct form of the verb to complete this story.

EXAMPLE: When I ___*sell*___ this milk, I ___*will buy*___ some eggs.
           (sell)   (buy)

1. When the eggs ___hatch___, I'll ___have___ many chickens.
                  (hatch)   (have)

2. I'll ___sell___ the chickens when they ___are___ big.
        (sell)   (be)

3. When I ___sell___ the chickens, I'll ___have___ money
          (sell)   (have)
   to buy a pretty new dress.

4. I'll ___go___ to a party when I ___have___ my new
        (go)   (have)
   dress.

5. All the young men ___notice___ me when I'll ___wear___
                      (notice)   (wear)
   the dress.

6. When the men ___see___ how pretty I am, they'll ___want___
                 (see)   (want)
   to marry me.

Suddenly the young woman drops the milk pail and all the milk spills. What lesson does this story try to teach us?

EXERCISE **14** Complete each statement.

EXAMPLES: When this class is over, ___I'll go home.___
             When this class is over, ___I'm going to get something to eat.___

1. When this semester is over, I'm going to take vacation.
2. When this class is over, I'm going to restaurant to dinner
★ 3. When I get home today, I'll go to take a nap.
4. When I graduate (or finish my courses at this school), I'll go do my registration to start summer curse
5. When I return to my country/become a citizen, I'll be happy.
6. When I retire, I'm going buy a farm.
7. When I speak English better, I'll go do a tour in the

[4] A *fable* is an old story. It usually teaches us a lesson, called a moral.

EXERCISE 15 Complete each statement.

EXAMPLES: If I drink too much coffee, _I won't sleep tonight._

If I drink too much coffee, _I'm going to feel nervous._

1. If I practice English, _I'm going to improve my speech_

2. If I don't study, _I won't grow in my career._

3. If I don't pay my rent, _I won't stay in my apartament_

4. If I pass this course, _I'm get next one free._

5. If we have a test next week, _I'm going to study a lot._

6. If the teacher is absent tomorrow, _We won't have class._

7. If I find a good job, _I'm going to make mor money._

EXERCISE 16 On the first day of class, a teacher is explaining the course to the students. Fill in the blanks to complete this conversation between a teacher (T) and his students (S).

T: In this course, you ___are going to study___ English grammar.
(example: study)

You'll ___write___ a few short compositions. Tomorrow, I
(1 write)

___will give___ you a list of assignments. Do you have any ques-
(2 give)
tions about this course?

S: Yes. How many tests ___we'll have___?
(3 have)

T: You will have 13 tests, one for each lesson in the book. If you're absent

from a test, you can make it up.[5] If you ___won't take___ the test,
(4 not take)

you'll ___get___ an F on that test.
(5 get)

S: ___You'll tell___ us about the tests ahead of time?
(6 tell)

[5] If you are absent on the day of a test, the teacher expects you to take it at a later time.

T: Oh, yes. I'll always tell you about a test a few days before.

S: When ___I'll give___ the midterm exam?
       (7 give)

T: I'm going to give you the midterm exam in April.

S: ___It'll be___ very hard?
     (8 be)

T: If you ___study___, it won't be hard.
           (9 study)

S: What ___we'll study___ in this course?
         (10 study)

T: You'll study verb tenses, count and noncount nouns, and comparison of adjectives.

S: ___We'll finish___ everything in this book?
     (11 finish)

T: Yes, I think we'll finish everything.

S: ___When will the semester be___ over?
     (12 be)

T: The semester will be over[6] in June. Tomorrow I ___'ll give___
                                                    (13 give)
you a course outline with all this information.

EXERCISE 17 Write two questions to ask your teacher about this course.

EXAMPLES:
Will there be a test on this lesson?

When will you give us the next test?

When will we finish this curse are we going
If no, why won't ?

EXERCISE 18 A young woman (A) is going to leave her country to go to the U.S. Her friend (B) is asking her questions. Fill in the blanks to complete this conversation.

A. I'm so happy! I'm going to the U.S.

B. When *are you going to leave?*
          (example: leave)

A. I'm going to leave next month.

B. So soon? ___Will you buy___ anything before you ___leave___?
             (1 buy)   (2 leave)

[6] To *be over* means to be finished.

A. Yes. I'm going to buy warm clothes for the winter. I hear the winter there is very cold.

B. Where _____?
(3 be)

A. I'll be in Ann Arbor, Michigan.

B. Where _____?
(4 live)

A. I'm not sure. When I _____ there, I _____
(5 get)   (6 decide)
where to live.

B. _____ in the U.S.?
(7 work)

A. No, I'm not going to work. I have a scholarship. I'm going to study at the University of Michigan.

B. What _____?
(8 study)

A. I'm going to study to be a computer analyst.

B. When _____ to our country?
(9 return)

A. I _____ when I _____.
(10 return)   (11 graduate)

B. When _____?
(12 you/graduate)

A. In four years.

B. That's a long time! _____ me?
(13 miss)

A. Of course, I'll miss you.

B. _____ to me?
(14 write)

A. Of course. I _____ to you when I _____
(15 write)   (16 find)
a place to live.

EXERCISE 19 A young woman is planning to get married. Her friend is asking her questions about her plans. Fill in the blanks to complete this conversation.

A. I'm getting married!

B. That's wonderful! Congratulations. _Are you going to have_____ a
(example: have)
big wedding?

A. No, we're going to have a small wedding. We'll invite ___ (we're going to invite ~~crossed out~~) **we'll invite** _(1 invite)_ about 50 people.

B. Where __will it be__? _(2 be)_

A. It'll be at St. Peter's Church. We're going to have _(3 have)_ a reception[7] at a Korean restaurant after the wedding.

B. __Are you going to buy__ a wedding dress? _(4 buy)_

A. No, I'll __use__ my sister's dress for the wedding. Then, for _(5 use)_ the reception, I'll __wear__ a traditional Korean dress. _(6 wear)_

B. Where __will you live__ after you get married? _(7 live)_

A. For a few years, we're going to live _(8 live)_ with Kim's parents. When Kim __finishes the__ college and __gets__ a job, _(9 finish)_ _(10 get)_ we're going to get _(11 get)_ our own apartment.

B. You're going to live with your in-laws? I can't believe it.

A. In my country, it's common. My in-laws are very nice. I'm sure it __won't be__ a problem. We __won't have__ children _(12 not/be)_ _(13 not/have)_ right away.

B. __Are your parent going to come__ here for the wedding? _(14 come)_

A. No, my parents aren't going to come. But a month after the wedding, we're going to take _(15 take)_ a trip to Korea, and Kim can meet my parents there.

B. __When are you going to get__ married? _(16 get)_

A. On May 15. I hope you'll be able to attend. We're are going to send _(17 send)_ you an invitation.

B. I'll __be__ glad to attend. _(18 be)_

---

[7] A *reception* is a party.

1. Do you think life is hard for newlyweds? In what way?
2. In your community, do parents help their children after they get married?

Read the following article. Pay special attention to verb tenses: simple present, present continuous, and future.

Jason and Katie—Starting a Married Life

Jason and Katie are newlyweds. The wedding is over, the honeymoon was great, the gifts are opened, and their life as a married couple **is beginning**. They **are learning** that they have many responsibilities as a married couple.

Katie **works** as a nurse full time. She **doesn't work** in a hospital. She **goes** to people's homes and **helps** them there. Jason **isn't working** now. He**'s** still **attending** college. He's in his last year. He**'s studying** to be a lawyer. After classes every day, he **studies** at home or **goes** to the law library at his college. He**'s going to graduate** next June. When he **graduates**, he **will have** to take a special exam for lawyers. If he **passes** it, he**'ll get** a good job and **make** good money. But when he **starts** to work, he**'ll have** to pay back student loans. For now, they**'re** both **living** on Katie's salary.

Katie and Jason **are saving** money little by little. They**'re planning** to buy a house some day. They **are** also **thinking** about having two children in the future. But they want to be financially stable before they **have** children. Their parents **offer** to help them, but they **don't want** to depend on their parents. Because Jason is so busy with his studies and Katie is so busy with her job, they rarely **go** out. Staying at home **helps** them save money.

SIMPLE PRESENT TENSE

Forms	Uses of the Simple Present Tense
Jason **studies** law. He **doesn't study** medicine. **Does** he **study** every day? Yes, he **does**. Where **does** he **study**? Why **doesn't** he **study** medicine? Who **studies** medicine?	• With facts Law school **costs** a lot of money. • With customs Grown children **don't like** to depend on their parents. • With habits and regular activities Jason **goes** to the library almost every day.

PRESENT CONTINUOUS TENSE

Forms	Uses of the Present Continuous Tense
They **are saving** money to buy a house. They **aren't saving** to buy a new car. **Are** they **saving** for a vacation? No, they **aren't**. How **are** they **saving** money? Why **aren't** they **saving** to buy a car? Who **is saving** money?	• With an action in progress now, at this moment We **are reviewing** verb tenses now. • With a long-term action that is in progress. It may not be happening at this exact moment. They **are saving** money.

FUTURE

Forms—*Will*	Uses of the Future with *Will*
Jason **will graduate** next year. He **won't graduate** this year. **Will** he **graduate** in January? No, he **won't**. When **will** he **graduate**? Why **won't** he **graduate** in January? Who **will graduate** in January?	• With predictions I think they **will be** happy together. • With facts The law exam **will be** in March. • With plans They **will buy** a house. • With promises "I'll **always** love you, Katie," says Jason. • With an offer to help "I'll **help** you in the kitchen."

(continued)

Forms—*Be Going To*	Uses of the Future with *Be Going To*

They **are going to buy** a house.
They **aren't going to buy** a new car.
Are they **going to buy** a house in the city?
No, they **aren't**.
Where **are** they **going to buy** a house?
Why **aren't** they **going to buy** a house in the city?
Who **is going to buy** a house?
	• With predictions
	  I think they **are going to have** a wonderful life.
	• With facts
	  They **are going to receive** bills for student loans.
	• With plans
	  Jason **is going to look** for a job next year.

LANGUAGE NOTES

1. Don't use the future in *if* or time clauses.
   When Jason *graduates*, he *will look* for a job.
   If they have children, they *will need* a bigger house.
2. Don't use the present continuous with nonaction verbs.
   They *have* a lot of responsibilities now.

EXERCISE 20 Fill in the blanks with the correct tense and form of the verb in parentheses ( ).

EXAMPLE: Jason ___*is going to graduate*___ next year.
            (graduate)

1. He's ~~going to have~~ He'll a good job when he __graduates.__
   (have)   (graduate)

2. He __often studies__ in the library.
   (often/study)

3. Jason and Katie __rarely go__ out.
   (rarely/go)

4. They're __thinking__ about buying a house.
   (think)

5. They're __saving__ their money now.
   (save)

EXERCISE 21 Fill in the blanks with the negative form of the underlined verb.

EXAMPLE: They are young. They __*aren't*__ old.

1. They have an apartment now. They __don't have__ a house.

2. They want children, but they __don't want__ children right now.

3. Katie is working. Jason _isn't working_ .

4. They depend on each other. They _don't depend_ on their parents.

5. Jason will graduate in June. He _won't graduate_ in January.

EXERCISE 22 Read each statement. Then write a *yes/no* question with the words in parentheses ( ). Write a short answer.

EXAMPLE: Katie works as a nurse. (in a hospital)
Does she work in a hospital? No, she doesn't.

1. Jason is a student. (Katie)
   Is Katie a student? Yes, she is.

2. They are thinking about buying a house. (about having children)
   Are they thinking about having children? Yes,

3. Jason will have a job. (a good job)
   Will Jason have a good job. Yes, he will.

4. Jason is attending college now. (Katie)
   Is Katie attending college now? Yes she is

X 5. They are going to have children. (five children)
   Are they going to have five children? No they a

EXERCISE 23 Read each statement. Then write a *wh-* question about the words in parentheses ( ). An answer is not necessary.

EXAMPLE: Katie works as a nurse. (Where)
Where does she work as a nurse?

1. They are saving their money. (why)

   _____

2. They don't want to depend on their parents. (why)

   _____

3. Jason will make good money. (when)

   _____

4. Jason <u>wants</u> to be a lawyer. (why)

Why does want to be a lawyer?

5. Katie <u>isn't going to work</u> when her children are small. (why)

_____

6. Jason <u>will pay</u> back his student loans. (when)

When will Jason pay back his student loans?

7. They <u>don't go</u> out very much. (why)

Why don't they go out very much?

8. Jason <u>is attending</u> college. (what college)

What college is Jason attending?

9. He <u>is going to graduate</u>. (when)

When is he going to graduate?

✗10. Jason <u>isn't earning</u> money now. (who)

Who isn't earning money now?

11. Someone <u>wants</u> to help them. (who)

Who wants to help them?

12. They <u>are learning</u> about responsibilities. (how)

How are they learning about responsibilities?

SUMMARY OF LESSON 7

1. Future patterns with **will**.
AFFIRMATIVE:	He **will buy** a car.
NEGATIVE:	He **won't buy** a Japanese car.
YES/NO QUESTION:	**Will** he **buy** an American car?
SHORT ANSWER:	Yes, he **will**.
WH- QUESTION:	When **will** he **buy** a car?
NEGATIVE QUESTION:	Why **won't** he **buy** a Japanese car?
SUBJECT QUESTION:	Who **will buy** a car?

2. Future patterns with **be going to**.

AFFIRMATIVE:	He **is going to buy** a car.
NEGATIVE:	He **isn't going to buy** a Japanese car.
YES/NO QUESTION:	**Is** he **going to buy** an American car?
SHORT ANSWER:	Yes, he **is**.
WH- QUESTION:	When **is** he **going to buy** a car?
NEGATIVE QUESTION:	Why **isn't** he **going to buy** a Japanese car?
SUBJECT QUESTION:	Who **is going to buy** a car?

3.   Uses of **be going to** and **will**.

Use	*Will*	*Be Going To*
Prediction	You **will become** rich and famous.	You **are going to become** rich and famous.
Fact	The sun **will set** at 6:32 p.m. tonight.	The sun **is going to set** at 6:32 p.m. tonight.
Plan		**I'm going to buy** a new car next month.
Promise	I **will help** you.	
Offer to help	A. I can't open the door. B. **I'll open** it for you.	

4.   Review the simple present tense and the present continuous tense on pages 173–174.

EDITING ADVICE ✏️

1.   Don't use *be* with a future verb.

   I will ~~be~~ go.

2.   You need *be* in a future sentence that has no other verb.

   He will ^be^ angry.

   There will ^be^ a party soon.

3.   Don't combine *will* and *be going to*.

   He ~~will~~ ^is^ going to leave.   *Or   He will leave.*

4.   Don't use the present tense for a future action.

   I'm going home now. I ^'ll^ see you later.

5. Don't use the future tense after *when* or *if*.

   When they ~~will~~ go home, they will watch TV.

6. Use a form of *be* with *going to*.

   He $\overset{is}{\wedge}$ going to help me.

7. Use *to* after *going*.

   I'm going $\overset{to}{\wedge}$ study on Saturday.

8. Use correct word order for questions.

   Why ~~you aren't~~ $\overset{aren't\ you}{}$ going to eat lunch?

LESSON 7 TEST / REVIEW

PART 1   Find the mistakes with the underlined words and correct them. Not every sentence has a mistake. If the sentence is correct, write C.

EXAMPLES: I $\overset{am}{\underset{}{\text{~~will~~}}}$ going to buy a newspaper.

   If you're too tired to cook, I'll do it.   C

1. When $\overset{will\ you}{\underline{\text{~~you will~~}}}$ write your composition?

2. We will ~~be~~ buy a new car soon.   C

3. <u>Will you going to eat</u> dinner tonight?   *Are you going to eat dinner tonight?*

4. When he <u>will leave,</u> he will turn off the light.   *When he leaves he will turn off the light.*

5. I <u>going to take</u> a vacation soon.   *I'm going to take a vacation soon.*

6. <u>Is he going to use</u> the computer?   C

7. <u>They're going graduate soon.</u>   *They're going to graduate soon.*

8. I <u>will happy</u> when I will <u>know</u> more English.   *I'll be happy when I know more English.*

9. I'm going on vacation. I <u>will going to leave</u> next Friday.   *I'm going to leave next Friday.*

10. I'll write you a letter when I <u>arrive.</u>   C

11. There ~~will~~ a test soon.   *There will be a test soon.*

12. <u>I'll help</u> you tomorrow.   C

PART 2

Fill in the blanks with *will* or a form of *be* + *going to*. In some cases, both answers are possible.

EXAMPLES: I believe the next president _____will be_____ OR _____is going to_____ be a Democrat.

You can't move your piano alone. I _____'ll_____ help you do it.

1. We're going to eat in a new restaurant tomorrow. Do you want to go with us?

2. My friend is planning her wedding. She's going to invite 150 guests to her wedding.

3. I promise I _____will_____ clean my room tomorrow.

4. If you come to work late every day, you _____will_____ lose your job.

5. You don't know anything about computers? Come to my house. I _____will_____ teach you.

6. The teacher is going to give a test next Friday.

7. Next week we'll _____ begin Lesson Eight.

8. Mother: Please call me when you arrive.

   Daughter: Don't worry, Mom. I'_____ll_____ call you as soon as I arrive.

9. We're planning a picnic, but I think it's going to rain tomorrow.

PART 3

Fill in the blanks with the negative form of the underlined word.

EXAMPLE: She <u>will get</u> married in church. She _____won't get_____ married at home.

1. She <u>is going to invite</u> all her relatives. She _____isn't going to invite_____ all her friends.

2. He <u>will wear</u> a new suit. He _____won't wear_____ old clothes.

3. I <u>am going to buy</u> a gift. I'm not going to buy dishes.

4. I'll <u>help</u> you tomorrow. I _____won't help_____ you today.

5. You <u>are going to meet</u> my parents. You aren't going to meet my brothers.

PART 4

Read each statement. Then write a *yes/no* question about the words in parentheses ( ). Write a short answer.

EXAMPLE: She <u>will write</u> a letter. (a postcard) (no)
Will she write a postcard? No, she won't.

1. They will send a gift. (money) (no)
   Will they send money? No, they won't.

2. You're going to invite your friends. (relatives) (yes)
   Are you going to ivinte your relatives? Yes, I am.

3. They are going to receive gifts. (open the gifts) (yes)
   Are they going to open the gifts? Yes, they are.

4. They will need things for their kitchen. (for their bathroom) (yes)
   Will they need thing for their bathroom? Yes, they will.

5. There will be a party after the wedding. (food at the party) (yes)
   Will there be food at the party? Yes, they will

PART 5

Read each statement. Then write a question with the words in parentheses ( ). No answer is necessary.

EXAMPLE: I'm going to buy something. (What)
What are you going to buy?

1. They will use the money. (How)
   How will they use the money?

2. I'm going to send a gift. (What kind of gift)
   What kind of gift are you going to send?

X 3. They will thank us. (When)
   When will they thank us.?

4. They're going to get married. (Where)
   Where are they going to get married.?

5. They aren't going to open the gifts at the wedding. (Why)
   Why aren't they going to open the gifts at the wedding.?

6. There will be a lot of people at the wedding. (How many people)
   How many people will be there at the wedding.?

7. Some people will give money. (Who)
   Who will give money?

Future Tenses; Comparison of Tenses   **205**

TEST ON COMPARISON OF TENSES

PART 1   Read the following letter. Fill in the blanks with the simple present, the present continuous, or the future tenses.

Dear Judy,

Please excuse me for not writing sooner. I rarely _have_ time to sit and
(have)

write a letter. My husband _is working_ on his car now, and the baby _is sleeping_.
     (1 work)   *(2 sleep)*

So now I _have_ a few free moments.
     (3 have)

I _am_ a student now. I _go_ to Kennedy College twice a
   (4 be)   *(5 go)*

week. The school _is_ a few blocks from my house. I usually _walk_
         (6 be)   *(7 walk)*

to school, but sometimes I _drive_. My mother usually _watchs_ the
              (8 drive)   *(9 watch)*

baby when I'm in school. This semester I'm _studying_ English and math. Next
                                    (10 study)

semester I'll _take_ a computer course, I _think_ knowledge about
        (11 take)   *(12 think)*

computers _will help_ me find a good job.
          (13 help)

When the semester _is_ over, we're _going_ to Canada for vaca-
                 (14 be)   *(15 go)*

tion. We'll _visit_ my husband's sister. She _lives_ in Montreal.
        (16 visit)   *(17 live)*

We'll _spend_ Christmas with her family this year. When we _get_ to
    (18 spend)   *(19 get)*

Montreal, I'll _send_ you a postcard.
          (20 send)

Please write and tell me what is happening in your life.

Love,

Barbara

PART 2   Fill in the blanks with the negative form of the underlined verb.

EXAMPLE: Barbara's a student. She _isn't_ a teacher.

1.   She's writing a letter now. She _isn't writing_ a composition.

2.   Her mother sometimes <u>takes</u> care of her baby. Her father _doesn't_ care
     of her baby.

3.   They're going to visit her husband's sister. They _aren't going to visit_ her mother.

4.   She <u>goes</u> to Kennedy College. She _doesn't go_ to Truman College.

5. Barbara and her husband live in the U.S. They _don't live_ in Canada.

6. Her family will go to Montreal. They _won't go_ to Toronto.

PART 3 Read each statement. Then write a *yes/no* question with the words in parentheses ( ). Write a short answer, based on the letter.

EXAMPLE: Barbara's studying English. (math)
Is she studying math? Yes, she is.

1. The baby's sleeping. (her husband)
   Is her husband sleeping? No, he isn't.

2. She sometimes drives to school. (ever/walk to school)
   Does she ever walk to school? Yes, sometimes.

3. She's going to take a computer course next semester. (a math class)
   Is she going to take a math class next semester?
   Yes, she is.

4. She'll go to Canada. (Montreal)
   Will she go to Montreal? Yes, she will.

5. She's going to send Judy a postcard. (a letter)
   Is she going to send Judy a letter?
   No, she isn't. Yes, she is.

× 6. She sometimes writes letters. (write a letter/now)
   Does she write a letter now? Yes, she does.
   Is she writing a letter now?

7. Her sister-in-law lives in Canada. (in Toronto)
   Does live her sister-in-law in toronto.
   No, she doesn't.

PART 4 Read each statement. Then write a *wh-* question with the words in parentheses ( ). Write an answer, based on the letter.

EXAMPLE: She goes to college. (Where)
A. _Where does she go to college?_
B. _She goes to Kennedy College._

1. Her baby's sleeping. (What/her husband/do)
   A. _What does her husband do?_
   B. _He works in his car._

2. She's taking two courses this semester. (What courses)

   A. _____

   B. _____

3. Someone watches her baby. (Who)

   A. _____

   B. _____

4. She's going to take a course next semester. (What course)

   A. _____

   B. _____

5. They'll go on vacation for Christmas. (Where)

   A. _____

   B. _____

6. Her husband's sister lives in another city. (Where/she)

   A. _____

   B. _____

7. She doesn't usually drive to school. (Why)

   A. _____

   B. _____

EXPANSION ACTIVITIES

CLASSROOM ACTIVITIES

1. Check (√) the activities that you plan to do soon. Find a partner. Ask your partner for information about the items he or she checked off. Report something interesting to the class about your partner's plans.

EXAMPLE:

    __√__ move
    When are you going to move?
    Why are you going to move?
    Are your friends going to help you?
    Are you going to rent a truck?
    Where are you going to move to?

    a. _____ get married

    b. _____ go back to my country

    c. _____ spend a lot of money

    d. _____ write a letter

e. _____ buy something (a computer, a VCR, a TV, an answering machine, etc.)

f. _____ go to a party

g. _____ have a job interview

h. _____ transfer to another college

i. _____ become a citizen

j. _____ eat in a restaurant

2. Role play the following characters. Practice the future tense.

   a. Fortune teller and young woman. The woman wants to know her future.

   b. Man proposing marriage to a woman. The man is making promises.

   c. Teenager and parents. The teenager wants to go to a party on Saturday night.

   d. Politician and voter. The politician wants votes.

   e. Landlord and a person who wants to rent an apartment. (The person wants to know what the landlord will do to fix up the apartment.)

3. What are your concerns and plans for the future? Write two sentences (statements or questions) for each of the categories in the box below. Then find a partner. Discuss your concerns and plans with your partner.

Job/Career	*Where will I work if I lose my present job?*
Money	
Learning English	
Home	
Family and children	
Health	
Fun and recreation	
Other	

4. Imagine that you are going to buy a gift for someone in the following circumstances. What gift would you buy? Find a partner and compare your list of gifts to your partner's list.

    a. a friend in the hospital after surgery _____

    b. a couple with a new baby _____

    c. a nephew for high school graduation _____

    d. a friend getting married for the first time _____

    e. a friend getting married for the second time _____

    f. a friend moving into a new apartment _____

    g. a family that invites you to dinner at their house _____

DISCUSSION

1. In a small group or with the entire class, talk about gift giving customs in your native culture. What kind of gifts do people give for weddings? How much money do they spend? Do newlyweds open presents at the wedding? Do they send thank-you cards? What kind of gifts do people give for other occasions?

2. In your native culture, does a woman ever support a man?

OUTSIDE ACTIVITY

Use the third classroom activity on the previous page to interview an American about his or her concerns about the future. What is he or she worried about?

Internet Activity

Find a bridal or wedding registry on the Internet. What kind of gifts can a couple register for? What are the prices?

GRAMMAR

The Simple Past Tense

CONTEXT

The Wright Brothers
Charles Lindbergh and Amelia Earhart
Robert Goddard

LESSON FOCUS

We use the simple past tense to talk about an action that is completely in the past.

World War II *started* in 1939.
Many people *lost* their lives during the war.
It *ended* in 1945.
It *was* a very tragic time.

The Wright Brothers and an assistant with their first plane at Kitty Hawk

Wilbur Wright
1867–1912

Orville Wright
1871–1948

Read the following article. Pay special attention to simple past tense verbs.

The Wright Brothers—Men with a Vision

Wilbur Wright **was** born in 1867 and his brother Orville **was** born in 1871. In 1878, they **received** a paper flying toy from their father. From that time, they **dreamed** about flying. They **played** with kites and **studied** everything they could about glider planes.

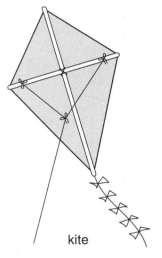

kite

When they were older, they **started** a bicycle business in Dayton, Ohio. They **used** the bicycle shop to design their airplanes. They **studied** three aspects of flying: lift, control, and power. In 1899, they **constructed** their first flying machine—a kite made of wood, wire, and cloth. It had no pilot. Because of wind, it was difficult to control. They **continued** to study aerodynamics.[1] Finally Wilbur **designed** a small machine with a gasoline engine. Wilbur **tried** to fly the machine, but it **crashed**. They **fixed** it and flew it for the first time on December 17, 1903, with Orville as the pilot. The airplane **remained** in the air for 12 seconds. It **traveled** a distance of 120

[1] *Aerodynamics* is the branch of mechanics that deals with the motion of air and its effect on things.

Did you know...?

The Wright Brothers never married. Their only love was aviation.

feet. It was over 600 pounds. This historic flight **changed** the world. However, only four newspapers in the U.S. **reported** this historic moment.

The Wright Brothers **offered** their invention to the U.S. government, but the government **rejected**[2] their offer at first. The government **didn't believe** that these men **invented** a flying machine. Finally, President Theodore Roosevelt **investigated** their claims and **offered** the inventors a contract to build airplanes for the U.S Army.

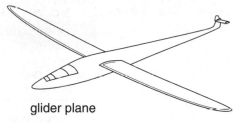

glider plane

8.1 The Simple Past Tense of Regular Verbs

Examples	Explanation
The Wright Brothers **dreamed** about flying. They **started** a bicycle business. They **invented** the airplane.	For regular verbs, the simple past tense ends in *-ed*. BASE FORM PAST FORM dream dream**ed** start start**ed** invent invent**ed**

LANGUAGE NOTES

1. The past form is the same for all persons.
   I worked.
   He worked.
   They worked.
   You worked.
2. The verb after *to* does not use the past form.
   The Wright Brothers wanted *to fly*.
3. We often use *ago* with sentences about the past.
   The Wright Brothers *invented* the airplane about 100 years *ago*.
   We *studied* the future tense a week *ago*.
   We *learned* about the Wright Brothers a few minutes *ago*.

[2] *Reject* means not accept.

8.2 Spelling of the Past Tense of Regular Verbs

Rule	Base Form	Past Form
Add *-ed* to most regular verbs.	start rain	start**ed** rain**ed**
When the base form ends in *e*, add *-d* only.	die live	die**d** live**d**
When the base form ends in a consonant + *y*, change *y* to *i* and add *-ed*.	carry study	car**ried** stu**died**
When the base form ends in a vowel + *y*, add *-ed*. Do not change the *y*.	stay enjoy	stay**ed** enjoy**ed**
When a one-syllable verb ends in a consonant-vowel-consonant, double the final consonant and add *-ed*.	stop hug	stop**ped** hug**ged**
Do not double final *w* or *x*.	fix show	fix**ed** show**ed**
When a two-syllable verb ends in a consonant-vowel-consonant, double the final consonant and add *-ed* only if the last syllable is stressed.	occúr permít	occur**red** permit**ted**
When the last syllable of a two-syllable verb is not stressed, do not double the final consonant.	ópen óffer	open**ed** offer**ed**

EXERCISE 1 Write the past tense of these regular verbs. (Accent marks show you where a word is stressed.)

EXAMPLES: learn _____ *learned* _____   clap _____ *clapped* _____

love _____ *loved* _____   listen _____ *listened* _____

1. play _____   8. stop _____

2. study _____   9. háppen _____

3. decide _____   10. carry _____

4. want _____   11. enjoy _____

5. like _____   12. drag _____

6. show _____   13. drop _____

7. look _____   14. start _____

15. follow _____   18. mix _____

16. prefér _____   19. admít _____

17. like _____   20. devélop _____

8.3 Pronunciation of -ed Past Forms

Pronounce /t/	Pronounce /d/	Pronounce /əd/
jump—jumped	rub—rubbed	wait—waited
cook—cooked	drag—dragged	hate—hated
cough—coughed	love—loved	want—wanted
kiss—kissed	bathe—bathed	add—added
wash—washed	use—used	decide—decided
watch—watched	massage—massaged	
	charge—charged	
	name—named	
	learn—learned	
	bang—banged	
	call—called	
	care—cared	
	free—freed	

LANGUAGE NOTES

1. We pronounce /t/ after voiceless sounds: /p, k, f, s, š, č/
2. We pronounce /d/ after voiced sounds: /b, g, v, đ, z, ž, ǰ, m, n, ŋ, l, r/ and all vowels.
3. We pronounce /əd/ after /d/ or /t/ sounds.

EXERCISE 2 Go back to Exercise 1 and pronounce the base form and past form.

EXERCISE 3 Fill in the blanks with the past tense of the verb in parentheses ( ). Use the correct spelling.

EXAMPLE: The Wright Brothers __received__ a flying toy from their father.
(receive)

1. They _____ about flying.
(dream)

2. They _____ everything they could about flying.
(study)

3. They _____ a bicycle business.
(start)

4. They _____ the bicycle shop to design airplanes.
(use)

5. They _____ to fly their first plane in 1899.
   (try)

6. In 1903, their plane _____ in the air for 12 seconds.
   (stay)

7. They _____ their invention to the U.S. government.
   (offer)

8. The government _____ to offer them a contract.
   (decide)

9. Wilbur Wright _____ in 1912.
   (die)

10. Orville Wright _____ for many more years.
    (live)

11. Their invention _____ the world.
    (change)

Before You Read
1. When was the first time you traveled by airplane?
2. Do you recognize the people in these photos?

Charles Lindbergh
1902–1974

Amelia Earhart
1897–1937

Read the following article. Pay special attention to the past forms of *be*.

Charles Lindbergh and Amelia Earhart

Charles Lindbergh loved to fly. He **was** born in 1902, one year before the Wright Brothers' historic flight. In 1927, a man offered a $25,000 reward for the first person to fly from New York to Paris nonstop. Lindbergh **was** a pilot for the United States Mail Service at that time. He wanted to win the prize. He became famous because he **was** the first person to fly alone across the Atlantic Ocean. His plane **was** in the air for 33 hours. The distance of the flight **was** 3,600 miles. There **were** thousands of people in New York to welcome him home. He **was** an American hero. He **was** only 25 years old.

Another famous American aviator[3] **was** Amelia Earhart. She **was** the first woman to fly across the Atlantic Ocean alone. She wanted to land in Paris, but her flight **was** difficult and she had to land in Ireland. She **was** 34 years old. Americans **were** in love with Earhart. In 1937, however, she **was** on a flight around the world when her plane disappeared somewhere in the Pacific Ocean. No one really knows what happened to Earhart.

8.4   Past Tense of *Be*

AFFIRMATIVE STATEMENTS

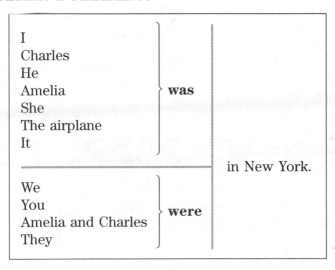

I	
Charles	
He	
Amelia	**was**
She	
The airplane	
It		in New York.

We	
You	**were**
Amelia and Charles	
They	

NEGATIVE STATEMENTS

Subject	*Be*	*Not*	Complement
Charles and Amelia	**were**	**not**	inventors.
Earhart	**was**	**not**	alone.

LANGUAGE NOTES

1. The verb *be* uses two forms in the past: *was* and *were*.
2. To make a negative statement, put *not* after *was* or *were*. The contraction for *was not* is *wasn't*. The contraction for *were not* is *weren't*.

---

[3] *Aviator* means pilot.

Fill in the blanks with *was* or *were*.

EXAMPLE: Lindbergh and Earhart ___*were*___ very famous.

1. The Wright Brothers _____ the inventors of the airplane.

2. The first airplane _____ in the air for 12 seconds.

3. Lindbergh and Earhart _____ aviators.

4. There _____ thousands of people in New York to welcome Lindbergh home.

5. Earhart _____ the first woman to fly across the Atlantic Ocean.

6. I _____ interested in the story about Earhart and Lindbergh.

7. _____ you surprised that Earhart was a woman?

8. Lindbergh _____ in Paris.

9. We _____ in school last week.

8.5 Uses of *Be*

Examples	Explanations
Lindbergh **was** an aviator.	Classification of the subject
Lindbergh **was** brave.	Description of the subject
Lindbergh **was** in Paris.	Location of the subject
Earhart **was** from Kansas.	Place of origin of the subject
She **was** born in 1897.	With *born*
There **were** thousands of people in New York to welcome Lindbergh.	With *there*

EXERCISE 5 Read each statement. Then write a negative statement with the words in parentheses ( ).

EXAMPLE: The Wright Brothers were inventors. (Earhart and Lindbergh)
Earhart and Lindbergh weren't inventors.

1. The train was common transportation in the early 1900s. (the airplane)

_____

2. Earhart was from Kansas. (Lindbergh)

_____

3. Lindbergh's last flight was successful. (Earhart's last flight)

_____

4. Lindbergh's plane was in the air for many hours. (the Wright brothers' first plane)

_____

5. The Wright brothers were inventors. (Earhart)

_____

6. There were a lot of trains 100 years ago. (planes)

_____

7. Lindbergh was born in the twentieth century. (the Wright brothers)

_____

8.6 Questions with *Was/Were*

Compare statements and questions with *was* and *were*.

Wh-Word	Was/Were Wasn't/Weren't	Subject	Was/Were Wasn't/Weren't	Complement	Short Answer
	Were	Americans **were**		in love with Lindbergh.	
Why	**were**	Americans		in love with Earhart?	Yes, they **were**.
		Americans		in love with them?	
Why	**wasn't**	Earhart	**wasn't**	alone.	
		she		alone?	
		Someone	**was**	with Earhart.	
		Who	**was**	with Earhart?	

EXERCISE 6 Read each statement. Then write a *yes/no* question with the words in parentheses ( ). Give a short answer.

EXAMPLE: The Wright Brothers were inventors. (Lindbergh)
Was Lindbergh an inventor? No, he wasn't.

_____

1. The airplane was an important invention. (the telephone)

_____

2. Thomas Edison was an inventor. (the Wright brothers)

_____

3. Amelia Earhart was American. (Lindbergh)

   _____

4. Travel by plane is common now. (100 years ago)

   _____

5. There were telephones 100 years ago. (airplanes)

   _____

6. You are in class today. (yesterday)

   _____

7. I was interested in the story about the aviators. (you)

   _____

8. I wasn't born in the U.S. (you)

   _____

EXERCISE 7   With a partner or in a small group, discuss your answers to these questions.

1. Where were you born?

2. Were you happy or sad when you left your hometown?

3. Who was with you on your trip to the U.S.?

4. Were you happy or sad when you arrived in the U.S.?

5. What was your first impression of the U.S.?

6. Were you tired when you arrived?

7. Who was at the airport to meet you?

8. How was the weather on the day you arrived?

EXERCISE 8   Read each statement. Then write a *wh-* question with the words in parentheses ( ). Answer the question.

EXAMPLE: Lindbergh was very famous. (why)

   A. _Why was Lindbergh famous?_____

   B. _He was one of the first aviators._____

1. Lindbergh was a hero. (why)

   A. _____

   B. _____

2. Lindbergh was American. (what nationality/Earhart)

   A. _____

   B. _____

3. Earhart was thirty-four years old when she crossed the ocean. (Lindbergh)

   A. _____

   B. _____

4. Earhart's last flight wasn't successful. (why)

   A. _____

   B. _____

5. Lindbergh was a famous aviator. (who/the Wright brothers)

   A. _____

   B. _____

6. Lindbergh was born in 1902. (Earhart) (answer: 1897)

   A. _____

   B. _____

7. The Wright Brothers were famous. (why)

   A. _____

   B. _____

8.7 Simple Past Tenses of Irregular Verbs

Verbs with No Change		Final *d* Changes to *t*	
bet—bet	hurt—hurt	bend—bent	send—sent
cost—cost	let—let	build—built	spend—spent
cut—cut	put—put	lend—lent	
fit—fit	quit—quit		
hit—hit	shut—shut		

(continued)

Verbs with a Vowel Change

feel—felt keep—kept leave—left	lose—lost mean—meant[4] sleep—slept	bring—brought buy—bought catch—caught	fight—fought teach—taught think—thought
break—broke choose—chose freeze—froze	steal—stole speak—spoke wake—woke	begin—began drink—drank ring—rang	sing—sang sink—sank swim—swam
dig—dug hang—hung	spin—spun win—won	drive—drove ride—rode	shine—shone write—wrote
blow—blew draw—drew fly—flew	grow—grew know—knew throw—threw	bleed—bled feed—fed lead—led	meet—met read—read[5]
sell—sold	tell—told	find—found	wind—wound
shake—shook take—took	mistake—mistook	lay—laid say—said[6]	pay—paid
tear—tore	wear—wore	bite—bit light—lit	hide—hid
become—became come—came	eat—ate	fall—fell	hold—held
give—gave forgive—forgave	lie—lay	run—ran sit—sat	see—saw
forget—forgot shoot—shot	get—got	stand—stood understand—understood	

Miscellaneous Changes

be —was/were do—did	go—went have—had	hear—heard make—made	

LANGUAGE NOTES

1. An irregular verb does not use the *-ed* ending for the past tense.
2. For an alphabetical list of irregular verbs, see Appendix D.

---

[4] There is a change in the vowel sound. *Meant* rhymes with *sent*.
[5] The past form of *read* is pronounced like the color *red*.
[6] *Said* rhymes with *bed*.

Robert Goddard with early rocket

Apollo 11 on the moon

Read the following article. Pay special attention to past tense verbs.

Robert Goddard

Robert Goddard **was** born in 1882. When he **was** a child, he **became** interested in firecrackers and **believed** in the possibility of rocket travel. He **became** a professor of physics. He **built** rockets and carried them to a field, but they **didn't fly**. In 1920, the *New York Times* **heard** about his ideas and **wrote** an article about him. The article **said** that space travel **was** impossible and that Goddard **was** a fool. Goddard's colleagues **laughed** at him. Goddard **was** angry, but he **didn't stop** his research.

In 1926, he **built** a ten-foot rocket, **put** it into an open car, and **drove** to his aunt's nearby farm. He **put** the rocket in a field and **lit** the fuse. Suddenly the rocket **went** into the sky. It **traveled** at 60 m.p.h. to an altitude of 41 feet. Then it **fell** into the field. The flight **lasted** 2½ seconds, but Goddard **was** happy about his achievement. Over the years, his rockets **grew** to eighteen feet and **flew** to 9,000 feet in the air. No one **made** fun of him after he was successful.

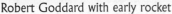

firecracker

Did you know...?

The first woman in space was a Russian, Valentina Tereshkova, in 1963.

When Goddard **died** in 1945, his work **did not stop**. Scientists **continued** to build bigger and better rockets. In 1969, when the American rocket Apollo 11 **took** the first men to the moon, the *New York Times* **wrote**: "The *Times* regrets[7] the error."

---

[7] *Regret* means to be sorry for a mistake you made.

1920	Goddard **published** a paper on rockets.
1926–1939	Goddard **built** and **flew** rockets.
1944	Germany **used** the first rockets in World War II.
1957	The Russians **sent** up their first satellite, "Sputnik 1."
1958	The Americans **sent** up their first satellite, "Explorer 1."
1961	Yuri Gagarin, a Russian, **became** the first person in space.
1961	Alan Shepard **became** the first American in space.
1969	The United States **put** the first men on the moon.

EXERCISE 9 Fill in the blanks with the past tense of one of the words from the box below.

fly	think	drive	be	fall
write	put	√become	see	

EXAMPLE: Goddard ___*became*___ interested in rockets when he was a child.

1. He _____ a professor of physics.

2. People _____ that space travel was impossible.

3. Goddard _____ his first rocket in a car and _____ to his aunt's farm.

4. The rocket _____ for 2½ seconds and then it _____ to the ground.

5. Goddard never _____ the first moon landing.

6. The *New York Times* _____ about their mistake 49 years later.

EXERCISE 10 Fill in the blanks with the past tense of the verb in parentheses ( ).

EXAMPLE: The Wright brothers' father ___*gave*___ them a toy airplane.
                                        (give)

1. They _____ a dream of flying.
          (have)

2. They _____ interested in flying after seeing a flying toy.
          (become)

3. They _____ many books on flight.
          (read)

4. They _____ bicycles.
          (sell)

5. They _____ the first airplane.
   (build)

6. At first they _____ problems with wind.
   (have)

7. They _____ some changes to the airplane.
   (make)

8. They _____ for the first time in 1903.
   (fly)

9. Only a few people _____ the first flight.
   (see)

10. President Theodore Roosevelt _____ about their airplane.
    (hear)

11. The airplane was an important invention because it _____ people
    (bring)
    from different places closer together.

8.8   Negative Forms of Past Tense Verbs

Affirmative Statement	Negative Statement
Lindbergh **returned** from his famous flight.	Earhart **didn't return** from her last flight.
Goddard **became** a professor.	He **didn't become** a pilot.
People **thought** that space travel was foolish.	They **didn't think** that space travel was possible.
The Wright Brothers **flew** in their plane.	Goddard **didn't fly** in his rocket.
People **laughed** at Goddard's theories.	They **didn't laugh** when they saw the rocket in the sky.

LANGUAGE NOTES

For the negative of past tense verbs, use *didn't* (*did not*) + the base form for all verbs, regular and irregular.

EXERCISE 11   Fill in the blanks with the negative form of the underlined words.

EXAMPLE: Goddard <u>believed</u> in space flight. Other people ___*didn't believe*___ in space flight.

1. In 1926 his rocket <u>flew</u>. Before that time, his rockets _____.

2. He <u>wanted</u> to build rockets. He _____ to build airplanes.

3. In 1920, a newspaper <u>wrote</u> that he was foolish. The newspaper
   _____ about the possibility of rocket travel.

4. The first rocket <u>stayed</u> in the air for 2½ seconds. It _____ in the air for a long time.

5. Goddard <u>thought</u> his ideas were important. His colleagues _____ his ideas were important.

6. Goddard <u>saw</u> his rockets fly. He _____ rockets go to the moon.

7. A rocket <u>went</u> to the moon in 1969. A rocket _____ to the moon during Goddard's lifetime.

8. In 1957, the Russians <u>put</u> the first man in space. The Americans _____ the first man in space.

9. In 1969, the first Americans <u>walked</u> on the moon. Russians _____ on the moon.

10. The Wright brothers <u>dreamed</u> about flying. They _____ about rockets.

11. They <u>sold</u> bicycles. They _____ cars.

12. Their 1903 airplane <u>had</u> a pilot. Their first airplane _____ a pilot.

13. The Wright brothers <u>built</u> the first airplane. They _____ the first rocket.

14. The Wright brothers <u>wanted</u> to show their airplane to the U.S. government. The government _____ to see it at first.

EXERCISE 12 Fill in the blanks with the affirmative or negative form of the verb in parentheses to tell about the time before you came to the U.S. Add some specific information to tell more about each item.

EXAMPLES: I ___*studied*___ English before I came to the U.S. *I studied with a*
               (study)
private teacher for three months.

                    OR

I ___*didn't study*___ English before I came to the U.S. *I didn't have*
               (study)
enough time.

1. I _____ my money for dollars before I came to the U.S.
      (change)

2. I _____ a passport.
      (get)

3. I _____ for a visa.
   (apply)

4. I _____ English.
   (study)

5. I _____ some things (house, furniture, etc.).
   (sell)

6. I _____ goodbye to my friends.
   (say)

7. I _____ an English dictionary.
   (buy)

8. I _____ a clear idea about life in the U.S.
   (have)

9. I _____ afraid about my future.
   (be)

10. I _____ to another country first.
    (go)

11. I _____ English well.
    (understand)

12. I _____ a lot about Americans.
    (know)

EXERCISE 13 Tell if these things happened or didn't happen after you moved to this city. Add some specific information to tell more about each item.

EXAMPLE: find an apartment
I found an apartment two weeks after I arrived in this city.
OR
I didn't find an apartment right away. I lived with my cousins for two months.

1. find a job
2. register for English classes
3. rent an apartment
4. buy a car
5. get a Social Security card
6. get a driver's license
7. visit a museum
8. see a relative
9. buy clothes
10. go to the bank

EXERCISE 14 Tell if you did or didn't do these things in the past week. Add some specific information to tell more about each item.

EXAMPLE: go to the movies
I went to the movies last weekend with my brother. We saw a great movie.
OR
I didn't go to the movies this week. I didn't have time.

1. receive a letter
2. write a letter
3. go to the library
4. do my laundry
5. buy groceries
6. make a long-distance phone call
7. buy a magazine
8. work hard
9. look for a job
10. rent a video
11. send an e-mail
12. read a newspaper

8.9 Questions with Past Tense Verbs

Compare statements and questions with the simple past tense.

Wh-Word	Did/Didn't	Subject	Verb	Complement	Short Answer
		Goddard	**studied**	physics.	
	Did	he	**study**	hard?	Yes, he **did**.
Why	**did**	he	**study**	physics?	
		Lindbergh	**flew**	across the Atlantic.	
	Did	he	**fly**	alone?	Yes, he **did**.
When	**did**	he	**fly**	across the Atlantic?	
Why	**didn't**	he	**fly**	with someone?	

LANGUAGE NOTES

1. For all *yes/no* questions of past tense verbs, regular or irregular, we use *did* + the base form.
2. For most *wh-* questions, we use *did* + the base form.

EXERCISE 15 Use these questions to ask another student about the time when he or she lived in his or her country. (You may work with a partner.)

1. Did you study English in your country?

2. Did you live in a big city?

3. Did you live with your parents?

4. Did you know a lot about the U.S.?

5. Were you happy with the political situation?

6. Did you finish high school?

7. Did you own a car?

8. Did you have a job?

9. Did you think about your future?

10. Were you happy?

EXERCISE 16 Read each statement. Write a *yes/no* question about the words in parentheses ( ). Write a short answer.

EXAMPLE: The Wright Brothers had a dream. (Goddard) (yes)
Did Goddard have a dream? Yes, he did.

1. Wilbur Wright died in 1912. (his brother) (no)

   _____

2. The Wright Brothers built an airplane. (Goddard) (no)

   _____

3. Earhart loved to fly. (Lindbergh) (yes)

   _____

4. Lindbergh crossed the ocean. (Earhart) (yes)

   _____

5. Lindbergh worked for the U.S. Mail Service. (Earhart) (no)

   _____

6. Lindbergh became famous. (Earhart) (yes)

   _____

7. Earhart disappeared. (Lindbergh) (no)

   _____

8. Lindbergh was born in the twentieth century. (Earhart) (no)

   _____

9. Lindbergh won money for his first flight. (the Wright Brothers) (no)

   _____

10. People didn't believe the Wright Brothers at first. (Goddard) (no)

    _____

11. The Wright Brothers dreamed about flight. (Goddard) (yes)

    _____

12. The Russians sent a rocket into space in 1957. (the Americans) (no)

    _____

13. The Russians put a man in space in 1961. (Americans) (yes)

_____

14. Americans saw the first moon landing. (Goddard) (no)

_____

EXERCISE 17 Fill in the blanks with the correct words.

EXAMPLE: What kind of engine _did the first airplane have?_

The first airplane had a gasoline engine.

1. Where _____?
   The Wright brothers built their plane in their bicycle shop.

2. Why _____?
   The first plane crashed because of the wind.

3. Why _____ difficult to control?
   The plane was difficult to control because of the wind.

4. Why _____ the first flight in 1903?
   Newspapers didn't report it because they didn't believe it.

5. Where _____?
   Lindbergh worked for the U.S. Mail Service.

6. Why _____?
   He crossed the ocean to win the prize money.

7. How much money _____?
   He won $25,000.

8. How old _____ when he crossed the ocean?
   Lindbergh was 25 years old when he crossed the ocean.

9. Where _____?
   His plane landed in Paris.

10. When _____?
    Lindbergh died in 1974.

11. Why _____?
    Nobody knows why Earhart didn't return.

12. Where _____?
    Earhart was born in Kansas.

13. Where _____?
    She disappeared in the Pacific Ocean.

14. Who _____ with?
    Earhart was with a copilot.

15. When _____?
    The first man walked on the moon in 1969.

16. Why _____ the first moon landing?
    Goddard didn't see the first moon landing because he died in 1945.

EXERCISE 18 Read each statement. Then write a question with the words in parentheses ( ). Answer with a complete sentence. (The answers are at the bottom of the page.)

EXAMPLE: The Wright Brothers were born in the nineteenth century. (Where)
Where were they born? They were born in Ohio.

_____

1. The Wright Brothers were born in the nineteenth century. (When/Lindbergh)

_____

2. Their father gave them a toy. (What kind of toy)

_____

3. They had a shop. (What kind of shop)

_____

4. They designed airplanes. (Where)

_____

5. They flew their first plane in North Carolina. (When)

_____

6. The first plane stayed in the air for a few seconds. (How many seconds)

_____

7. The U.S. government didn't want to see the airplane at first. (Why)

_____

8. The Wright Brothers invented the airplane. (What/Goddard)

_____

ANSWERS TO EXERCISE 18:
1) 1902, 2) a flying toy, 3) a bicycle shop, 4) in their bicycle shop, 5) in 1903, 6) 12 seconds, 7) they didn't believe it, 8) the rocket, 9) to see if it would fly, 10) they didn't believe him (they thought he was a fool)

9. Goddard took his rocket to his aunt's farm. (Why)

_____

10. People laughed at Goddard. (Why)

_____

EXERCISE 19 Check (√) all statements that are true for you. Then read aloud one statement that you checked. Another student will ask a question with the words in parentheses ( ). Answer the question.

EXAMPLES:
A. __√__ I did my homework. (where)
B. Where did you do your homework?
A. I did my homework in the library.

A. __√__ I got married. (when)
B. When did you get married?
A. I got married six years ago.

1. ____ I graduated from high school. (when)

2. ____ I studied biology. (when)

3. ____ I bought an English dictionary. (where)

4. ____ I left my country. (when)

5. ____ I came to the U.S. (why)

6. ____ I brought my clothes to the U.S. (what else)

7. ____ I rented an apartment. (where)

8. ____ I started to study English. (when)

9. ____ I chose this college. (why)

10. ____ I found my apartment. (when)

11. ____ I needed to learn English. (when)

12. ____ I got married. (when)

EXERCISE 20 Check (√) which of these things you did when you were a child. Make an affirmative or negative statement about one of these items. Another student will ask a question about your statement.

EXAMPLE: _____ I attended public school.
A. I didn't attend public school.
B. Why didn't you attend public school?
A. My parents wanted to give me a religious education.

1. _____ I participated in a sport.

2. _____ I enjoyed school.

3. _____ I got good grades in school.

4. _____ I took music lessons.

5. _____ I lived with my grandparents.

6. _____ I got an allowance.[8]

7. _____ I had a pet.

8. _____ I lived on a farm.

9. _____ I played soccer.

10. _____ I studied English.

11. _____ I had a bike.

12. _____ I thought about my future.

8.10 Questions about the Subject

Subject Questions	Questions with *Did*
Who **invented** the airplane? The Wright Brothers did?	When **did** the Wright Brothers **invent** the airplane? They invented it in 1903.
Who **laughed** at Goddard? His colleagues did.	Why **did** they **laugh** at Goddard? They laughed at him because they didn't believe in rocket travel.
How many people **went** to see Lindbergh in Paris? Thousands of people did.	When **did** Lindbergh **go** to Paris? He went there in 1927.
What **happened** to Earhart's plane? It disappeared.	When **did** the accident **happen**? It happened in 1937.

[8] An *allowance* is money children get from their parents, usually once a week.

LANGUAGE NOTES

When we ask a question about the subject, we use the past form, not the base form in the question. We don't use *did* in the question. We can use *did* in the short answer.

EXERCISE 21 Choose the correct word to answer these questions about the subject.

EXAMPLE: Who invented the airplane? ((The Wright Brothers,) Goddard, Lindbergh)

1. Who landed on the moon? (Yuri Gagarin, Neil Armstrong, John Glenn)

2. Who crossed the ocean in 1927? (Wilbur Wright, Orville Wright, Charles Lindbergh)

3. Who sent up the first rocket? (The Wright Brothers, Goddard, Lindbergh)

4. Who disappeared in 1937? (Earhart, Goddard, Lindbergh)

5. Who won money to fly across the Atlantic Ocean? (Earhart, Lindbergh, Goddard)

6. Which president showed interest in the Wright Brothers' airplane? (T. Roosevelt, Lincoln, Wilson)

7. Which newspaper said that Goddard was a fool? (*The Chicago Tribune, The Washington Post, The New York Times*)

EXERCISE 22 Read one of the *who* questions below. Someone will volunteer an answer. Then ask a related question to the person who answered "I did."

EXAMPLE: A. Who went to the bank last week?
B. I did.
A. Why did you go to the bank?
B. I went there to buy a money order.

1. Who brought a dictionary to class today?

2. Who drank coffee this morning?

3. Who wrote a composition last night?

4. Who watched TV this morning?

5. Who came to the U.S. alone?

6. Who made a long distance call last night?

7. Who studied English before coming to the U.S.?

8. Who bought a newspaper today?

EXERCISE 23 Fill in the blanks in this conversation between two students about their past.

A. I ___was born___ in Mexico. I _____ to the U.S. ten years ago.
      (born)   (1 come)

   Where _____ born?
         (2 be)

B. In El Salvador. But my family _____ to Guatemala when
                (3 move)

   I _____ 10 years old.
     (4 be)

A. Why _____ to Guatemala?
        (5 move)

B. We _____ afraid to stay in El Salvador.
      (6 be)

A. Why _____ afraid?
       (7 be)

B. Because there _____ a war in El Salvador.
        (8 be)

A. How long _____ in Guatemala?
        (9 stay)

B. We stayed there for about five years. Then I _____ to the U.S.
                (10 come)

A. What about your family? _____ to the U.S. with you?
            (11 come)

B. No, they _____. I _____ a job, _____ my money,
        (12)   (13 find)   (14 save)

   and _____ them here later.
      (15 bring)

A. My parents _____ with me either. But my older brother did.
        (16 not/come)

   I _____ to go to school as soon as I _____.
     (17 start)   (18 arrive)

B. Who _____ you while you were in school?
     (19 support)

A. My brother _____.
        (20)

B. I _____ to school right away because I _____ to work.
   (21 not/go)   *(22 have)*

  Then I _____ a grant and _____ to go to City College.
     (23 get)   *(24 start)*

A. Why _____ City College?
     (25 choose)

B. I chose it because it has a good ESL program.

A. Me too.

SUMMARY OF LESSON 8

The Simple Past Tense

1. **Be**

I He She It	was in Paris	We You They	were in Paris
There was a problem.		There were many problems.	

AFFIRMATIVE:	He **was** in Poland.	They **were** in France.
NEGATIVE:	He **wasn't** in Russia.	They **weren't** in England.
YES/NO QUESTION:	**Was** he in Hungary?	**Were** they in Paris?
SHORT ANSWER:	No, he **wasn't**.	No, they **weren't**.
WH- QUESTION:	Where **was** he?	When **were** they in France?
NEGATIVE QUESTION:	Why **wasn't** he in Russia?	Why **weren't** they in Paris?
SUBJECT QUESTION:	Who **was** in Russia?	How many people **were** in France?

2. Other Verbs

	Regular Verb *(work)*	Irregular Verb *(buy)*
AFFIRMATIVE:	She **worked** on Saturday.	They **bought** a car.
NEGATIVE:	She **didn't work** on Sunday.	They **didn't buy** a motorcycle.
YES/NO QUESTION:	**Did** she **work** in the morning?	**Did** they **buy** an American car?
SHORT ANSWER:	Yes, she **did**.	No, they **didn't**.
WH- QUESTION:	Where **did** she **work**?	What kind of car **did** they **buy**?
NEGATIVE QUESTION:	Why **didn't** she **work** on Sunday?	Why **didn't** they **buy** an American car?
SUBJECT QUESTION:	Who **worked** on Sunday?	How many people **bought** an American car?

1. Use the base form, not the past form, after *to*.

        buy
    I wanted to ~~bought~~ a new car.

2. Review the spelling rules for adding *-ed*, and use correct spelling.

        studied
    I ~~studyed~~ for the last test.

        dropped
    He ~~droped~~ his pencil.

3. Use the base form after *did* or *didn't*.

        know
    She didn't ~~knew~~ the answer.

        come
    Did your father ~~came~~ to the U.S.?

4. Use correct word order in a question.

        your mother go
    Where did ~~go your mother~~?

        did your sister buy
    What ~~bought your sister~~?

5. Use *be* with *born*. (Don't add *-ed* to *born*.) Don't use *be* with *died*.

        was born
    Her grandmother ~~borned~~ in Russia.

    She ~~was~~ died in the U.S.

        was
    Where ~~did~~ your grandfather born?

        did
    Where ~~was~~ your grandfather died?

6. Check your list of verbs for irregular verbs.

        brought
    I ~~bringed~~ my photos to the U.S.

        saw
    I ~~seen~~ the accident yesterday.

7. Use *be* with an age.

        was
    My grandfather ~~had~~ 88 years old when he died.

---

8. Don't confuse *was* and *were*.

Where ~~was~~ *were* you yesterday?

9. Don't use *did* in a question about the subject.

Who ~~did take~~ *took* my pencil?

LESSON 8 TEST / REVIEW

PART 1

Find the mistakes with the underlined words, and correct them. Not every sentence has a mistake. If the sentence is correct, write **C**.

EXAMPLES: Lindbergh ~~were~~ *was* famous.

Lindbergh was born in 1902.   C

1. Lindbergh decided to flew across the Atlantic.

2. The first plane stay in the air for 12 seconds.

3. When Lindbergh crossed the ocean?

4. Earhart borned in 1897.

5. Who invented the first rocket?

6. When did Goddard invented the rocket?

7. When was Goddard died?

8. When was Goddard born?

9. Lindbergh won $25,000.

10. Thousands of people seen Lindbergh in Paris.

11. Lindbergh had 25 years old when he made his historic flight.

12. Who did walk on the moon in 1969?

13. How many people walked on the moon?

14. Earhart didn't returned from her flight across the Pacific.

15. The Wright Brothers' father gave his sons a flying toy.

16. Goddard's colleagues didn't believed him.

17. The first rocket flight <u>lasted</u> 2½ seconds.

18. When <u>landed men</u> on the moon?

19. What <u>happened</u> to Earhart's plane?

20. Who <u>saw</u> the first moon landing?

PART 2 Write the past tense of each verb.

EXAMPLES: live _____lived_____   feel _____felt_____

1. eat _____   11. drink _____

2. see _____   12. build _____

3. get _____   13. stop _____

4. sit _____   14. leave _____

5. hit _____   15. buy _____

6. make _____   16. think _____

7. take _____   17. run _____

8. find _____   18. carry _____

9. say _____   19. sell _____

10. read _____   20. stand _____

PART 3 Fill in the blanks with the negative form of the underlined verb.

EXAMPLE: Lindbergh <u>worked</u> for the U.S. Mail Service. Earhart ____didn't work____ for the U.S. Mail Service.

1. There <u>were</u> trains in 1900. There _____ any airplanes.

2. The Wright Brothers <u>flew</u> a plane in 1903. They _____ a plane in 1899.

3. Charles Lindbergh <u>was</u> an aviator. He _____ a president.

4. The Wright Brothers <u>invented</u> the airplane. They _____ the telephone.

5. Wilbur Wright <u>died</u> of typhoid fever. He _____ in a plane crash.

6. Lindbergh <u>went</u> to Paris. Earhart _____ to Paris.

7. Lindbergh <u>came</u> back from his flight. Earhart _____ back from her last flight.

8. Goddard <u>was</u> born in the nineteenth century. He _____ in the twentieth century.

9. Goddard <u>built</u> a rocket. He _____ an airplane.

10. He <u>became</u> a physics professor. He _____ a pilot.

PART **4**   Read each statement. Write a *yes/no* question about the words in parentheses ( ). Write a short answer.

EXAMPLE: Lindbergh crossed the ocean. (Earhart) (yes)
Did Earhart cross the ocean? Yes, she did.

1. Wilbur Wright became famous. (Orville Wright) (yes)

   _____

2. Lindbergh was an aviator. (Goddard) (no)

   _____

3. Lindbergh flew across the Atlantic Ocean. (Earhart) (yes)

   _____

4. Lindbergh was born in the U.S. (Goddard) (yes)

   _____

5. Goddard wrote about rockets. (the Wright Brothers) (no)

   _____

6. The Russians sent a man into space. (the Americans) (yes)

   _____

7. Goddard died in 1945. (Wilbur Wright) (no)

   _____

8. The U.S. put men on the moon in 1969. (Russia) (no)

   _____

9. People laughed at Goddard's ideas in 1920. (in 1969) (no)

   _____

10. Goddard thought about rockets. (about computers) (no)

   _____

Write a *wh-* question about the words in parentheses ( ). It is not necessary to answer the questions.

EXAMPLE: The Wright Brothers became famous for their first airplane. (why/Lindbergh)
Why did Lindbergh become famous?

1. Earhart was born in 1897. (when/Lindbergh)

   _____

2. Thomas Edison invented the phonograph. (what/the Wright Brothers)

   _____

3. Thomas Edison invented the phonograph. (who/the airplane)

   _____

4. Lindbergh crossed the ocean in 1927. (when/Earhart)

   _____

5. Lindbergh got money for his flight. (how much)

   _____

6. Earhart wanted to fly around the world. (why)

   _____

7. Many people saw Lindbergh in Paris. (how many people)

   _____

8. Goddard's colleagues didn't believe his ideas. (why)

   _____

9. Wilbur Wright died in 1912. (when/Orville Wright)

   _____

10. A president examined Goddard's ideas. (which president)

   _____

EXPANSION ACTIVITIES

CLASSROOM ACTIVITIES

1. In a small group or with the entire class, discuss your first experiences in the U.S. What were your first impressions? What did you do in your first few days in the U.S.?

EXAMPLE:

I lived with my cousins. They helped me find an apartment. I didn't have money to buy furniture. They lent me money. At first I wasn't happy. I didn't go out of the house much. . . .

2. Find a partner to interview. Ask questions about the circumstances that brought him or her to the U.S. and the conditions of his/her life after he/she arrived. Write your conversation. Use Exercise 23 as your model.

EXAMPLE:

A. When did you leave your country?
B. I left Ethiopia five years ago.
A. Did you come directly to the U.S.?
B. No. First I went to Sudan.
A. Why did you leave Ethiopia?

3. Game: Who and When

Part A. On left side of the page, there are questions about famous people. On the right side of the page are some names of famous people. Work with a partner and see how many you can match. (You can find the answers at the end of the chapter.) The first one has been done for you.

a) Who invented the rocket?   *4*   1. Leonardo da Vinci
b) Who discovered America?   2. Yuri Gagarin
c) Who painted the Mona Lisa?   3. William Shakespeare
d) Who wrote *Romeo and Juliet*?   4. Robert Goddard
e) Who was the first person to walk on the   5. Thomas Edison
    moon?   6. George Washington
f) Who was the first person in space?   7. George Bush
g) Which president freed the slaves?   8. Pablo Picasso
h) Who composed *The Magic Flute*?   9. Alexander Graham Bell
i) Who invented the phonograph?   10. Johann Sebastian Bach
j) Who was the first president of the U.S.?   11. Christopher Columbus
k) Who became president after Reagan and   12. Neil Armstrong
    before Clinton?   13. Wolfgang Mozart
l) Who invented the telephone?   14. Abraham Lincoln

Part B. Take each question from above and write a question using *when*. Try to guess the answer by choosing one of the years given.

EXAMPLE:

When did Goddard invent the rocket?

a) 1903   1914   (1926)   1935
b) 1215   1385   1492   1620
c) 1325   1503   1625   1788
d) 1596   1675   1801   1865

e) 1957	1960	1969	1972
f) 1957	1960	1969	1970
g) 1834	1850	1865	1899
h) 1623	1688	1699	1791
i) 1877	1899	1902	1920
j) 1620	1724	1789	1825
k) 1985	1989	1990	1992
l) 1845	1877	1910	1935

4. Finish these statements five different ways. Then find a partner and compare your sentences to your partner's sentences. Did you have any sentences in common?

EXAMPLE: When I was a child, _I didn't like to do my homework._

When I was a child, _my parents gave me a bicycle for my tenth birthday._

When I was a child, _my nickname was "Curly"_

a. When I was a child, _____

b. Before I came to the U.S., _____

OUTSIDE ACTIVITIES

1. Interview an American about a vacation he or she took. Find out where he or she went, with whom, for how long, and other related information.

2. Interview an American about a famous person he or she admires. Ask what this famous person did.

Internet Activity

Using the Internet, find out something about one of the following famous people. What did he or she do? When did he or she do it? When was he/she born? Is he/she still alive? If not, when did he/she die?

a. Marie Curie
b. Alexander Fleming
c. Thomas Edison
d. Alexander Graham Bell
e. Bill Gates
f. Henry Ford
g. Jonas Salk
h. Edwin Hubble
i. Enrico Fermi
j. John Von Neumann
k. Leo Baekeland
l. Ian Wilmut

ANSWERS TO CLASSROOM ACTIVITY 3:
Part A: b=11, c=1, d=3, e=12, f=2, g=14, h=13, i=5, j=6, k=7, l=9
Part B: a=1926, b=1492, c=1503, d=1596, e=1969, f=1957, g=1865, h=1791, i=1877, j=1789, k=1989, l=1877

Lesson Nine

GRAMMAR

Imperatives
Infinitives
Modals

CONTEXT

Application for Check Cashing
Getting the Best Price
Smart Shopping: Coupons, Rebates, and Rain Checks
At the Customer Service Counter

LESSON FOCUS

We use imperative sentences to make requests or give commands and instructions to other people.

Stay here.   *Be* good.   *Open* your book.

The infinitive is *to* + the base form of the verb.

I want *to leave*.   I need *to go* home.

We use modal auxiliaries to add certain meanings to verbs. The modal auxiliaries are: *can, could, should, may, might, must, will, would*.

I *can* read this paragraph easily.
You *should* help your roommate.

1. Where do you shop for food?
2. What services do supermarkets have for customers?

Read the following article. Pay special attention to imperative forms.

Application for Check Cashing

You can cash checks at a supermarket near your house. **Ask** for an application at the customer service counter. **Read** the instructions carefully and **fill out** the form.

On this form, **print** all information, except for the last line. **Sign** your name on the last line and **write** the date.

Some forms ask you to put your last name before your first name. On this form, however, **put** your first name before your last. Then **fill in** all parts of section one. If you are married and want a card for your spouse,[1] **fill out** the second part.

Do not write anything in the space that says "For Office Use Only." **Do not fill out** anything where you see "Dominick's Use Only."

---

[1] A *spouse* is a husband or a wife.

When you finish filling out the form, **return** it to the customer service desk. **Show** your driver's license or state ID card.

9.1 Using Imperatives

Examples	Use
Get an application. **Print** your name on the first line. **Sign** your name on the bottom line. **Don't print** your name on the bottom line. **Don't write** in the box that says, "For Office Use Only."	To give instructions
Please **show** me your driver's license. **Take** this card to front desk, please.	To make a request
Don't open my mail. **Stand** at attention! **Don't be** late.	To make a command
Watch out! **Be** careful! **Don't be** late for the meeting. **Don't move!** You're under arrest.	To give a warning
Have a nice day. **Have** a good time. **Make** yourself at home. **Drive** safely.	In certain polite conversational expressions
Shut up! **Mind** your own business!	In some angry, impolite expressions

LANGUAGE NOTES

1. To form the imperative, use the base form. The subject of the imperative is *you*, but we don't include *you* in the sentence.
2. A negative imperative is *do not* + base form. The contraction is *don't*.

Fill in the blanks with an appropriate imperative verb (affirmative or negative) to give instructions.

EXAMPLE: ___Go___ to the customer service desk for an application.

1. _Write_ out the application in pen.

2. _Do not_ a pencil to fill out an application.

3. _Fill_ all the information in clear letters.

4. If you have a middle name, _Write_ your middle initial.

5. _____ anything in the box in the lower right corner.

6. If you are not married, _____ out the second part.

7. When you give your telephone number, always _____ your area code.

8. _____ your last name before your first name on this application.

9. _____ the application to a person at the customer service counter.

EXERCISE 2   Parents often give their children rules with imperatives. Fill in the blanks with an imperative, either affirmative or negative. (You may work with a partner.)

EXAMPLES: _Do_ your homework.

             Don't eat so much candy.

1. _____ to strangers.

2. _____ after school.

3. _____ before dinner.

4. _____ before you cross the street.

5. _____ your brothers and sisters.

6. _____ with matches.

7. _____ your grandparents.

8. _____ before you go to bed.

EXERCISE 3   Choose one of the activities from the following list (or choose a different one, if you like). Use imperatives to give instructions on how to do the activity. (You may work with a partner.)

EXAMPLE: how to get from school to your house
             Take the number 53 bus north on the corner of Elm Street. Ask the driver for a transfer. Get off at Park Avenue. Cross the street and wait for a number 18 bus.

1. hang a picture
2. change a tire
3. fry an egg
4. prepare your favorite recipe
5. hem a skirt
6. write a check
7. make a deposit at the bank
8. tune a guitar
9. get a driver's license
10. use a washing machine
11. prepare for a job interview
12. get from school to your house
13. get money from a cash machine (automatic teller)
14. record a TV show on your VCR

EXERCISE 4 Work with a partner. Write a list of command forms that the teacher often uses in class. Read your sentences to the class.

EXAMPLES:
Open your books to page 10.

Don't come late to class.

1. _____
2. _____
3. _____

9.2 *Let's*

Examples	Explanation
Let's go to the supermarket. **Let's** hurry. **Let's** not spend a lot of money.	We use *let's* + a base form to make an invitation or suggestion. *Let's* includes the speaker in the invitation.

LANGUAGE NOTES

1. *Let's* is a contraction for *let us*.
2. For a negative, put *not* after *let's*.

Fill in the blanks with an appropriate verb to complete this conversation.

A. I need to cash a check.

B. We need to get some groceries. Let's ____*go*____ to the supermarket.
   (example)

A. Do you want to drive there?

B. The supermarket is not so far. Let's _____.
   (1)

A. It looks like rain.

B. No problem. Let's _____ an umbrella.
   (2)

A. Let's _____. It's late and the store will close soon.
   (3)

B. Don't worry. This store is open 24 hours a day.

A. We're almost out of dog food. Let's _____ a 20-pound bag.
   (4)

B. Let's _____ then. I don't want to carry a 20-pound bag home.
   (5)

   Let's _____ instead.
   (6)

EXERCISE **6** Work with a partner. Write a few suggestions for the teacher or other students in this class. Read your suggestions to the class.

EXAMPLES: *Let's review verb tenses.*

Let's not speak our native languages in class.

1. _____

2. _____

3. _____

Before You Read 1. Do you like to shop for new things such as TVs, VCRs, computers, microwave ovens?
2. Do you try to compare prices in different stores before you buy an expensive item?

Read the following article. Pay special attention to infinitives.

Getting the Best Price

Are you planning **to buy** a new appliance, such as a TV or microwave oven? Do you want **to get** the best price? Of course! Every shopper wants **to save** money. But what do you do if you go to one store and see a VCR for $275 and then go to another store and see the same VCR for $300? You probably think it's necessary **to go** back to the first store **to get** the lower price. But usually it isn't. You can simply tell the salesperson in the second store that you saw the VCR at a better price. Usually the salesperson will try **to match**[2] the other store's price. However, you need **to prove** that you can buy it cheaper elsewhere. The proof can be the advertisement from the newspaper. If you don't have the ad, the salesperson can call the other store **to check** the price. The salesperson doesn't want you **to leave** the store without buying anything. He wants **to give** you the best price. He wants his store **to make** money. Some salespeople are happy **to call** the other store **to check** the price.

What happens if you buy something and a few days later see it cheaper at another store? Some stores will give you the difference in price for a limited period of time (such as 30 days). It's important **to keep** the receipt **to show** when you bought the item and how much you paid.

[2] To *match* a price means to give you an equal price.

9.3 Verbs Followed by an Infinitive

Subject	Verb	Infinitive	Complement
I	want	**to get**	the best price.
The salesperson	hopes	**to make**	a sale.
We	are planning	**to buy**	a new TV.

LANGUAGE NOTES

1. An infinitive is *to* + the base form of a verb: *to go, to be, to have.*
2. We often use an infinitive after the following verbs.

begin	hope	prefer
continue	like	promise
decide	love	start
expect	need	try
forget	plan	want

3. An infinitive never has an ending. It never shows the tense. Only the first verb shows the tense.

   He needs *to buy* a new TV.

   We wanted *to get* the best price.

   I'm planning *to compare* prices at several stores.

4. In an infinitive, we often pronounce *to* like "ta," or, after a *d* sound or vowel sound, like "da." Listen to your teacher pronounce these sentences.

   Do you like *to dance*?

   I try *to exercise* every day.

   I decided *to leave*.

   I need *to talk* to you.

5. In fast, informal speech, *want to* is often pronounced "wanna." Listen to your teacher pronounce these sentences.

   I *want to* go home. = I "wanna" go home.

   Do you *want to* leave now? = Do you "wanna" leave now?

EXERCISE 7 Make a sentence about yourself with the words given. Use an appropriate tense. You may find a partner, and compare your sentences to your partner's sentences.

EXAMPLES: like/eat

I like to eat pizza.

learn/speak

I learned to speak German when I was a child.

---

try/find

I'm trying to find a bigger apartment.

1. love/go

_____

2. like/play

_____

3. need/have

_____

4. expect/get

_____

5. want/go

_____

6. plan/buy

_____

7. need/understand

_____

8. not need/have

_____

9. try/learn

_____

EXERCISE 8 Ask a question with the words given in the present tense. Another student will answer.

EXAMPLE: like/travel
A. Do you like to travel?
B. Yes, I do. OR No, I don't.

1. expect/pass this course

2. plan/graduate soon

3. plan/transfer to another college

4. like/read

5. like/study grammar

6. try/understand Americans

7. try/learn idioms

8. expect/return to your country

EXERCISE 9 Ask a question with "Do you want to . . . ?" and the words given. Another student will answer. Then ask a *wh-* question with the words in parentheses ( ) whenever possible.

EXAMPLE: buy a car (why)
A. Do you want to buy a car?
B. Yes, I do.   OR   No, I don't.
A. Why do you want to buy a car?
B. I don't like public transportation.

1. take a computer course next semester (why)

2. move (why) (when)

3. return to your country (why) (when)

4. get a job/get another job (what kind of job)

5. become an American citizen (why)

6. transfer to a different school (why)

7. take another English course next semester (which course)

8. learn another language (which language)

9. review the last lesson (why)

9.4 *It* + *Be* + Adjective + Infinitive

It	*Be (+ Not)*	Adjective	Infinitive Phrase
It	is	important	**to save** your receipt.
It	isn't	necessary	**to go** back to the first store.
It	is	easy	**to shop**.

LANGUAGE NOTES

We can use an infinitive after the following adjectives:

dangerous	good	possible	expensive
difficult	hard	necessary	impossible
easy	important	fun	

EXERCISE 10 Complete each statement.

EXAMPLE: It's expensive to own _a big car._ _____

1. It's important to learn _____

2. It's hard to pronounce _____

3. It's hard to lift _____

4. It's necessary to have _____

5. It's easy to learn _____

6. It's hard to learn _____

7. It isn't important to know _____

EXERCISE 11 Complete each statement with an infinitive phrase.

EXAMPLE: It's easy _to ride a bike._ _____

1. It's fun _____

2. It's impossible _____

3. It's possible _____

4. It's necessary _____

5. It's dangerous _____

6. It's hard _____

7. It isn't good _____

8. It isn't necessary _____

9.5 Be + Adjective + Infinitive

Subject	*Be*	Adjective	Infinitive (Phrase)
I	am	happy	**to call** the other store.
She	is	ready	**to buy** a new TV.
We	are	glad	**to help** you.

LANGUAGE NOTES

We can use an infinitive after these adjectives:

afraid	happy	prepared	ready
glad	lucky	proud	sad

EXERCISE 12 Fill in the blanks.

EXAMPLE: I'm lucky _to be in the U.S._

1. Americans are lucky _____

2. I'm proud _____

3. I'm happy _____

4. I'm sometimes afraid _____

5. I'm not afraid _____

6. Are the students prepared _____

7. Is the teacher ready _____

EXERCISE 13 Answer the following questions. (You may work with a partner and ask and answer with your partner.)

1. Are you happy to be in this country?

2. Is it important to know English or another language in your country?

3. Are you afraid to make a mistake when you speak English?

4. Is it possible to find a job without knowing any English?

5. Is it easy to learn English grammar?

6. Is it important to wear a seat belt when you are a passenger in a car?

7. Is it necessary to have a computer?

8. Were you sad to leave your country?

9. Are you prepared to have a test on this lesson?

9.6 Using the Infinitive to Show Purpose

Examples	Explanation
I went to the store **to buy** a VCR. I bought a VCR **to record** my favorite programs. The saleswoman called another store **to check** the price.	We use the infinitive to show the purpose of an action. We can also say *in order to*: I bought a VCR **in order to** record my favorite programs.

EXERCISE 14 Fill in the blanks to show purpose.

EXAMPLE: I bought a phone card to ___*call my friends*___.

1. I use my dictionary to _____.
2. At the end of a concert, people applaud to _____.
3. He went to the customer service counter to _____.
4. She worked overtime to _____.
5. I bought the Sunday newspaper to _____.
6. You need to show your driver's license to _____.
7. You can use a hammer to _____.
8. Some people join a health club to _____.
9. On a computer, you use the mouse to _____.
10. When you return an item to a store, take your receipt to _____.

9.7 Overview of Modals

List of Modals	Facts about Modals

can
could
should
will
would
may
might
must
	1. Modals are different from other verbs because they don't have an -*s*, -*ed*, or -*ing* ending.
	    He **can** drive. (NOT: He *cans* drive.)
	
	2. Modals are different from other verbs because we don't use an infinitive after a modal.[3] We use the base form.
	    COMPARE:
	    He wants **to leave**. He likes to **swim**.
	    He **must leave**. He **can swim**.
	
	3. To form the negative, put *not* after the modal.
	    He **should not** drive.
	    You **must not** talk during a test.
	
	4. Some verbs are like modals in meaning: *have to, be able to*
	    He **must** sign the lease. = He **has to** sign the lease.
	    He **can** pay the rent. = He **is able to** pay the rent.

Observe statements and questions with a modal verb.

Wh- Word	Modal (+ *Not*)	Subject	Modal (+ *Not*)	Main Verb	Complement	Short Answer
		Mario	**should**	study	English.	
		He	**shouldn't**	study	literature.	
	Should	he		study	grammar?	Yes, he **should**.
Why	**should**	he		study	grammar?	
Why	**shouldn't**	he		study	literature?	
		Who	**should**	study	literature?	

[3] Exception: *ought to*. *Ought to* means *should*.

1. Do you see coupons in magazines and newspapers? Do you use them?
2. Do you see signs that say "rebate" on store products? Do you see signs that say "Buy one, get one free"?

MANUFACTURER'S COUPON | DO NOT DOUBLE | EXPIRES 12 / 12 / 00

Save 50¢
off next purchase of any
Best Choice Soup

CONSUMER: Limit one coupon per purchase.
RETAILER: Please redeem for face value as specified. Any Other Use Constitutes Fraud. Cash value 1/100 cent.

Read the following article. Pay special attention to modals and related expressions.

Smart Shopping: Coupons, Rebates, and Rain Checks

Manufacturers often send coupons to shoppers. They want people to try their products. If you always use the same toothpaste and the manufacturer gives you a coupon for a different toothpaste, you **might** try the new brand.[4] Coupons have an expiration date. You **should** pay attention to this date because you **cannot** use the coupon after this date.

Many supermarkets also have weekly specials. You **might** see a sign that says, "Buy one, get one free" or "Two for one." It's true: the supermarket **will** give you one item for free. There is usually a limit on sale items. For example, you **might** see a sign that says, "Eggs 49¢ a dozen. Limit 2." This means you **can** only buy two dozen at this price. If you see a sign that says, "3 for 99¢," you **don't have to** buy three items to get the special price. If you buy only one, you **will** pay 33¢.

If you see a sign that says "rebate," this means that you **can** get money back from the manufacturer. You **have to** mail the proof of purchase and the cash register receipt to the manufacturer to prove that you bought this product. Also you **have to** fill out a small form. The manufacturer **will** return

---

[4] The *brand* is the company name.

Sometimes the money you receive is very small. You **should** decide if it is worth it to spend money for a stamp in order to receive a check for $1.00 or less.

<table>
<tr><td colspan="2">

Rebate Form
_____

Name   Address
_____

City/State   Zip   Phone

Product Name: _____
Size/Weight: _____
Price: _____
Store where Purchased: _____
Date of Purchase: _____
Proof of Purchase attached: yes   /   no
</td></tr>
</table>

What **should** you do if a store has a special but you **can't** find this item on the shelf? If this item is sold out, you **can** go to the customer service desk and ask for a rain check. A rain check allows you to buy this item at the sale price even after the sale is over. A rain check usually has an expiration date. You **must** buy this item by the expiration date if you want to receive the sale price.

There are many ways to save money when shopping.

9.8   *Can*

Examples	Explanation
I **can** drive.	Ability
If you use coupons, you **can** save money.	Possibility
The sign says, "Eggs 49¢. Limit Two." You **can** only buy two cartons of eggs at the special price.	Permission
That sign says "Cash only." You **can't** use a credit card.	

LANGUAGE NOTES

1. The negative of *can* is *cannot* (one word). The contraction is *can't*.
2. In affirmative statements, we usually pronounce *can* /kən/. In negative statements, we pronounce *can't* /kænt/. Sometimes it is hard to hear the final **t**, so we must pay attention to the vowel sound and the stress to hear the difference between *can* and *can't*. Listen to your teacher pronounce these sentences:

    I *can* gó. /kən/
    I *cán't* go. /kænt/

3. In a short answer, we pronounce *can* /kæn/.
   Can you help me later?
   Yes, I *can*. /kæn/
4. We use *can* in the following idiomatic expression:
   I *can't afford* to buy a new car. I don't have enough money.
   I saved my money, and now I *can afford* to take a vacation.

EXERCISE 15 Fill in the blanks with *can* or *can't* to tell about your abilities.

EXAMPLES: I ____*can*____ drive a car.

I ____*can't*____ fly a plane.

1. I _____ read without glasses.

2. I _____ speak Spanish.

3. I _____ drive a car.

4. I _____ play tennis.

5. I _____ sing well.

6. I _____ change a tire.

7. I _____ save money.

8. I _____ program a VCR.

EXERCISE 16 Ask a question about a classmate's abilities with the words given. Another student will answer.

EXAMPLE: speak Spanish
A. Can you speak Spanish?
B. Yes, I can. OR No, I can't.

1. write with your left hand
2. type 60 words per minute
3. use a computer
4. play chess
5. ski
6. play the piano
7. speak Arabic
8. bake a cake
9. play the guitar
10. sew

EXERCISE 17 Write down one thing that you can do well. Share your answers with a partner or with the entire class.

_____

EXERCISE 18 These sentences are true about an American supermarket. Check (√) which ones are true about a supermarket in your country.

1. _____ You can use coupons.

2. _____ You can sometimes buy two items for the price of one.

3. _____ You can cash a check.

4. _____ You can buy stamps.

5. _____ You can get money back from a manufacturer.

6. _____ You can pay by check or credit card.

7. _____ You can't bargain⁵ for the price.

8. _____ You can return an item if you're not satisfied. You can get your money back.

9. _____ You can get free bags (paper or plastic).

10. _____ You can use a shopping cart. Small children can sit in the cart.

11. _____ If you have a small number of items, you can go to a special lane.

12. _____ You can shop 24 hours a day (in some supermarkets).

9.9 Should

Examples	Explanation
You **should** look at the date on a coupon. You **should** decide if it's worth it to mail in the rebate.	Advice
That milk is old. You **should not** use it. You **should** throw it away.	Warning

⁵ To _bargain_ for a price means to make an offer lower than the price the seller is asking.

LANGUAGE NOTES

The contraction for *should not* is *shouldn't.*

EXERCISE 19 What should a person do with each of the following health problems? Write a sentence of advice for each one. (You may work with a partner.)

EXAMPLE: He has a headache.

He should take an aspirin and lie down.

1. He has a stomachache. _____

2. She has a cut. _____

3. He has a burn. _____

4. She has a cold. _____

5. He has a fever. _____

6. She has a toothache. _____

7. He's always nervous. _____

8. She has a backache. _____

EXERCISE 20 A father is giving his son advice. What advice do you think he is giving? Write sentences with *should.* (You may work with a partner.)

EXAMPLES: You eat hot dogs, fries, and colas all the time.

You should eat more fruits and vegetables.

You shouldn't eat so much junk food.

1. You spend too much time at the computer.

_____

2. You always ask me for money.

_____

3. You always wait until the last minute to study for a test.

_____

4. Your hair is too long.

_____

5. Your clothes look dirty.

_____

6. You talk for hours on the phone with your friends.

_____

7. You never clean your room. It's a mess!⁶

_____

8. You never listen to your mother when she tells you something.

_____

9. You want your driver's license, but you're not responsible.

_____

EXERCISE 21 Check (√) if you agree or disagree about what schoolchildren should or shouldn't do. Discuss your answers with the whole class or in a small group.

	I agree.	I disagree.
1. Children should go to a teacher with a family problem.		
2. They should play video games.		
3. They should select their own TV programs.		
4. They should not trust all adults.		
5. They should always tell the truth.		
6. They should be responsible for taking care of younger sisters and brothers.		
7. They should select their own friends.		
8. They should always obey their parents and teachers.		
9. They should learn to use a computer.		
10. They should study a foreign language.		
11. They should help their parents with small jobs in the house.		

EXERCISE 22 Read each statement. Then ask a question with the word in parentheses ( ). Another student will answer.

EXAMPLE: The students should do the homework (why)
             A. Why should they do the homework?
             B. It helps them understand the lesson.

⁶ A *mess* is a disorganized place.

1. The students should study the lessons. (why)

2. The teacher should take attendance. (when)

3. The students should bring their textbook to class. (what else)

4. I should study modals. (why)

5. We should register for classes early. (why)

6. The teacher should speak clearly. (why)

7. The students shouldn't talk during a test. (why)

8. We shouldn't do the homework in class. (where)

9. The teacher should announce a test ahead of time. (why)

9.10 *Must*

Examples	Explanation
You **must** send a proof of purchase for a rebate. You **must** include your receipt.	Rules
You **must** have a license plate on the back of your car. A driver **must** stop at a red light.	Laws
You **must not** park at a fire hydrant.	Prohibition

LANGUAGE NOTES

1. The contraction for *must not* is *mustn't*.
2. *Must not* and *cannot* are very close in meaning.
    You *must not* park at a fire hydrant. (It's against the law.)
    You *cannot* park at a fire hydrant. (It is not permitted.)

EXERCISE 23 Fill in the blanks with *must* or *must not* for driving rules.

EXAMPLES: You _____*must*_____ stop at a red light.

You _____*must not*_____ drive slowly on the expressway.

1. You _____ pass a driving test if you want a driver's license.

2. If a school bus stops in front of you, you _____ stop.

3. You _____ park at a bus stop.

4. You _____ put money in a parking meter during business hours.

---

5. You _____ drive over the speed limit.

6. You _____ use your turn signal before you make a turn.

EXERCISE 24 Name something.

EXAMPLE: Name something you must have if you want to drive.
You must have a license.

1. Name something you must do or have if you want to leave the country.

2. Name something you must not carry onto an airplane.

3. Name something you must not do in the classroom.

4. Name something you must not do during a test.

5. Name something you must not do or have in your apartment.

6. Name something you must do or have to enter an American university.

9.11 *Must* vs. *Have To*

	Examples	Explanation
Affirmative	You **must** use a coupon by a certain date. = You **have to** use a coupon by a certain date.	It is a rule.
	I **have to** buy groceries tomorrow.	It is a personal obligation or necessity.
Negative	You **must not** steal.	It is against the law.
	If a sale says, "3 for $1.00," you **don't have to** buy 3 items.	It's not necessary to buy three items to get the sale price. You can buy one or two.

LANGUAGE NOTES

1. In affirmative statements, *have to* and *must* are very similar in meaning. They both show necessity. *Have to* is more common than *must* with a personal necessity or obligation. *Must* is stronger and usually tells about rules.

    I *have to* go to the bank today.
    I *must* go to court next week.

2. In negative statements, *must* and *have to* are very different. *Must not* shows that something is prohibited, against the rules. *Don't/Doesn't have to* shows that something is not necessary.

    You *must not* drive without a license.
    I *don't have to* drive to school. I can walk.

---

3. In fast speech, *have to* sounds like "hafta"; *has to* sounds like "hasta." Listen to your teacher pronounce these sentences:
I have to leave now. My friend has to leave too.

EXERCISE 25 Tell if you *have to* or *don't have to* do these things at this school. (Remember: *don't have to* means not necessary.)

EXAMPLES: study before a test
I have to study before a test.

study in the library
I don't have to study in the library. I can study at home.

1. wear a suit to school
2. come on time to class
3. stand up to ask a question in class
4. do homework
5. notify the teacher if I'm going to be absent
6. call the teacher "professor"
7. raise my hand to answer
8. take a final exam
9. wear a uniform
10. buy my own textbooks

EXERCISE 26 Ask your teacher what he or she *has to* or *doesn't have to* do.

EXAMPLE: work on Saturdays
A. Do you have to work on Saturdays?
B. Yes, I do.   OR   No, I don't.

1. take attendance
2. give the students a grade
3. call the students by their last names
4. wear a suit
5. work in the summer
6. have a master's degree
7. work on Saturdays
8. come to this school every day

EXERCISE 27 Write four sentences about students and teachers in your country. Tell what they *have to* or *don't have to* do. Use the ideas from the previous exercises. You may share your sentences with a small group or with the class.

EXAMPLE: *In my country, a student has to wear a uniform.*

1. _____
2. _____
3. _____
4. _____

EXERCISE 28 Tell what Judy *has to* or *doesn't have to* do in these situations.

EXAMPLE: Judy has a coupon for cereal. The expiration date is tomorrow. She has to *use it by tomorrow or she won't get the discount* .

1. The coupon for cereal says "Buy 2, get 50¢ off." She has to _____ in order to get the discount.

2. Judy has no milk in the house. She has to _____ more milk.

3. She has 26 items in her shopping cart. She can't go to a lane that says "10 items or fewer." She has to _____ another lane.

4. Eggs are on sale for 49¢, limit two. She has three cartons of eggs. She has to _____ one of the cartons of eggs.

5. She has a rebate application. She has to fill out the application if she wants to get money back. She also has to _____ the proof-of-purchase symbol and the receipt to the manufacturer.

6. She wants to pay by check. The cashier asks for her driver's license. She has to _____ .

9.12 *Might/May/Will*

Examples	Explanation
I have a coupon for a new toothpaste. I **might** buy it. I **may** like it and want to switch. A rebate check **might** take six to eight weeks. If you don't study, you **might** fail.	*May* and *might* have the same meaning. They show possibility.
If the price is 3 for 99¢, you **will** pay 33¢ for one. If the sign says "Two for one," the store **will** give you one item for free.	*Will* shows certainty about the future.

LANGUAGE NOTES

1. Compare *maybe* (adverb) and *may* or *might* (modal verbs):
   Maybe it will rain tomorrow.
   It *may rain* tomorrow.   OR   It *might rain* tomorrow.
2. We do not usually make a contraction for *may not* or *might not*.

Tell what may or might happen in the following situations.

EXAMPLE: Meg needs to go shopping. She's not sure what her kids want. They might
            want a new kind of
            _____ cereal.

1. She's not sure if she should buy the small size or the large size of
    cereal. The large size may _____ cheaper.

2. If she sends in the rebate form today, she might _____
    a check in four or five weeks.

3. The store sold all the coffee that was on sale. The clerk said, "We
    might _____ more coffee tomorrow."

4. Bananas are so expensive this week. If she waits until next week,
    the price may _____ .

5. The milk has an expiration date of June 27. Today is June 27. She's
    not going to buy the milk because it might _____ .

6. She's not sure what brand of toothpaste she should buy. She might
    buy the one she usually buys, or she might _____ .

EXERCISE **30** Tell what *may* or *might* happen in the following situations. If
you think the result is certain, use *will*.

EXAMPLES: If you don't put money in a parking meter, ___ *you might get a* ___
            parking ticket.
            _____

            If you are absent from tests, ___ *you may not pass the course.* ___

            If you don't pass the tests, ___ *you'll fail the course.* ___

1. If you drive too fast, _____

2. If you get a lot of tickets in one year, _____

3. If you don't water your plants, _____

4. If you don't take the final exam, _____

5. If you don't lock the door of your house, _____

6. If you eat too much, _____

7. If you work hard and save your money, _____

8. If the weather is nice this weekend, _____

1. Do you have a check cashing card at a local supermarket?
2. Do you pay with cash when you shop in a supermarket?

Read the following conversation between a store clerk (A) at the customer service counter and a store customer (B). Pay special attention to modals.

At the Customer Service Counter

A. **Can** I help you?

B. Yes. **I'd like** to cash a check.

A. Do you have a check-cashing card?

B. No, I don't.

A. You need to fill out an application. Here's one. **Would** you fill it out, please?

B. Yes. I don't have a pen. **Could** I use your pen?

A. Here's a pen.

B. Thanks.

. . . *A few minutes later* . . .

B. Here's my application.

A. **May** I see your driver's license?

B. Here it is. **Could** you cash my check now?

A. I'm sorry, sir. We have to wait for approval. We'll send you your check-cashing card in the mail.

9.13 Making Polite Commands and Requests with Modals

To request someone to do something	Explanation
Would **Could** } you cash my check, please?	These expressions are more polite than "Cash my check."

To ask permission	Explanation
May **Could** } I use your pen, please? **Can**	These expressions are more polite than "Give me your pen."

To request someone to do something	Explanation
I **would like** to cash a check. How **would** you **like** your change?	*Would like* has the same meaning as *want. Would like* is softer than *want*. The contraction of *would* after a pronoun is **'d**: I*'d* like to cash a check.

LANGUAGE NOTES

1. A command is very strong and is impolite in some situations. It is softer and more polite to use modals to make a request.
2. Some people consider *May I . . . ?* more polite than *Can I . . . ?* for permission.
3. Another way to make a soft request or suggestion is with *Why don't you/we . . . ?*

> Sit over there.
> *Why don't you* sit over there?
> Let's go to the bank.
> *Why don't we* go to the bank?

EXERCISE 31 Read the following conversation between a waiter (W) and a customer (C) in a restaurant. Change the underlined words to make the conversation more polite.

W. What <u>do you want</u> to order?   *would you like*

C. <u>I want</u> the roast chicken dinner.

W. Anything else?

C. Yes. <u>Bring</u> me a salad.

W. What kind of dressing <u>do you want</u>?

C. <u>Put</u> garlic dressing on my salad.

   . . .

W. Here's your salad, Miss.

C. Thanks. You know, it's a little cold at this table. <u>Let me sit</u> at another table.

W. Of course. There's a nice table in the corner. <u>Sit</u> over there.

C. Thanks, and <u>bring</u> me another glass of water.

W. Of course.

SUMMARY OF LESSON 9

1. Imperatives
   > **Sit** down. **Don't** be late.

2. *Let's*
   > **Let's** go to the movies. **Let's** not be late.

3. Infinitive Patterns

He wants **to go**.
It's necessary **to learn** English.
I'm afraid **to stay**.
I use coupons **to save** money.

4. Modals

Modal	Example	Explanation
can	He **can** speak English.	He has this ability.
	An 18-year-old **can** vote.	He has permission.
	Can I borrow your pen?	I'm asking permission.
can't	You **can't** park here. It's a bus stop.	It is not permitted.
	I **can't** help you now. I'm busy.	I am not able to.
should	You **should** eat healthy food.	It's good advice.
shouldn't	You **shouldn't** drive if you're sleepy.	It's a bad idea.
may	**May** I borrow your pen?	I'm asking permission.
	I **may** buy a new car.	This is possible.
may not	I **may not** be here tomorrow.	This is possible.
might	It **might** rain tomorrow.	This is possible.
might not	We **might not** have our picnic.	This is possible.
must	A driver **must** have a license.	This is a legal necessity.
	I'm late. I **must** hurry.	This is a personal necessity.
must not	You **must not** drive without a license.	This is against the law.
will	The manufacturer **will** send you a check.	This is in the future.
will not	You **will not** receive the check right away.	
would	**Would** you help me move?	I'm asking a favor.
would like	I **would like** to use your pen.	I want to use your pen.
could	**Could** you help me move?	I'm asking a favor.
have to	She **has to** leave.	It's necessary.
not have to	She **doesn't have to** leave.	It's not necessary.

1. Don't use *to* after a modal.

   I must ~~to~~ go.

2. Use *to* between verbs.

   They like _to_ play.
          ^

3. Always use the base form after a modal.

   He can swims.

   She can't ~~driving~~ *drive* the car.

4. Use the base form in an infinitive.

   He wants to goes.

   I wanted to worked.

5. We can introduce an infinitive with *it* + adjective.

   It i~~Is~~ important to get exercise.
   ^

6. Don't put an object between the modal and the main verb.

   She can ~~the lesson understand.~~ *understand the lesson.*

7. Use the correct word order in a question.

   Why ~~you can't~~ *can't you* stay?

8. Use an infinitive after some adjectives.

   I'm happy _to_ meet you.
            ^

   It's necessary _to_ have a job.
                 ^

9. Use *not* after *let's* to make a negative.

   Let's ~~don't~~ *not* go to the party.

10. Use *don't* to make a negative imperative.

    ~~Not~~ *Don't* come home late.

11. Use *to*, not *for*, to show purpose.

    We went to the theater ~~for~~ *to* see a play.

PART 1   Find the **grammar** mistakes with the underlined words and correct them. Not every sentence has a mistake. If the sentence is correct, write **C**.

EXAMPLES: You should ~~to~~ study more.

I don't have to work on Saturday.   **C**

1. I need cash a check.

2. What I can do for you?

3. I'm afraid to walk alone at night.

4. She has to leave early today.

5. We wanted to went home early last night.

6. Is necessary to have a car.

7. You must to go to court next week.

8. She can English speak very well.

9. Don't to walk so fast.

10. What I must do to get a driver's license?

11. He should study harder.

12. We want learn English quickly.

13. My brother can speaks English very well.

14. It's impossible learn English in one month.

15. She likes to swim in the ocean.

16. Let's don't make a lot of noise. Dad is sleeping.

17. I was glad to met him yesterday.

18. Don't worry. Everything will be all right.

19. She went to the school for talk to her daughter's teacher.

20. You should <u>looking</u> for a new job.

21. The teacher always says, "<u>Not</u> talk during a test."

22. I use spell check <u>to checking</u> my spelling.

PART **2**

Fill in the first blank with *to* or nothing (*X*). Then write the negative form in the second blank.

EXAMPLES: I'm ready _____*to*_____ study Lesson 10. I _____*'m not ready to study*_____ Lesson 11.

You should _____*X*_____ drive carefully. You _____*shouldn't drive*_____ fast.

1. I need _____ learn English. I _____ Polish.

2. You must _____ stop at a red light. You _____ on the highway.

3. The teacher expects _____ pass most of the students. She _____

_____ all of the students.

4. We want _____ study grammar. We _____ literature.

5. The teacher has _____ give grades. He _____ an A to everyone.

6. We might _____ have time for some questions later. We _____

_____ time for a discussion.

7. It's important _____ practice American pronunciation now. It _____

_____ British pronunciation.

8. It's easy _____ learn one's native language. It _____

_____ a foreign language.

9. Let's _____ speak English in class. _____ our native languages in class.

10. Please attend the meeting. _____ be here at six o'clock, please.

_____ late.

PART 3

Change each sentence to a question.

EXAMPLES: I'm afraid to drive.

Why _are you afraid to drive?_

He can help you.

When _can he help me?_

1. You should wear a seat belt.

   Why _____

2. I want to buy some grapes.

   Why _____

3. He must fill out the application.

   When _____

4. She needs to drive to New York.

   When _____

5. You can't park at a bus stop.

   Why _____

6. It's necessary to eat vegetables.

   Why _____

7. She has to buy a car.

   Why _____

8. They'd like to see you.

   When _____

PART **4**   This is a phone conversation between a woman (W) and her mechanic (M). Choose the correct words to fill in the blanks.

W. This is Cindy Fine. I'm calling about my car.

M. I _____ _can't_ _____ hear you. _____ you speak louder, please?
    <small>(example: can't, may not)</small>   <small>(1 could, might)</small>

W. This is Cindy Fine. Is my car ready yet?

M. We're working on it now. We're almost finished.

W. When _____ I pick it up?
    <small>(2 would, can)</small>

M. It will be ready by four o'clock.

W. How much will it cost?

M. $375.

W. I don't have that much money right now. _____ I pay by credit card?
    (3 Can, Might)

M. Yes. You _____ use any major credit card.
    (4 may, might)

Later, at the mechanic's shop:

M. Your car's ready, ma'am. The engine problem is fixed. But you _____
    (5 may, should)
    change your brakes. They're not so good.

W. _____ do it right away?
    (6 Do I have to, May I)

M. No, you _____ do it immediately, but you _____
    (7 must not, don't have to)   *(8 would, should)*
    do it within a month or two. If you don't do it soon, you _____ have
    (9 may, would)
    an accident.

W. How much will it cost to change the brakes?

M. It _____ cost about $200.
    (10 would, will)

W. I _____ like to make an appointment to take care of the brakes next
    (11 will, would)
    week. _____ I bring my car in next Monday?
    (12 Can, Will)

M. Yes, Monday is fine. You _____ bring it in early because we get very
    (13 could, should)
    busy later in the day.

W. OK. See you Monday morning.

PART 5   Decide if the sentences have the same meaning or different meanings. Write S for same, D for different.

EXAMPLES: Would you like to go to a movie? Do you want to go to a movie?   S
            We will not go to New York. We should not go to New York.   D

1. You should go to the doctor. You can go to the doctor.

2. I may buy a new car. I must buy a new car.

3. Could you help me later? Would you help me later?

4. She must not drive her car. She doesn't have to drive her car.

5. She has to leave immediately. She must leave immediately.

6. We will have a test soon. We may have a test soon.

7. I can't go to the party. I might not go to the party.

8. You shouldn't buy a car. You don't have to buy a car.

9. May I use your phone? Could I use your phone?

10. He might not eat lunch. He may not eat lunch.

11. I should go to the doctor. I must go to the doctor.

12. I have to take my passport with me. I should take my passport with me.

EXPANSION ACTIVITIES

CLASSROOM ACTIVITIES

1. Imagine that a friend of yours is getting married. You are giving him or her advice about marriage. Write some advice for this person. (You may work with a partner or compare your advice to your partner's advice when you are finished.)

It's important	It's not important
It's important to be honest.	It's not important to do everything together.

2. Imagine that a friend of yours is going to travel to the U.S. You are giving him/her advice about the trip and life in the U.S. Write as many things as you can in each box. Then find a partner and compare your advice to your partner's advice.

It's necessary OR It's important OR You should	It's difficult OR You shouldn't
It's necessary to have a passport.	It's difficult to understand American English.

3. Working in a small group, write a list to give information to a new student or to a foreign student.

should or shouldn't	must or have to	don't have to	might or might not	can or can't
You should bring your transcripts to this college.				

4. With a partner, write a few instructions for one of the following situations.

EXAMPLE: using a microwave oven
You shouldn't put anything metal in the microwave.
You can set the power.
You should rotate the dish in the microwave. If you don't, the food might not cook evenly.

a. preparing for the TOEFL[7]

b. taking a test in this class

c. preparing for the driver's test in this state

5. Bring in an application. (Bring two of the same application, if possible.) It can be an application for a job, driver's license, license plate, apartment rental, address change, check cashing, rebate, etc. Work with a partner. One person will give instructions. The other person will fill it out.

6. Bring in ads from different stores. You can bring in ads from supermarkets or any other store. See what is on sale this week. Find a partner and discuss the products and the prices. Compare prices at two different stores, if possible. What do these products usually cost in your country? Do you have all of these products in your country?

DISCUSSION

In your country, do shoppers use coupons, rebates, or rain checks?

WRITING

Write about differences in shopping between your country and the U.S.

[7] The *TOEFL* is the Test of English as a Foreign Language.

Internet Activities

1. Use the Internet to compare the prices of a product, such as a VCR, TV, or computer.

2. Use the Internet to find application forms. (Examples: change of address form from the post office; application for a checking account from a bank; application for a credit card; application for a frequent flyer program from an airline; motor vehicle registration form in your state)

GRAMMAR

Count and Noncount Nouns
Quantity Words

CONTEXT

A Healthy Diet

LESSON FOCUS

We can classify nouns into two groups: count nouns and noncount nouns.

A count noun is something we can count. It has a singular form and a plural form.

one egg	five eggs	one American	a thousand Americans
one book	six books	a child	six children

A noncount noun is something we don't count. It has no plural form.

bread	sugar	cheese
milk	oil	rice

We can use quantity words with count and noncount nouns.

I bought *a few* apples

I bought *a lot of* rice.

1. What kind of food do you like to eat? What kind of food do you dislike?
2. What are some popular dishes from your country or native culture?

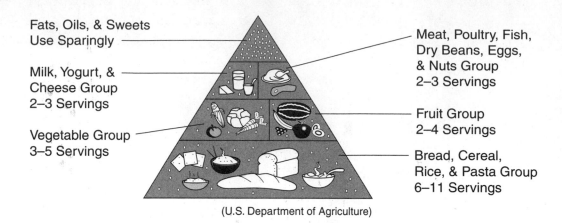

Fats, Oils, & Sweets
Use Sparingly

Milk, Yogurt, &
Cheese Group
2–3 Servings

Vegetable Group
3–5 Servings

Meat, Poultry, Fish,
Dry Beans, Eggs,
& Nuts Group
2–3 Servings

Fruit Group
2–4 Servings

Bread, Cereal,
Rice, & Pasta Group
6–11 Servings

(U.S. Department of Agriculture)

Read the following article. Pay special attention to count and noncount nouns.

A Healthy Diet

Good **nutrition** is extremely important. Eating the right kinds of **food** can keep you healthy. It is important to get enough **vitamins** and **minerals**. Vitamin and mineral supplements are important, but it is necessary to eat a well-balanced diet, too.

There are different food **groups**. It is important to eat some **food** from each group daily. The first group includes **bread**, **cereal**, **rice**, and **pasta**. You should eat more **foods** from this group than from any other group. The second group includes **vegetables.** The third group includes **fruit**. The fourth group includes **milk, yogurt**, and **cheese**. The fifth group includes **meat, poultry,**[1] **fish, beans, eggs**, and **nuts**. It is also important to drink a lot of water. Nutritionists recommend eight glasses of water a day.

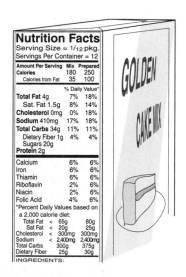

Nutrition Facts
Serving Size = 1/12 pkg.
Servings Per Container = 12

Amount Per Serving	Mix	Prepared
Calories	180	250
Calories from Fat	35	100

	% Daily Value*	
Total Fat 4g	7%	18%
Sat. Fat 1.5g	8%	14%
Cholesterol 0mg	0%	18%
Sodium 410mg	17%	18%
Total Carbs 34g	11%	11%
Dietary Fiber 1g	4%	4%
Sugars 20g		
Protein 2g		

Calcium	6%	6%
Iron	6%	6%
Thiamin	6%	6%
Riboflavin	2%	6%
Niacin	2%	6%
Folic Acid	4%	6%

*Percent Daily Values based on a 2,000 calorie diet:

Total Fat	<	65g	80g
Sat Fat	<	20g	25g
Cholesterol	<	300mg	300mg
Sodium	<	2,400mg	2,400mg
Total Carbs		300g	375g
Dietary Fiber		25g	30g

INGREDIENTS:

[1] *Poultry* includes domestic birds, such as chickens, turkeys, and ducks.

You should avoid **foods** that contain a lot of **fat**, **oil**, and **sugar**. Also avoid **foods** that are high in **cholesterol**. Cholesterol is a substance found in animal **foods**. A little cholesterol is good for the body, but high levels of cholesterol can be bad for the heart. Red **meat**, **eggs**, **cheese**, and **whole milk** contain a lot of cholesterol, and large quantities of these foods are not good for you. Foods from **plants** don't contain any cholesterol.

As people age, they need to make changes in their diet. People over 50 need to eat less to keep the same body weight. They also need to eat more fiber.[2] Foods which contain fiber are **fruits**, **vegetables**, **beans**, and **rice**. Women over 50 need more calcium. Foods which contain calcium are **milk**, **yogurt**, and **cheese**.

Good **nutrition** and **exercise** help prevent disease and give us longer, healthier lives.

10.1 Noncount Nouns

Group A: Nouns that have no distinct, separate parts. We look at the whole.		
milk	yogurt	soup
oil	air	bread
water	pork	meat
coffee	cholesterol	butter
tea	paper	poultry

Group B: Nouns that have parts that are too small or insignificant to count.		
rice	snow	hair
sugar	sand	grass
salt	corn	popcorn

Group C: Nouns that are classes or categories of things. The members of the category are not the same.

money (nickels, dimes, dollars)
food (vegetables, meat, spaghetti)
candy (chocolates, mints, candy bars)
furniture (chairs, tables, beds)
clothing (sweaters, pants, dresses)
mail (letters, packages, postcards)
fruit (cherries, apples, grapes)
makeup (lipstick, rouge, eye shadow)
homework (compositions, exercises, reading)

(continued)

---

[2] *Fiber* is the part of food that resists digestion.

Group D: Nouns that are abstractions.

love	advice	happiness
life	knowledge	education
time	nutrition	experience
truth	intelligence	crime
beauty	unemployment	music
luck	patience	art
fun	noise	work
help	information	health

LANGUAGE NOTES

1. Count and noncount are grammatical terms, but they are not always logical. Rice is very small and is a noncount noun. Beans and peas are also very small but are count nouns.
2. You sometimes see the plural forms *foods* and *fruits*. *Foods* means kinds of food. *Fruits* means kinds of fruit.
   Oranges and lemons are *fruits* that contain Vitamin C.
   Foods that contain a lot of cholesterol are not good for you.
3. When you talk about candy in general, *candy* is noncount. When you look at individual pieces of candy, you can use the plural form.
   Children like to eat *candy*.
   There are three *candies* on the table.

EXERCISE 1   Fill in the blanks with a noncount noun.

EXAMPLE: _____*Bread*_____ is in the first food group.

1. People should drink a lot of _____ every day.

2. _____ contains a lot of calcium.

3. Food from animals contains _____ .

4. Children like to eat _____, but it's not good for their teeth.

5. Food packages have information about _____ .

6. Some people put _____ in their coffee.

7. Women over 50 need a lot of _____ .

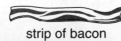
strip of bacon

By container	By portion	By measurement	By shape or whole piece	Other
a bottle of water a carton of milk a jar of pickles a bag of flour a can of soda (pop)[3] a bowl of soup a cup of coffee a glass of milk	a slice (piece) of bread a piece of meat a piece of cake a strip of bacon a piece (sheet) of paper a slice of pizza a piece of candy	a spoonful of sugar a scoop of ice cream a quart of oil a pound of meat a gallon of gasoline	a loaf of bread an ear of corn a piece of fruit a head of lettuce a candy bar a roll of film a tube of toothpaste a bar of soap	a piece of mail a piece of furniture a piece of advice a piece of information a work of art

LANGUAGE NOTES

1. We cannot put a number before a noncount noun. With a noncount noun, we use a unit of measure, which we can count.
   > one cup of coffee
   > five cups of coffee

2. For a list of conversions from the American system of measurement to the metric system, see Appendix G.

EXERCISE 2 Think of a logical measurement for each of these noncount nouns.

EXAMPLES: She bought ___*one pound of*___ coffee.

She drank ___*two cups of*___ coffee.

1. She ate _____ meat.

2. She bought _____ meat.

3. She bought _____ bread.

4. She ate _____ bread.

5. She bought _____ rice.

6. She ate _____ rice.

7. She bought _____ sugar.

8. She put _____ sugar in her coffee.

[3] Some Americans say "soda"; others say "pop."

9. She bought _____ gas for her car.

10. She put _____ motor oil into her car's engine.

11. She used _____ paper to do her homework.

12. She took _____ film on her vacation.

13. She ate _____ soup.

14. She ate _____ corn.

10.3 A Lot Of, Much, Many

	Count (plural)	Noncount
Affirmative	He baked **many** cookies. He baked **a lot of** cookies.	He baked **a lot of** bread.
Negative	He didn't bake **many** cookies. He didn't bake **a lot of** cookies.	He didn't bake **much** bread. He didn't bake **a lot of** bread.
Question	Did he bake **many** cookies? Did he bake **a lot of** cookies? **How many** cookies did he bake?	Did he bake **much** bread? Did he bake **a lot of** bread? **How much** bread did he bake?

LANGUAGE NOTES

1. We rarely use *much* in affirmative statements. We usually use it with questions and negatives. In affirmative statements, we use *a lot of*.
    Did he drink *much* coffee?
    No, he didn't drink *much* coffee.
    He drank *a lot of* water.
2. When the noun is omitted, we say *a lot*, not *a lot of*.
    Did he bake *a lot of* bread?
    No, he didn't bake *a lot* because he didn't have time.

EXERCISE 3 Fill in the blanks with *much, many,* or *a lot of*. In some cases, more than one answer is possible.

EXAMPLES: She doesn't eat _____*much*_____ pasta.

_____*Many*_____ American supermarkets are open 24 hours a day.

_____*A lot of*_____ sugar is not good for you.

1. In the summer in the U.S., there's _____ corn.

2. Children usually drink _____ milk.

3. _____ American people have an unhealthy diet.

4. I drink coffee only about once a week. I don't drink _____ coffee.

5. There are _____ places that sell fast food.

6. It's important to drink _____ water.

7. How _____ glasses of water did you drink today?

8. How _____ fruit did you eat today?

9. How _____ cholesterol is there in one egg?

10. It isn't good to eat _____ candy.

10.4 A Few, A Little

Count (plural)	Noncount
I bought **a few** bananas.	I spent **a little** money.
She ate **a few** cookies.	She put **a little** sugar in her tea.

LANGUAGE NOTES

We use *a few* and *a little* to show a small quantity. We use *a few* with count nouns. We use *a little* with noncount nouns.

EXERCISE 4 Fill in the blanks with *a few* or *a little*.

EXAMPLES: He has _____*a few*_____ good friends.

He has _____*a little*_____ time to help you.

1. Every day we study _____ grammar.

2. We do _____ exercises in class.

3. The teacher gives _____ homework every day.

4. We do _____ pages in the book each day.

5. _____ students always get an A on the tests.

6. It's important to eat _____ fruit every day.

7. It's important to eat _____ pieces of fruit every day.

8. I use _____ milk in my coffee.

9. I receive _____ mail every day.

10. I receive _____ letters every day.

10.5 Some, Any, and A

	Singular Count	Plural Count	Noncount
Affirmative	I ate **an** apple.	I ate **some** grapes.	I ate **some** rice.
Negative	I didn't eat **an** apple.	I didn't eat **any** grapes.	I didn't eat **any** rice.
Question	Did you eat **an** apple?	Did you eat **any** grapes?	Did you eat **any** rice?

LANGUAGE NOTES

1. We sometimes use *some* for questions.
    Do you want *some* fruit? = Do you want *any* fruit?
2. To make a negative statement with both plural count and noncount nouns, we can use *any* with a negative verb, or we can use *no* with an affirmative verb.
    COMPARE: I didn't buy *any* apples.
    I bought *no* apples.
    I don't have *any* fruit at home.
    I have *no* fruit at home.

EXERCISE 5 Fill in the blanks with *a*, *an*, *some*, or *any*.

EXAMPLE: I ate ____*an*____ apple.

1. I ate _____ corn.

2. I didn't buy _____ potatoes.

3. Did you eat _____ watermelon?

4. I don't have _____ sugar.

5. There are _____ apples in the refrigerator.

6. Do you want _____ orange?

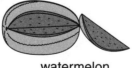
watermelon

7. Do you want _____ cherries?

---

8. I ate _____ banana.

9. I didn't eat _____ strawberries.

EXERCISE 6 Make a statement about people in this class with the words given and an expression of quantity. Practice count nouns.

EXAMPLES: Vietnamese student(s)
There are a few Vietnamese students in this class.

Cuban student(s)
There's one Cuban student in this class.

1. Polish student(s)
2. Spanish-speaking student(s)
3. American(s)
4. child(ren)
5. woman/women

6. man/men
7. teacher(s)
8. American citizen(s)
9. senior citizen(s)
10. teenager(s)

EXERCISE 7 Fill in the blanks with an appropriate expression of quantity. In some cases, more than one answer is possible. Practice noncount nouns.

EXAMPLE: I can't eat eggs because they have _____*a lot of*_____ cholesterol.

1. You shouldn't eat so much red meat because meat has _____ cholesterol.

2. Only animal products contain cholesterol. There is _____ cholesterol in fruit.

3. Diet colas use a sugar substitute. They don't have _____ sugar.

4. There is _____ sugar in a cracker, but not much.

5. Plain popcorn is healthy, but buttered popcorn has _____ fat.

6. Coffee has caffeine. Tea has _____ caffeine too, but not as much as coffee.

7. She doesn't drink _____ tea. She only drinks tea occasionally.

8. I usually put _____ butter on a slice of bread.

9. I'm going to put some sugar in my coffee. Do you want _____ sugar in your coffee?

10. My sister is a vegetarian. She doesn't eat _____ meat at all. She eats _____ fish or chicken either.

EXERCISE 8 Ask a question with *much* and the words given. Use *eat* or *drink*. Another student will answer. Practice noncount nouns.

EXAMPLES:
candy
A. Do you eat much candy?
B. No. I don't eat any candy.

fruit
A. Do you eat much fruit?
B. Yes, I eat a lot of fruit.

Eat	Drink
1. rice	7. apple juice
2. fish	8. lemonade
3. chicken	9. milk
4. pork	10. tea
5. bread	11. coffee
6. cheese	12. soda or pop

EXERCISE 9 Ask a question with "Do you have . . ." and the words given. Another student will answer. Practice both count and noncount nouns.

EXAMPLES:
American friends
A. Do you have any American friends?
B. Yes. I have a lot of American friends.

free time
A. Do you have any free time?
B. No. I don't have any free time.

1. money with you now	5. orange juice in your refrigerator
2. credit cards	6. plants in your apartment
3. bread at home	7. family pictures in your wallet
4. bananas at home	8. time to relax

EXERCISE 10 This is a conversation between a husband (H) and wife (W). Choose the correct word to fill in the blanks.

H. Where were you today? I called you from work ___many___
(example: much, many)
times, but there was no answer.

W. I went to the supermarket today. I bought _____ things.
(1 a little, a few)

H. What did you buy?

W. There was a special on coffee, so I bought _____ coffee.
(2 a lot of, much)

I didn't buy _____ fruit, because the prices were very
(3 any, no)
high.

H. How _____ money did you spend?
(4 much, many)

W. I spent _____ money because of the coffee. I bought 10
(5 much, a lot of)
one-pound bags.

H. It took you a long time.

W. Yes. The store was very crowded. There were _____
(6 much, many)
people in the store. And there was _____ traffic at that
(7 a lot of, much)
hour, so it took me _____ time to drive home.
(8 a lot of, much)

H. There's not _____ time to cook.
(9 much, many)

W. Maybe you can cook today and let me rest?

H. Uh . . . I don't have _____ experience. You do it better.
(10 much, no)
You have _____ experience.
(11 a lot of, much)

W. Yes. I have _____ because I do it all the time!
(12 a lot of, a lot)

EXERCISE 11 This is a conversation between a waitress (W) and a customer (C). Fill in the blanks with an appropriate quantity word. (In some cases, more than one answer is possible.)

SPECIALS TODAY
Eggs......scrambled
.........sunny side up
.............hardboiled
Waffles_____
Pancakes_____
Side Orders......bacon
.............sausage
.............home fries

W. Would you like ___*any (or some)*___ coffee, sir?
(example)

C. Yes, and please bring me _____ cream too. I don't need
(1)
_____ sugar. And I'd like a _____ of orange juice, too.
(2)   (3)

A few minutes later:

W. Are you ready to order, sir?

C. Yes, I'd like the scrambled eggs with three _____ of bacon. And
(4)
some pancakes, too.

W. Do you want _____ syrup with your pancakes?
(5)

C. Yes. What kind do you have?

Count and Noncount Nouns; Quantity Words   **291**

W. We have _____ different kinds: strawberry, cherry, blueberry,
(6)
maple . . .

C. I'll have the strawberry syrup. And bring me _____ butter too.
(7)

After the customer is finished eating:

W. Would you like _____ dessert?
(8)

C. Yes, I'd like a _____ cherry pie. And put _____ ice cream
(9)   (10)
on the pie. And I'd like _____ more coffee, please.
(11)

After the customer eats dessert:

W. Would you like anything else?

C. Just the check. I don't have _____ cash with me. Can I pay by
(12)
credit card?

W. Of course.

10.6   *A Lot Of* vs. *Too Much/Too Many*

A lot of = **Large quantity** **No problem is presented**	*Too much/Too many* = **Excessive quantity** **A problem is presented**
I eat **a lot of** fruit. I baked **a lot of** cookies.	If you put **too much** sugar in my tea, I can't drink it. She invited **too many** people to the party, and there was not enough food.

LANGUAGE NOTES

1. *A lot of* shows a large quantity. It is a neutral term. *Too much* and *too many* show that the quantity is excessive for a specific purpose.
2. In some cases, *too much/too many* and *a lot of* are interchangeable.
    He eats *a lot of* cookies. He's getting fat.
    OR
    He eats *too many* cookies. He's getting fat.

EXERCISE **12** Fill in the blanks with *much* or *many*, and complete each statement.

EXAMPLE: If I drink too ___*much*___ coffee, _I won't be able to sleep tonight._

1.   If the teacher gives too _____ homework, _____

2. If I take too _____ classes, _____

3. If I eat too _____ candy, _____

4. If I'm absent too _____ days, _____

5. Too _____ cholesterol _____

10.7 Too Much/Too Many vs. Too

Too + Adjective or Adverb	Too Much + Noncount Noun Too Many + Count Noun
I don't eat ice cream. It is **too** fattening.	I don't eat ice cream. It has **too many** calories. It has **too much** sugar.

LANGUAGE NOTES

Too comes before adjectives and adverbs. *Too much* and *too many* come before nouns.

EXERCISE 13 Fill in the blanks with *too, too much*, or *too many*.

Situation A. Some students are complaining about the school cafeteria. They are giving reasons why they don't want to eat there.

EXAMPLE: It's ___*too*___ noisy.

1. The food is _____ greasy.

2. There are _____ students. I can't find a place to sit.

3. The lines are _____ long.

4. The food is _____ expensive.

5. There's _____ noise.

Situation B. Some students are complaining about their class and school.

1. The classroom is _____ small.

2. There are _____ students in one class.

3. We have to write _____ compositions.

4. The teacher gives _____ homework.

5. There are _____ tests.

EXERCISE 14 Write a few sentences to complain about something: your apartment, your roommate, this city, this college, etc. Use *too*, *too much*, or *too many* in your sentences.

EXAMPLE: My roommate spends too much time in the bathroom in the morning. He's too messy.[4]

_____

_____

_____

EXERCISE 15 Fill in the blanks with *too, too much*, or *too many* if a problem is presented. Use *a lot of* if no problem is presented.

EXAMPLE: Most people can't afford to buy a Mercedes because it costs ___*too much*___ money.

1. There are _____ noncount nouns in English.

2. "Rice" is a noncount noun because the parts are _____ small to count.

3. If this class is _____ hard for you, you should go to a lower level.

4. Good students spend _____ time doing their homework.

5. If you spend _____ time watching TV, you won't have time for your homework.

6. It takes _____ time to learn English, but you can do it.

7. Oranges have _____ vitamin C.

8. If you are on a diet, don't eat ice cream. It has _____ calories and _____ fat.

9. Babies drink _____ milk.

10. If you drink _____ coffee, you won't sleep.

EXERCISE 16 A doctor (D) and patient (P) are talking. Fill in the blanks with an appropriate quantity word or unit of measurement to complete this conversation. (In some cases, more than one answer is possible.)

[4] A *messy* person does not put his or her things in order.

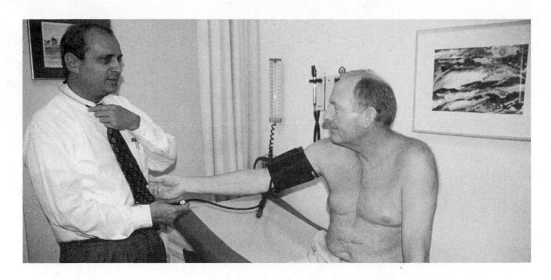

D. I'm looking at your lab results and I see that your cholesterol level is very high. Also your blood pressure is ___*too*___ high. Do _(example)_ you use ___ salt on your food? _(1)_

P. Yes, doctor. I love salt. I eat ___ potato chips and _(2)_ popcorn.

D. That's not good. You're overweight too. You need to lose 50 pounds. What do you usually eat?

P. For breakfast I usually grab ___ of coffee and a doughnut. _(3)_ I don't have ___ time for lunch, so I eat ___ _(4)_ _(5)_ of potato chips and drink ___ of soda while I'm work- _(6)_ ing. I'm so busy that I have ___ time to cook at all. So _(7)_ for dinner, I usually stop at a fast-food place and get a burger and fries.

D. That's a terrible diet! How ___ exercise do you do? _(8)_

P. I never exercise. I don't have ___ time at all. I own my _(9)_ own business and I have ___ work. Sometimes I work _(10)_ 80 hours a week.

D. I'm going to give you an important ___ advice. You're _(11)_ going to have to change your lifestyle.

P. I'm ___ old to change my habits. _(12)_

D. You're only 45 years old. You're _____ young to die. And
(13)
if you don't change your habits, you're going to have a heart attack.
I'm going to give you a booklet about staying healthy. It has

_____ information that will teach you about diet and
(14)
exercise. Please read it and come back in six months.

SUMMARY OF LESSON 10

Words that we use before count and noncount nouns

Word	Count (singular) Example: *book*	Count (plural) Example: *books*	Noncount Example: *tea*
the	x	x	x
a	x		
one	x		
two, three, etc.		x	
some (affirmatives)		x	x
any (negatives and questions)		x	x
a lot of		x	x
much (negatives and questions)			x
many		x	
a little			x
a few		x	

EDITING ADVICE ✎

1. Don't put *a* or *an* before a noncount noun.

            some
I want to give you ~~an~~ advice.

2. Noncount nouns are always singular.

   a lot of

   My mother gave me ~~many~~ advices.

   pieces of

   He received three ^mails today.

3. Don't use a double negative.

   any

   He doesn't have ~~no~~ time.   OR   *He has no time.*

4. Don't use *much* with an affirmative statement.

   Uncommon: There was much rain yesterday.
   Common: There was a lot of rain yesterday.

5. Use *a* or *an*, not *any*, with a singular count noun.

   a

   Do you have ~~any~~ computer?

6. Don't use *a* or *an* before a plural noun.

   She has a blue eyes.

7. Use the plural form for plural count nouns.

   s

   He has a lot of friend.^

8. Omit *of* after *a lot* when the noun is omitted.

   In my country, I have a lot of friends, but in the U.S. I don't have
   a lot ~~of~~.

9. Use *of* with a unit of measure.

   of

   I ate three pieces^bread.

10. Don't use *of* after *many, much, a few, a little* if a noun follows directly.

    She has many ~~of~~ friends.

    He put a little ~~of~~ sugar in his coffee.

11. Only use *too much/too many* if there is a problem.

    a lot of

    He has a good job. He earns ~~too much~~ money.

12. Don't use *too much* before an adjective or adverb.

    I don't want to go outside today. It's too ~~much~~ hot.

PART 1   Find the mistakes with the underlined words, and correct them. Not every sentence has a mistake. If the sentence is correct, write **C**.

EXAMPLES: My dog doesn't get enough exercise. He's <u>too much</u> fat.

You can be happy if you have <u>a few</u> good friends.   **C**

1. He doesn't have <u>no</u> money with him at all.

2. He's a lucky man. He has <u>too many</u> friends.

3. There are a lot of tall buildings in a big city. There aren't <u>a lot of</u> in a small town.

4. I don't have <u>much</u> time to help you.

5. A 14-year-old person is <u>too much</u> young to get a driver's license.

6. <u>A few</u> students in this class are from Pakistan.

7. I don't have <u>some</u> time to help you.

8. I don't have <u>any</u> car. I use public transportation.

9. Did we have <u>many</u> snow last winter?

10. <u>Many</u> people would like to have <u>a lot of</u> money in order to travel.

11. He doesn't have <u>any</u> time to study at all.

12. I'd like to help you, but I have <u>too many</u> things to do this week. Maybe I can help you next week.

13. She drinks <u>two cups of coffee</u> every morning.

14. I drink <u>four milks</u> a day.

15. He bought five <u>pounds sugar</u>.

16. <u>How much</u> bananas did you buy?

17. <u>How much</u> money did you spend?

18. This building doesn't have <u>a</u> basement.

19. I have <u>much</u> time to read because I'm on vacation now.

20. She gave me <u>a good advice</u>.

21. The piano is <u>too much</u> heavy. I can't move it.

22. I have a lot of cassette, probably over 200.

23. I don't have much experience with cars.

24. There are many of books in the library.

25. I have a little time, so I can help you.

PART 2

Fill in the blanks with an appropriate measurement of quantity.

EXAMPLE: a _____*cup*_____ of coffee

1. a _____ of soda   6. a _____ of advice
2. a _____ of sugar   7. a _____ of bread
3. a _____ of milk   8. a _____ of paper
4. a _____ of furniture   9. a _____ of meat
5. a _____ of mail   10. a _____ of soup

Read the following composition. Choose the correct quantity word or indefinite article.

I had _____*some*_____ problems when I first came to the U.S. First, I
(example: some, any, a little)

didn't have _____ money. _____ friends of mine lent
(1 much, a, some)   (2 A few, A little, A few of)

me _____ money, but I didn't feel good about borrowing it.
(3 some, a, any)

Second, I couldn't find _____ apartment. I went to see
(4 a, an, no)

_____ apartments, but I couldn't afford _____ of
(5 some, a little, an)   (6 an, any, none)

them. For _____ months, I had to live with my uncle's family, but
(7 a little, a few of, a few)

the situation wasn't good.

Third, I started to study English, but soon found _____ job
(8 a, any, some)

and didn't have _____ time to study. As a result, I was failing my
(9 no, much, a few)

course.

However, little by little my life started to improve, and I don't need

_____ help from my friends and relatives anymore.
(10 no, some, much)

CLASSROOM ACTIVITIES

1. Make a list of unhealthy things that you eat. Make a list of things that you need to eat for a healthy diet.

Unhealthy things I eat	Things I should eat

2. These are some popular foods in the U.S. Put a check (√) in the column that describes your experience of this food. Then find a partner and compare your list to your partner's list.

submarine sandwich

pretzels

tortilla chips

Food	I like	I don't like	I never tried
pizza		√	
hot dogs			
hamburgers			
tacos			
breakfast cereal			
peanut butter			
cheesecake			
potato chips			
popcorn			
submarine sandwiches			
chocolate chip cookies			
fried chicken			
pretzels			
tortilla chips			

3. Take something from your purse, pocket, or book bag. Say, "I have _____ with me." Then ask the person next to you if he or she has this.

EXAMPLE: I have some keys in my pocket. Do you have any keys in your pocket?

I have a picture of my daughter in my purse. Do you have any pictures of your family in your purse?

4. Cross out the phrase that doesn't fit and fill in the blanks with an expression of quantity to make a true statement about the U.S. or another country. Find a partner and compare your answers.

EXAMPLE: There are/~~There aren't~~ _____many_____ foreigners in _____the U.S._____

a. There's/There isn't _____ interest in soccer in _____ .

b. There's/There isn't _____ opportunity to make money in

_____ .

c. People in _____ eat/don't eat _____ natural foods.

d. There are/There aren't _____ single mothers in _____ .

e. Most people in _____ have/don't have _____ education.

f. Parents in _____ give/don't give their children _____ advice.

g. People in _____ drink/don't drink _____ tea.

DISCUSSION

1. Look at the dialog that takes place in a restaurant on pages 291–292. Do you think this man is eating a healthy breakfast? Why or why not?

2. Americans often eat some of these foods for breakfast:
   cereal and milk, toast and butter or jelly, orange juice, eggs, bacon, coffee
   Describe a typical breakfast for you.

3. Most American stores sell products in containers: bags, jars, cans, etc. How do stores in other countries sell products?

4. Do stores in other countries give customers bags for their groceries, or do customers have to bring their own bags to the store?

5. Some things are usually free in an American restaurant: salt, pepper, sugar, cream or milk for coffee, mustard, ketchup, napkins, water, ice, coffee refills, and sometimes bread. Are these things free in a restaurant in another country?

SAYING

The following saying is about food. Discuss the meaning. Do you have a similar saying in your native language?

You are what you eat.

OUTSIDE ACTIVITY

1. Bring to class a package of a food or drink you enjoy. Read the label for "Nutrition Facts." Look at calories, grams of fat, cholesterol, sodium, protein, vitamins, and minerals. Do you think this is a nutritious food? Why or why not?

2. Bring a favorite recipe to class. Explain how to prepare this recipe.

WRITING

Describe shopping for food in the U.S. or in another country. You may include information about the following:

- packaging
- open market vs. stores
- self-service vs. service from sales people
- shopping carts
- fixed prices vs. negotiable prices
- freshness of food

Internet Activities

1. Go to the Department of Agriculture web site. Find the food pyramid chart and brochure. Fill out the form called "How to Rate Your Diet."

2. Use the Internet to find a recipe for something you like to eat. Bring the recipe to class.

Lesson Eleven

GRAMMAR
    Adjectives
    Noun Modifiers
    Adverbs

CONTEXT
    Helen Keller
    Grandma Moses

LESSON FOCUS

An adjective describes a noun.
    That's a *red* light.

A noun can also describe a noun.
    That's a *traffic* light.

An adverb can describe a verb.
    She stopped *quickly*.

Helen Keller 1882–1968

1.   In your country, are there special schools for handicapped people?
2.   Do you know of a famous person who was handicapped?

k
American Sign language   Braille

Read the following article. Pay special attention to adjectives and adverbs.

Helen Keller

Helen Keller was a **healthy** baby. But when she was 19 months old, she had a **sudden** fever. The fever disappeared, but she became **blind** and **deaf**. Because she couldn't hear, it was difficult for her to learn to speak. As she grew up, she was **angry** and **frustrated** because she couldn't understand or communicate with people. She became **wild**, throwing things and kicking and biting.

When Helen was 7 years old, a teacher, Anne Sullivan, came to live with Helen's family. First, Anne taught Helen how to talk with her fingers. Helen was **excited** when she realized that things had names. Then Anne taught Helen to read by the Braille system. Helen learned these skills **quickly**. However, learning to speak was harder. Anne continued to teach Helen **patiently**. Finally, when Helen was 10 years old, she could speak **clearly** enough for people to understand her.

Helen was very **intelligent**. She went to an institute for the blind, where she did very **well** in her studies. Then she went to college,[1] where she graduated with honors when she was 24 years old. Helen traveled **extensively** with Anne. She worked **tirelessly**, traveling all over America, Europe, and Asia to raise money to build schools for **blind** people. Her **main** message was that **handicapped** people are like everybody else. They want to live life **fully** and **naturally**. Helen wanted all people to be treated **equally**.

While she was in college, Helen wrote her first of many books, *The Story of My Life*, in 1903.

Did you know...?

In Washington, D.C., there is a special college for deaf students— Gallaudet University.

---

[1] In the U.S., the words *college* and *university* usually have the same meaning.

Examples	Explanation
Helen was a **healthy** baby. She seemed **intelligent**. She became **blind**. Anne Sullivan was a **wonderful** teacher.	Adjectives describe nouns. We can use adjectives before nouns or after the verbs *be, become, look, seem,* and other sense-perception verbs.
She felt **frustrated**. She was **excited** when she learned her first word. **Handicapped** people are like everybody else.	Some *-ed* words are adjectives: *married, divorced, excited, frustrated, handicapped, worried, finished, located, tired, crowded*
Helen had a **college** education. Helen wrote her **life** story.	We sometimes use a noun to describe another noun.
Anne taught Helen **patiently**. Helen learned **quickly**. People want to live life **fully**.	Adverbs of manner tell how or in what way we do things. We form most adverbs of manner by putting *-ly* at the end of an adjective.

EXERCISE 1 Choose the correct word to complete each sentence.

EXAMPLE: Helen was a (*healthy*) / *sick* baby.

1. She was *happy / frustrated* when she couldn't communicate.

2. She learned sign language when she was *5 / 7* years old.

3. It was *easy / hard* for Helen to learn how to speak.

4. She *graduated / didn't graduate* from college.

5. She wanted handicapped people to be treated *differently / equally*.

EXERCISE 2 Fill in the blanks with an appropriate adjective. Change *a* to *an* if the adjective begins with a vowel.

EXAMPLE: This is a ___*n*___ *interesting* _____ class.

1. This classroom is _____.

2. English is a _____ language.

3. The U.S. is a _____ country.

4. This book is very _____.

5. I come from a _____ city.

6. The story about Helen Keller was _____.

7. Helen Keller had a _____ life.

8. I don't like _____ food.

11.2 Adjectives

Examples	Explanation
Anne was a **good** friend. I have many **good** friends.	Adjectives are always singular.
Helen was a **normal**, **healthy** baby.	Sometimes we put two adjectives before a noun. We sometimes separate the two adjectives with a comma.
Some people have an easy childhood. Helen had a hard **one**. We read a short story about Helen. We didn't read a long **one**. Do you like serious stories or funny **ones**?	After an adjective, we can substitute a singular noun with *one* and a plural noun with *ones*.

EXERCISE 3 Ask a question of preference with the words given. Follow the example. Use *one* or *ones* to substitute for the noun. Another student will answer.

EXAMPLES: an easy exercise/hard
A. Do you prefer an easy exercise or a hard one?
B. I prefer a hard one.

funny movies/serious
A. Do you prefer funny movies or serious ones?
B. I prefer funny ones.

1. a big city/small
2. an old house/new
3. a cold climate/warm
4. a small car/big
5. a soft mattress/hard
6. green grapes/red
7. red apples/yellow
8. strict teachers/easy
9. noisy children/quiet
10. used textbooks/new

11.3 Noun Modifiers

Adjective + Noun	Noun + Noun
She had a **good** education.	She had a **college** education.
She wrote an **interesting** story.	She wrote her **life** story.

LANGUAGE NOTES

1. When two nouns come together, the second noun is more general than the first.
   A department store is a store.
   A shoe department is a department.
2. When two nouns come together, the first is always singular.
   A *shoe* department is a department that sells shoes.
   A *rose* garden is a garden of roses.
3. When a noun describes a noun, the first noun usually receives the greater emphasis in speaking. Listen to your teacher pronounce the following:
   I need a wínter coat.
   She works in a shóe store.

EXERCISE 4 Fill in the blanks by putting the two nouns in the correct order. Remember to take the *s* off the plural nouns.

EXAMPLES: People need a ___*winter coat*___ in cold climates.
(coat/winter)

We buy groceries in a ___*grocery store.*___
(groceries/store)

1. A _____ delivers the mail.
(letters/carrier)

2. You have an important _____ .
(phone/call)

3. Do you own a _____ ?
(phone/cell)

4. We use a _____ to paint the walls.
(brush/paint)

5. If you want to drive, you need a _____ .
(driver's/license)

6. A lot of women like to wear _____ .
(rings/ears)

7. A married person usually wears a _____ on his or her left hand.
(wedding/ring)

8. Please put your garbage in the _____.
(can/garbage)

9. The college is closed during _____.
(vacation/winter)

10. There's a good _____ at 7 p.m.
(program/TV)

11. I'm taking a _____ this semester.
(course/math)

12. I bought some flowers at the _____.
(flowers/shop)

13. My _____ is green.
(teeth/brush)

11.4   Adverbs of Manner

Adjectives	Adverbs	Explanation
Anne was a **patient** teacher. Helen was a **quick** learner. She had a **clear** voice. She had a **full** life.	She taught **patiently**. She learned **quickly**. She spoke **clearly**. She lived life **fully**.	We form most adverbs of manner by putting -ly at the end of an adjective.
This is a **fast** car. I have a **late** class. We had a **hard** test. I have an **early** appointment.	He drives **fast**. I arrived **late**. I studied **hard**. I need to wake up **early**.	Some adjectives and adverbs have the same form.
Helen was a **good** student.	She did **well** in school.	This adverb is completely different from the adjective form.

LANGUAGE NOTES

1. Adverbs of manner usually follow the verb phrase.

SUBJECT	VERB PHRASE	ADVERB
My friend	did his homework	quickly.

2. You can use *very* before an adverb of manner.
   She types *very* quickly.

EXERCISE 5 Check (√) if the sentence is true or false.

	True	False
1. Helen lost her hearing slowly.		√
2. Anne taught Helen patiently.		
3. Helen learned quickly.		
4. Helen never learned to speak clearly.		
5. Helen didn't do well in college.		
6. Helen wanted deaf people to be treated differently from hearing people.		

11.5 Spelling of -ly Adverbs

Adjective Ending	Examples	Adverb Ending	Adverb
y	easy lucky happy	Change y to i and add -ly.	eas**ily** luck**ily** happ**ily**
consonant + le	simple double comfortable	Drop the -e and add -ly.	simp**ly** doub**ly** comfortab**ly**
e	nice free brave	Just add -ly.	nice**ly** free**ly** brave**ly**

LANGUAGE NOTES

There is one exception for the last rule: *true—truly*

EXERCISE 6 Fill in the blanks with the correct form of the word in parentheses ( ) to give advice about driving.

EXAMPLE: It is important to drive ____*carefully*____ .
          (careful)

1. Don't follow the car in front of you _____ .
   (close)

2. Make sure your brakes are working _____ .
   (good)

3. Check your rearview mirror _____.
   (frequent)

4. Drive _____ on a curve.
   (slow)

5. Don't use your horn _____.
   (unnecessary)

6. Don't drive _____ in rain or snow.
   (fast)

7. If you have an accident, stop _____.
   (immediate)

EXERCISE 7 Fill in the blanks with the adverb form of the underlined adjective.

EXAMPLE: He's a <u>careful</u> driver. He drives *carefully* _____.

1. She has a <u>beautiful</u> voice. She sings _____.

2. You are a <u>responsible</u> person. You always act _____.

3. You have a <u>neat</u> handwriting. You write _____.

4. I'm not a <u>good</u> swimmer. I don't swim _____.

5. He is a <u>cheerful</u> person. He always smiles _____.

6. He is <u>fluent</u> in French. He speaks French _____.

7. You have a <u>polite</u> manner. You always talk to people _____.

8. Nurses are <u>hard</u> workers. They work _____.

9. She looks <u>sad</u>. She said goodbye _____.

10. You are a <u>patient</u> teacher. You explain the grammar _____.

11. My answers are <u>correct</u>. I filled in all the blanks _____.

EXERCISE 8 Tell how you do these things.

EXAMPLE: write
I write a composition carefully and slowly.

1. speak English
2. speak your native language
3. dance
4. walk
5. study
6. do your homework
7. drive
8. sing
9. type
10. work
11. dress for class
12. dress for a party

EXERCISE 9 Name something.

EXAMPLE: Name some things you do well.
I speak my native language well.
I swim well.
I sing well.

1. Name some things you do well.

2. Name some things you don't do well.

3. Name some things you do quickly.

4. Name some things you do slowly.

5. Name something you learned to do easily.

EXERCISE 10 The adjective is in parentheses ( ). Use the adjective or change it to an adverb to fill in the blanks.

A. I heard you moved last month.

B. Yes, we did. The move was _____*difficult*_____. We had
(example: difficult)

_____ movers. They didn't behave _____.
(1 terrible)   (2 responsible)

They arrived _____ and worked _____.
(3 late)   (4 slow)

So the move was very_____. And they didn't do
(5 expensive)

a _____ job.
(6 good)

A. What happened?

B. They were so _____ with the furniture. They broke
(7 careless)

a few of my _____ dishes.
(8 favorite)

A. You seem very _____ about this.
(9 upset)

B. Of course, I'm _____.
(10 upset)

A. Well, the move's over now. Are you _____ with your
(11 happy)

new apartment?

B. We like the apartment. It's very big and _____. All
(12 comfortable)

of our furniture fits _____. But we're not
(13 easy)

_____ with our _____ neighbors.
(14 happy)   (15 rude)

They have _____ fights. I can hear them _____
(16 loud)   (17 clear)

right through the walls. I think both of them are _____.
(18 crazy)

And they have a dog. The dog barks _____. I can't
(19 constant)

sleep _____ with all their noise.
(20 peaceful)

A. Are you going to talk to them about it?

B. I already did. I tried talking to them _____. They
(21 polite)

said that they would try to be more _____, but nothing
(22 quiet)

changed. I'm so _____.
(23 angry)

A. When you were _____, nothing changed. You need
(24 polite)

to speak to them more _____ and _____.
(25 direct)   (26 honest)

Tell them to be _____ or you're going to call the
(27 quiet)

police.

Before You Read

1. Do you know of any old people who have a healthy, good life?
2. Who is the oldest member of your family? Is he or she in good health?

Read the following article. Pay special attention to *very* and *too*.

Grandma Moses (1860–1961)

Anna Mary Moses was born in 1860. She had a **very** hard life working as a farmer's wife in New York state. She was always interested in art, but she was **too** busy working on the farm and raising her 5 children to paint. In her 70s, she became **too** weak to do hard farm work. She liked to do embroidery, but as she became older, she couldn't because of arthritis. It was easier for her to hold a paintbrush than a needle, so she started to paint. She painted pictures of farm life. A New York City

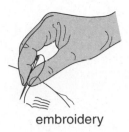

embroidery

art collector saw her paintings in a drugstore window and bought them. Some of her paintings are in major art museums.

When she was 92, she wrote her autobiography. At the age of 100, she illustrated a book. She was still painting when she died at age 101. Better known as "Grandma Moses," she created 1,600 pictures.

11.6 *Too* vs. *Very*

Examples	Explanation
Grandma Moses was **very** old when she wrote her autobiography. Her paintings became **very** popular.	*Very* shows a large degree. It doesn't indicate any problems.
She was **too** busy working on the farm to paint. She became **too** weak to do farm work.	*Too* shows that there is a problem. We often use an infinitive after *too*.

EXERCISE 11 Fill in the blanks with *very* or *too*.

EXAMPLES: Basketball players are ____*very*____ tall.

I'm ____*too*____ short to touch the ceiling.

1. In December, it's _____ cold to go swimming outside.

2. June is usually a _____ nice month.

3. Some old people are in _____ good health.

4. Some old people are _____ sick to take care of themselves.

5. It's _____ important to know English.

6. This textbook is _____ long to finish in three weeks.

7. The President has a _____ important job.

8. The President is _____ busy to answer all his letters.

9. Some Americans speak English _____ fast for me. I can't understand them.

10. I can speak my own language _____ well.

11. When you buy a used car, you should inspect it _____ carefully.

12. A turtle moves _____ slowly.

13. If you drive _____ slowly on the highway, you might get a ticket.

turtle

11.7   Too and Enough

Too + Adjective/Adverb	Adjective/Adjective + Enough	Enough + Noun
My mother is 60. She's **too young** to retire.	My father is 65. He's **old enough** to retire.	He rides a bicycle every day. He gets **enough exercise**.
Grandma Moses was **too old** to do farm work.	She was **talented enough** to catch the eye of an art dealer.	She had **enough time** to paint when she was older.
Some Americans talk **too fast** for me.	Our teacher speaks **clearly enough** for me.	I don't have **enough experience** with American English.

LANGUAGE NOTES

1. Put *too* before the adjective or adverb.
   too young   too slowly
2. Put *enough* after the adjective or adverb.
   young enough   fluently enough
3. Put *enough* before the noun.
   enough money   enough time

EXERCISE 12 Fill in the blanks with *too* or *enough* plus the word in parentheses ( ).

EXAMPLES: My son is 4 years old. He's ___*too young*___ to go to first grade.
                                                    (young)

My daughter is 18 years old. She's ___*old enough*___ to get a driver's
                                                 (old)
license.

1. I can't read Shakespeare in English. It's _____ for
                                                    (hard)
me.

2. My brother is 19 years old. He's _____ to get a driver's
                                        (old)
license.

314   Lesson Eleven

3. My grandfather is 90 years old and in bad health. My family takes care of him. He's _____ to take care of himself.
   (sick)

4. I saved $5,000. I want to buy a used car. I think I have _____
   _____.
   (money)

5. I'd like to get a good job, but I don't have _____.
   (experience)

6. She wants to move that piano, but she can't do it alone. She's not _____.
   (strong)

7. The piano is _____ for one person to move.
   (heavy)

8. I sit at my desk all day, and I don't get _____.
   (exercise)

SUMMARY OF LESSON 11

1. Adjectives and Adverbs:

ADJECTIVES	ADVERBS
She has a **beautiful** voice.	She sings **beautifully**.
She is **careful**.	She drives **carefully**.
She has a **late** class.	She arrived **late**.
She is a **good** driver.	She drives **well**.

2. Adjective Modifiers and Noun Modifiers:

ADJECTIVE MODIFIER	NOUN MODIFIER
a clean window	a store window
a new store	a shoe store
warm coats	winter coats
a new license	a driver's license

3. **Very/Too/Enough**:
   He's **very** healthy.
   He's **too** young to retire. He's only 55.
   He's old **enough** to understand life.
   He has **enough** money to take a vacation.

1. Don't make adjectives plural.

   Those are importants ideas.

2. Put the specific noun before the general noun.

   He is a ~~driver truck~~. *truck driver*

3. Some adjectives end in *-ed*. Don't omit the *-ed*.

   I'm finish *ed* with my project.

4. If the adjective ends in *-ed*, don't forget to include the verb *be*.

   He *is* married.

5. A noun modifier is always singular.

   She is a letters carrier.

6. Put the adjective before the noun.

   He had a *very important* meeting ~~very important~~.

7. Use *one(s)* after an adjective to substitute for a noun.

   He wanted a big wedding, and she wanted a small. *one*

8. Don't confuse *too* and *very*. *Too* indicates a problem.

   My father is ~~too~~ *very* healthy.

9. Don't confuse *too much* and *too*. *Too much* is followed by a noun. *Too* is followed by an adjective or adverb.

   It's too ~~much~~ hot today. Let's stay inside.

10. Put *enough* after the adjective.

    He's *old* enough ~~old~~ to drive.

11. Don't use *very* before a verb. *Very* is used only with adjectives and adverbs.

    He ~~very~~ likes the U.S. *very much.*

12. Put the adverb at the end of the verb phrase.

> _late_
> He ~~late~~ came home.
>   ^

>   _slowly_
> He opened ~~slowly~~ the door.
>   ^

13. Use an adverb to describe a verb. Use an adjective to describe a noun.

>   _ly_
> He drives careful.
>   ^

> That man is very ~~nicely~~.

LESSON 11 TEST / REVIEW

PART 1   **Find the mistakes with the underlined words and correct them. Not every sentence has a mistake. If the sentence is correct, write C.**

EXAMPLES: She is very <u>carefully</u> about money.

                 She drives very <u>carefully</u>.   **C**

1. I took my <u>olds</u> shoes to a <u>shoes</u> repair shop.

2. It's <u>too much</u> cold outside. Let's stay inside today.

3. Basketball players are <u>too</u> tall.

4. The <u>very rich</u> woman bought <u>an expensive birthday present</u> for her <u>beautiful daughter</u>.

5. She is only 16 years old. She's <u>too young</u> to get married.

6. I found a <u>wonderful job</u>. I'm <u>too</u> happy.

7. My father is only 50 years old. He is <u>too much</u> young to retire.

8. He speaks English very <u>good</u>.

9. You came home late last night. I was very <u>worry</u> about you.

10. He worked <u>very hard</u> last night.

11. He counted the money <u>very carefully</u>.

12. My sister is <u>marry</u>.

13. This college <u>located</u> downtown.

14. I prefer a <u>small car</u>. My wife prefers <u>a large</u>.

15. He won a prize. He seems very <u>happily</u>.

16. I <u>very</u> like my new apartment.

PART 2

Find the mistakes in word order and correct them. Not every sentence has a mistake. If the sentence is correct, write **C**.

EXAMPLES: He writes (very carefully) his compositions.

He has enough time to do his homework.   **C**

1. I got my license driver's last year.

2. My brother is only 15 years old. He's not enough old to drive.

3. He early ate breakfast.

4. She opened slowly the door.

5. She speaks English very fluently.

6. They are too young to retire.

PART 3

Fill in the blanks with the correct form, adjective or adverb, of the word in parentheses ( ).

EXAMPLES: Sue is a ___*patient*___ person. Don does everything ___*impatiently*___.
   (patient)   *(impatient)*

1. Sue has a _____ handwriting. Don writes _____.
   (neat)   *(sloppy)*
   I can't even read what he wrote.

2. She likes to drive _____. He likes to drive _____.
   (careful)   *(fast)*

3. She speaks English _____. He has a _____
   (fluent)   *(hard)*
   time with English.

4. She learns languages _____. Learning a new language
   (easy)

   is _____ for Don.
   (difficult)

5. She types _____. He makes a lot of mistakes. He needs
   (accurate)

   someone to check his work _____.
   (careful)

6. She has a very _____ voice. He speaks _____.
   (soft)   *(loud)*

7. She sings _____. He sings like a _____
   (beautiful)   *(sick)*
   chicken.

8. She is always very _____. He sometimes behaves
                          (responsible)

   _____.
      (childish)

9. She saves her money _____. He buys things he doesn't
                          (careful)

   need. He spends his money _____.
                                (foolish)

10. She exercises _____. He's very _____
                    (regular)   *(lazy)*
    about exercising.

EXPANSION ACTIVITIES

CLASSROOM ACTIVITIES

1. Circle the word that best describes your actions. Find a partner and compare your personality to your partner's personality. How many characteristics do you have in common?

a. I usually spend my money	carefully	foolishly
b. I do my homework	willingly	unwillingly
c. I write compositions	carefully	carelessly
d. I usually walk	slowly	quickly
e. I write	neatly	sloppily
f. I like to drive	fast	slowly
g. I write my language	well	poorly
h. Before a test, I study	hard	a little
i. I exercise	regularly	infrequently
j. I play tennis	well	poorly
k. I like to live	dangerously	carefully
l. I make important decisions	quickly	slowly and methodically
m. I learn languages	easily	with difficulty
n. I learn math	easily	with difficulty
o. I make judgments	logically	intuitively

Hello

neat

Hello

sloppy

2. Game: "In the manner of"

Teacher: Write these adverbs on separate pieces of paper or on index cards: gladly, suddenly, slowly, comfortably, simply, steadily, foolishly, efficiently, accurately, quietly, surprisingly, excitedly, promptly, fearlessly, fearfully, indecisively, carefully, carelessly, neatly, smoothly, repeatedly. Make sure the students know the meaning of each of these adverbs. Ask one student to leave the room. The other students pick one adverb. When the student returns to the room, he/she asks individuals to do something by giving imperatives. The others do this task in the manner of the adverb that was chosen. The student tries to guess the adverb.

EXAMPLE:
Edgar, write your name on the blackboard.
Sofia, take off one shoe.
Maria, open the door.
Elsa, walk around the room.
Nora, give me your book.

DISCUSSIONS

1. In a small group or with the entire class, discuss the situation of older people in your native culture. Who takes care of them when they are too old or too sick to take care of themselves? How does your family take care of its older members?

2. In a small group or with the entire class, discuss the situation of handicapped people in your home town. Are there special schools? Are there special facilities, such as parking, public washrooms, elevators?

QUOTE

Discuss the meaning of this quote by Grandma Moses:

"What a strange thing is memory, and hope. One looks backward, the other forward; one is of today, the other of tomorrow. Memory is history recorded in our brain. Memory is a painter. It paints pictures of the past and of the day."

WRITING

1. Write about a famous person you know about who accomplished something in spite of a handicap or age.

2. Write about a man or woman whom you admire very much. You may write about a famous person or any person you know (family member, teacher, doctor, etc.).

Internet Activity

Use the Internet to find more information about Anne Sullivan. Share this information with the class.

Lesson Twelve

GRAMMAR
Comparatives
Superlatives

CONTEXT
U.S. Geography
A Tale of Two Cities

LESSON FOCUS

Adjectives and adverbs have three forms: simple form, comparative form, and superlative form. Compare these sets of adjectives.

SIMPLE	San Francisco is a *big* city.
COMPARATIVE	Los Angeles is *bigger* than San Francisco.
SUPERLATIVE	New York is the *biggest* city in the U.S.

SIMPLE	She is *intelligent*.
COMPARATIVE	She is *more intelligent* than her sister.
SUPERLATIVE	She is the *most intelligent* person in her family.

Sears Tower,
Chicago, Illinois

321

1. What is the tallest building in this city?
2. In your opinion, what is the most interesting city? Why is it interesting?
3. What cities or regions have the best climate?

Read the following information. Pay special attention to comparative and superlative forms.

World Trade
Center,
New York

U.S. Geography

1. In area, the United States is the third **largest** country in the world (after Russia and Canada).
2. In population, the U.S. is the third **largest** country in the world (after China and India).
3. The **biggest** city in the U.S. in population is New York. Chicago used to be the second **largest** city, but now Los Angeles is **larger** than Chicago.
4. The **tallest** building in the U.S. is the Sears Tower in Chicago (1,450 feet or 442 meters tall). It is even **taller** than the World Trade Center in New York. However, the Sears Tower is not the **tallest** building in the world. That building is in Kuala Lumpur (1,483 feet or 452 meters tall).
5. New York City has the **highest** cost of living.
6. Hispanics are the **fastest** growing minority in the U.S. In 1990, there were 5.9 million Hispanics in the U.S. That number rose to 20.9 million in 1996.
7. Rhode Island is the **smallest** state in area.
8. Alaska is the **largest** state in area. Alaska is even **larger** than Colombia, South America.
9. The **least populated** state is Wyoming. It has **less** than half a million people.
10. California is the **most populated** state. It has about 30 million people. There are **more** people in California than in Peru.
11. Juneau, Alaska, gets the **most** snow, about 101 inches per year.
12. Phoenix, Arizona, gets the **most** sunshine. Eighty-five percent of the days have sunshine.
13. Mount McKinley is the **highest** mountain in the U.S. (20,320 feet or 6,178 meters). It is in Alaska.
14. There are five great lakes in the U.S. The **biggest** is Lake Superior. The others are Lake Huron, Lake Michigan, Lake Erie, and Lake Ontario.

Did you know...?

Before 1849, the population of California was very small. In 1849, gold was found in California and about 100,000 people rushed there to try to get rich.

12.1 Comparatives and Superlatives

Examples	Explanation
New York City is the **biggest** city in the U.S. California is the **most populated** state in the U.S.	We use the superlative form to point out the number–one item in a group of three or more.
Los Angles is **bigger** than Chicago. There are **more** people in California than in Peru.	We use the comparative form to compare two items.

EXERCISE 1 Circle the correct word to complete the statement.

EXAMPLE: Chicago is *bigger* / (*smaller*) than Los Angeles.

1. The tallest building in the world *is / isn't* in the U.S.
2. The most populated state is *Alaska / California*.
3. The U.S. *is / isn't* the largest country in the world in area.
4. *Alaska / California* has the largest area.
5. The fastest growing minority is *Hispanic / African-American*.

12.2 Comparative and Superlative Forms of Adjectives and Adverbs

	Simple	Comparative	Superlative
One-syllable adjectives and adverbs	tall fast	taller faster	the tallest the fastest
EXCEPTIONS:	bored tired	more bored more tired	the most bored the most tired
Two-syllable adjectives that end in *-y*	easy happy	easier happier	the easiest the happiest
Other two-syllable adjectives	frequent active	more frequent more active	the most frequent the most active
Some two-syllable adjectives have two forms.	simple common	simpler more simple commoner more common	the simplest the most simple the commonest the most common
(Other two-syllable adjectives that have two forms are *handsome, quiet, gentle, narrow, clever, friendly, angry, polite, stupid.*)			

(continued)

	Simple	Comparative	Superlative
Adjectives with three or more syllables	important difficult	more important more difficult	the most important the most difficult
-ly adverbs	quickly brightly	more quickly more brightly	the most quickly the most brightly
Irregular adjectives and adverbs	good/well bad/badly far little a lot	better worse farther less more	the best the worst the farthest the least the most

SPELLING RULES FOR SHORT ADJECTIVES AND ADVERBS

Rule	Simple	Comparative	Superlative
Add -er and -est to short adjectives and adverbs.	tall fast	taller faster	tallest fastest
For adjectives that end in y, change y to i and add -er and -est.	easy happy	easier happier	easiest happiest
For adjectives that end in e, add -r and -st.	nice late	nicer later	nicest latest
For words ending in consonant-vowel-consonant, double the final consonant, then add -er and -est. EXCEPTION: Do not double final w. new—newer—newest	big sad	bigger sadder	biggest saddest

---

EXERCISE 2   Give the comparative and superlative forms of the word.

EXAMPLES: fat   *fatter*   *the fattest*

important   *more important*   *the most important*

1. interesting   _____   _____

2. young   _____   _____

3. beautiful   _____   _____

4. good   _____   _____

5. common   _____   _____

6. thin   _____   _____

7. carefully _____ _____

8. pretty _____ _____

9. bad _____ _____

10. famous _____ _____

11. lucky _____ _____

12. simple _____ _____

13. high _____ _____

14. delicious _____ _____

15. far _____ _____

16. foolishly _____ _____

12.3   Superlative Adjectives

Examples	Explanation
New York is **the biggest** city in the U.S. California is **the most populated** state in the U.S.	We use the superlative form to point out the number one item of a group of three or more. Use *the* before a superlative form.

LANGUAGE NOTES

1. We sometimes put a prepositional phrase at the end of a superlative sentence.
   - in the world   in my family
   - in my class   in my country
2. We often say "one of the" before a superlative form. Then we use a plural noun.
   - San Francisco is *one of the* most beautiful *cities* in the U.S.
   - The Mississippi is *one of the* longest *rivers* in the world.

EXERCISE 3   Fill in the blanks with the superlative form of the word in parentheses ( ). Include *the* before the superlative form.

EXAMPLE: Alaska is ___*the largest*___ state in area.
(large)

1. _____ lake in the U.S. is Lake Superior.
(big)

2. _____ river in the U.S. is the Missouri.
   (long)

3. _____ mountain in the U.S. is Mount McKinley.
   (high)

4. The computer is one of _____ inventions in recent
   (important)
   years.

5. Johnson is one of _____ last names in the U.S.
   (common)

6. *Casablanca* is one of _____ American movies of all
   (popular)
   time.

7. *Titanic* is one of _____ American movies of all
   (expensive)
   time.

8. Marilyn Monroe was one of _____ American
   (beautiful)
   actresses.

9. Harvard is one of _____ universities in the U.S.
   (good)

10. The Sears Tower is _____ building in the U.S.
    (tall)

11. Crime is one of _____ problems in the U.S.
    (bad)

12. Boston is one of _____ cities in the U.S.
    (old)

EXERCISE 4   Talk about the number-one person in your family for each of these adjectives.

EXAMPLES: interesting
My aunt Rosa is the most interesting person in my family.

tall
The tallest person in my family is my brother Carlos.

1. intelligent	7. serious
2. kind	8. nervous
3. handsome/beautiful	9. strong
4. stubborn	10. funny
5. lazy	11. responsible
6. tall	12. neat

Write a superlative sentence, giving your opinion about each of the following items. (You may use "one of the . . ." plus a plural noun.)

EXAMPLE: big problem today

The biggest problem in the U.S. today is crime.

OR

One of the biggest problems in my native country today is the

economy.

1. exciting sport

   _____

2. bad war

   _____

3. bad tragedy in the world or in the U.S.

   _____

4. important invention of the last 100 years

   _____

5. interesting city in the world

   _____

6. big problem in the U.S. today

   _____

7. bad job

   _____

8. good job

   _____

9. hard teacher at this school

   _____

10. popular movie star

   _____

12.4 Superlatives and Word Order

Examples	Explanation
Which building is **the tallest**? The Sears Tower is **the tallest building**.	Put superlative adjectives after the verb *be* or before the noun.
The Hispanic population is growing **the most quickly**.	Put superlative adverbs after the verb phrase.
It snows **the most** in Juneau.	Put *the most, the least, the best, the worst* after a verb.
Phoenix gets **the most** sunshine.	Put *the most, the least, the best, the worst* before a noun.

EXERCISE 6 Name the person in your family who is the superlative in each of the following activities. (Put the superlative form after the verb.)

EXAMPLES: cook well
My mother cooks the best in the family.

eat a lot
My brother eats the most in my family.

1. talk a lot
2. drive well
3. walk fast
4. speak English well
5. stay up late
6. get up early
7. speak softly
8. eat a lot

EXERCISE 7 Name the person in your family who is the superlative in each of the following activities. (Put the superlative form before the noun.)

EXAMPLE: watch a lot of TV
My brother watches the most TV. He watches TV four hours a day.

1. spend a lot of money
2. get a lot of mail
3. drink a lot of coffee
4. spend a lot of time in the bathroom

5. spend a lot of time on the telephone

6. have a bad temper

7. use a lot of makeup (women)

Before You Read
1. Is this city similar or very different from your native city?
2. Do you have any friends or relatives in American cities? Do you visit them?

Look at the following chart. Then read the sentences that follow. Pay special attention to comparative forms.

A Tale of Two Cities

	Seattle	Minneapolis
Population	524,000	358,000
3 bedroom home	$172,000	$118,000
unemployment	3.1%	2.5%
dollar spent for each student	$3,400	$4,000
graduation rate	80%	60%
climate—rainfall	39 inches	26 inches
climate—snow	15 inches	46 inches
climate—sunny days	136	200

(continued)

	Seattle	Minneapolis
average high temp in July	75 degrees	82 degrees
average low temp in January	33 degrees	3 degrees
crime	914 per 100,000 people	1,850 per 100,000 people
job growth	8.8%	6.3%

- Seattle has a **larger** population than Minneapolis.
- A house in Seattle is **more expensive** than a house in Minneapolis.
- Unemployment in Seattle is **higher** than in Minneapolis.
- Minneapolis spends **more** on education than Seattle.
- Seattle has **more** high school graduates than Minneapolis.
- Seattle has **more** rain than Minneapolis.
- Minneapolis has **more** snow than Seattle.
- Minneapolis is **sunnier** than Seattle.
- Minneapolis is **warmer** in the summer.
- Minneapolis is **colder** in the winter.
- Minneapolis has **more** crime.
- Jobs in Seattle are growing **faster** than jobs in Minneapolis.

12.5 Comparisons

Examples	Explanation
Minneapolis is **sunnier than** Seattle. A house in Seattle is **more expensive than** a house in Minneapolis.	We use the comparative form to compare two items. We use *than* before the second item of comparison.

LANGUAGE NOTES

1. Omit *than* if the second item of comparison is not included.
   Minneapolis is *sunnier* than Seattle, but it is *colder*.
2. *Much* or *a little* can come before a comparative form.
   Minneapolis is *much* colder in the winter.
   Unemployment is *a little* higher in Seattle.
3. When a pronoun follows *than*, the most correct form is the subject pronoun (*he, she, I, etc.*). Sometimes an auxiliary verb follows (*is, are, do, did, etc.*). Informally, many Americans use the object pronoun (*him, her, me, etc.*) after *than*. An auxiliary verb does not follow.

FORMAL   INFORMAL
She is taller than he (*is*).   She is taller than *him*.
She is older than I (*am*).   She is older than *me*.

EXERCISE 8   Circle the correct words to complete the statement.

EXAMPLE: Minneapolis has (more)/ *less* crime than Seattle.

1. Minneapolis has a *larger / smaller* population than Seattle.

2. Minneapolis has *more / less* snow than Seattle.

3. Houses in Minneapolis are *more expensive / less expensive* than houses in Seattle.

4. Jobs in Minneapolis are growing *faster / slower* than jobs in Seattle.

5. Minneapolis is a *safer / more dangerous* place to live.

EXERCISE 9   Compare yourself to another person, or compare two people you know using these adjectives.

EXAMPLES: tall
My father is taller than I am.   (OR   than me.)

talkative
My mother is more talkative than my father.

1. tall	5. thin	9. successful
2. educated	6. quiet	10. strong
3. friendly	7. stubborn	11. nervous
4. lazy	8. patient	12. polite

EXERCISE 10   Compare men and women. Give your own opinion. Talk in general terms. Discuss your answers.

EXAMPLE: intelligent
In my opinion, women are more intelligent than men.
OR
In my opinion, men are more intelligent than women.

1. polite	5. kind	9. romantic
2. strong	6. friendly	10. sensitive
3. tall	7. talkative	11. logical
4. intelligent	8. patient	12. responsible

EXERCISE 11 Compare this city to your hometown.

EXAMPLES:
big
Tokyo is bigger than Boston.

crowded
Tokyo is more crowded than Boston.

1. crowded
2. modern
3. big
4. noisy
5. beautiful
6. interesting
7. cold in winter
8. safe
9. dirty
10. sunny

12.6 Word Order with Comparisons

Examples	Explanation
Houses in Seattle are **more expensive** than houses in Minneapolis. I want to move to a **warmer** climate.	Put comparative adjectives after the verb *be* or before a noun.
He found a job **more quickly** in Minneapolis. She speaks English **more fluently** than I do.	Put comparative adverbs after the verb phrase.
It rains **more** in Seattle. You drive **better** than I do.	Put *more, less, better, worse* after a verb.
Minneapolis has **more** sunshine than Seattle. Seattle has **less** snow.	Put *more, less, fewer, better, worse* before a noun.

EXERCISE 12 Compare men and women. Give your own opinion. Talk in general terms. Discuss your answers.

EXAMPLES:
work hard
In my opinion, women work harder than men.

talk a lot
In my opinion, women talk more than men.

1. run fast
2. gossip a lot
3. take care of children well
4. worry a lot

5. drive foolishly   9. think fast

6. work hard   10. live long

7. drive fast   11. get old fast

8. spend a lot on clothes   12. make decisions quickly

EXERCISE 13 Compare this city to your hometown. Use *better, worse,* or *more*.

EXAMPLES:

factories
Chicago has more factories than Ponce.

public transportation
Moscow has better public transportation than Chicago.

1. traffic	7. factories
2. climate	8. tall buildings
3. rain	9. people
4. crime	10. sunshine
5. pollution	11. snow
6. job opportunities	12. homeless people

EXERCISE 14 Make comparisons with the following words. Give your opinion and reasons. You may work with a partner or in a small group.

EXAMPLE:

men/women—have an easy life
In my opinion, men have an easier life than women. Women have to work two jobs—in the office and at home.

1. men/women—have responsibilities

_____

2. men/women—live long

_____

3. American women/women in my native culture—have an easy life

_____

4. American couples/couples in my native culture—have children

_____

5. married men/single men—are responsible

_____

6. American teenagers/teenagers in my native culture—have freedom

_____

7. American teenagers/teenagers in my native culture—have responsibilities

_____

8. American children/children in my native culture—have toys

_____

9. American children/children in my native culture—have a good education

_____

10. American teachers/teachers in my native culture—have high salaries

_____

11. American teachers/teachers in my native culture—get respect

_____

EXERCISE 15 Fill in the blanks with the comparative or superlative form of the word in parentheses ( ). Include *than* or *the* where necessary.

EXAMPLES: August is usually _____ *hotter than* _____ May.
(hot)

January is usually _____ *the coldest* _____ month of the year.
(cold)

1. A lion is _____ a dog.
(big)

2. A whale is _____ animal in the world.
(big)

3. A dog is _____ a bird.
(intelligent)

4. A dolphin is one of _____ animals in the world.
(intelligent)

5. New York is _____ Los Angeles.
(crowded)

6. Mexico City is one of _____ cities in the world.
(crowded)

7. New York is a crowded city, but Tokyo is _____ .
(crowded)

8. San Francisco is one of _____ cities in the U.S.
(beautiful)

9. _____ distance between two points is a straight line.
(short)

10. Line A is _____ line B.   A _____ B _____
(short)

EXERCISE 16 Two students in Seattle are talking. Fill in the blanks with appropriate words to make comparatives and superlatives.

A. I'm planning to visit Chicago.

B. You're going to love it. It's a beautiful city. In fact, it's one of
   the most beautiful cities in the U.S.
   _____
   (example)

A. It's the second largest city, isn't it?

B. Not any more. Los Angeles is now _____ Chicago.
   (1)

A. What should I see while I'm there?

B. You can visit the Sears Tower. It's _____ building in
   (2)
   the U.S. It has 110 stories. On a clear day, you can see many miles.

A. Did you go to the top when you were there?

B. When I was there, the weather was bad. It was raining. I hope you

   have _____ weather than I had. When are you going?
   (3)

A. In August.

B. Ugh! August is the _____ month of the year. It's often
   (4)
   90 degrees or more. If you get hot, you can always go to the beach
   and cool off.

A. Is Chicago near an ocean?

B. Of course not. It's near Lake Michigan.

A. Is it big like Lake Washington?

B. It's much _____ than Lake Washington. In fact, it's
   (5)
   one of the _____ lakes in the U.S.
   (6)

A. Is it very rainy?

B. Not in the summer. It's sunny. In fact, it's much _____
   (7)
   than Seattle.

A. What do you suggest that I see?

B. You should see the famous architecture downtown. The
   _____ architects in the U.S. built buildings in
   (8)
   Chicago.

A. Do I need to take taxis everywhere or does Chicago have a good public transportation system?

B. Taxis are so expensive! They're much _____ than (9) the buses and trains. You should use the public transportation. But remember there's a lot of crime in Chicago, so it's not safe to travel alone at night. It's _____ in the day time. (10)

A. Does Chicago have _____ crime than Seattle? (11)

B. Yes. But if you're careful, you'll be OK. I'm sure you'll enjoy it. It's an interesting place because it has people from all over the world.

In fact, I think it's one of the _____ cities in the U.S. (12)

SUMMARY OF LESSON 12

1. Comparison of Adjectives
   SHORT ADJECTIVES
   Chicago is a **big** city.
   Chicago is **bigger** than Boston.
   New York is **the biggest** city in the U.S.

   LONG ADJECTIVES
   Houston is a **populated** city.
   Chicago is **more populated** than Houston.
   New York is **the most populated** city in the U.S.

2. Comparison of Adverbs
   SHORT ADVERBS
   She drives **fast**.
   She drives **faster than** her husband.
   Her son drives **the fastest** in the family.

   -LY ADVERBS
   You speak English **fluently**.
   You speak English **more fluently than** your brother.
   Your sister speaks English **the most fluently** in your family.

3. Word Order
   VERB (PHRASE) + COMPARATIVE ADVERB
   She **speaks English more fluently** than her husband.
   She **talks more** than her husband.
   COMPARATIVE WORD + NOUN
   She has **more experience** than her husband.
   She has a **better accent** than her sister.

EDITING ADVICE

1. Don't use a comparison word when there is no comparison.

   California is a bigg~~er~~ state.

2. Don't use *more* and *-er* together.

   My new car is ~~more~~ better than my old one.

3. Use *than* before the second item in a comparison.

   He is younger ~~that~~ *than* his wife.

4. Use *the* before a superlative form.

   China has ˄ *the* biggest population in the world.

5. Use a plural noun after the phrase "one of the."

   Jim is one of the tallest boy˄ *s* in the class.

6. Use the correct word order.

   She ~~faster drives~~ *drives faster* than her husband.

   I have ˄ *more* responsibilities ~~more~~ than you.

   The U.S. is the ~~country~~ most powerful ˄ *country* in the world.

7. Don't use *the* with a possessive form.

   My ~~the~~ best friend lives in London.

8. Use correct spelling.

   She is ~~happyer~~ *happier* than her friend.

LESSON 12 TEST / REVIEW

PART 1   Find the mistakes with the underlined words, and correct them. Not every sentence has a mistake. If the sentence is correct, write C.

EXAMPLES: I am taller ˄ *than* my father.

I am tall, but my father is <u>taller</u>.   C

1. Paul is one of <u>the youngest student</u> in this class.

2. She is <u>more older than</u> her husband.

3. I'm <u>the most tall</u> person in my family.

4. My father is <u>more educated</u> my mother.

5. She is <u>the most intelligent</u> person in her family.

6. New York City is <u>biggest</u> city in the U.S.

7. My sister's <u>the oldest</u> son got married last month.

8. Houston is a very <u>big</u> city.

9. He is <u>much older</u> than his wife.

10. New York is <u>biger</u> than Los Angeles.

11. I speak English <u>more better than</u> I did a year ago.

12. Book One is <u>easyer</u> than Book Two.

PART **2**   Find the mistakes with word order and correct them. Not every sentence has a mistake. If the sentence is correct, write **C**.

EXAMPLES: You more know about the U.S. than I do.
Soccer is more interesting than football for me.   **C**

1. I have problems more than you.

2. I earlier woke up than you.

3. Paris is the city most beautiful in the world.

4. She speaks English more fluently than her brother.

5. You faster type than I do.

6. My father is the most intelligent person in the family.

7. Your car is expensive more than my car.

8. You sing more beautifully than I do.

9. I travel more than my friend does.

10. You have more money than I do.

Fill in the blanks with the comparative or the superlative of the word in parentheses ( ). Add *the* or *than* if necessary.

EXAMPLES: New York is ___*bigger than*___ Chicago.
(big)

New York is ___*the biggest*___ city in the U.S.
(big)

1. Mount Everest is _____ mountain in the world.
(high)

2. A D grade is _____ a C grade.
(bad)

3. Johnson is one of _____ last names in the U.S.
(common)

4. Tokyo is _____ Miami.
(populated)

5. June 21 is _____ day of the year.
(long)

6. The teacher speaks English _____ I do.
(well)

7. Lake Superior is _____ lake in the U.S.
(large)

8. Children learn a foreign language _____ adults.
(quickly)

9. Some people think that Japanese cars are _____
(good)
American cars.

10. A dog is _____ a cat.
(friendly)

11. Women drive _____ men.
(carefully)

12. Who is _____ student in this class?
(good)

13. The teacher speaks English _____ I do.
(fluently)

14. A dog is intelligent, but a monkey is _____ .
(intelligent)

EXPANSION ACTIVITIES

CLASSROOM ACTIVITIES

1. Form a small group of 3–5 students. Fill in the blanks to give information about yourself. Compare your list with the lists of other members of your group to make superlative statements.

EXAMPLE: Susana has the most relatives in the U.S.

a. Number of relatives I have in the U.S. _____

b. My height _____

c. Number of letters in my last name _____

d. Number of children I have _____

e. Number of sisters and brothers I have _____

f. Age of my car _____

g. Number of hours I watch TV per week _____

h. Number of hours I exercise per week _____

i. Money I spent today _____

j. Distance I traveled to come to the U.S. _____

k. Cups of coffee I drank today _____

l. Number of miles I usually drive per day _____

m. Number of movies I usually see per year _____

2. Work with a partner from the same native culture, if possible. Compare American men and men from your native culture. Compare American women and women from your native culture. Report some of your ideas to the class.

3. The manager of a company is interviewing two people for the same job: a younger woman (24 years old) and an older woman (55 years old). He can't decide which one to hire. Find a partner. One person (the manager) will make a statement. The partner will say, "Yes, but . . ." and follow with another statement.

EXAMPLES:
    A. Older people are wiser.
    B. Yes, but younger people are quicker.
    A. Older people have more experience.
    B. Yes, but younger people are more flexible.

4. Find a partner and choose one of the following pairs and decide which of the two is better. Write five reasons why it is better. One person will make a statement saying that one is better than the other. The other person will follow with, "Yes, but . . ." and give another point of view.

EXAMPLES:
    A. I think dogs are better pets than cats. They are more loyal.
    B. Yes, but dogs need more attention.

• cats and dogs
• big cities and small towns
• travel by train and travel by plane
• houses and condos
• spring and fall
• voice mail and answering machines

5. Pretend you and your friend are trying to decide where to go on vacation in July—to the mountains of Canada or to the coast of Mexico. Write a dialog presenting your reasons for choosing one place over the other.

EXAMPLE:
    A. Canada is cooler.
    B. Yes, but Mexico is more interesting.

WRITING

1. Choose one of the topics below to write a comparison:

   a. Compare your present car with your last car.

   b. Compare two cities you know well.

   c. Compare American women and women in your native culture.

   d. Compare American men and men in your native culture.

   c. Compare soccer and football.

   f. Compare your life in the U.S. and your life in your native country.

   g. Compare the place where you lived in your native country with the place where you live now.

2. Write about the biggest problem in the world (or in your native country, or in the U.S.) today. Why is this a problem? How can we solve the problem?

OUTSIDE ACTIVITIES

Interview an American. Get his or her opinion about the superlative of each of the following items. Share your findings with the class.

good car: What do you think is the best car?

a. good car

b. famous celebrity

c. good president in the last 25 years

d. beautiful city in the U.S.

e. good university in the U.S.

f. popular movie at this time

g. terrible tragedy in American history

h. big problem in the U.S. today

i. popular singer in the U.S.

j. best athlete

Internet Activity

1. Using the Internet, find a site that compares cities. Compare any two American cities that interest you.

2. Using the Internet, find out about the city where you live. Find out:

    *   the name of the mayor
    *   the population
    *   the annual rainfall
    *   the coldest month
    *   interesting places to visit in this city

GRAMMAR

Auxiliary Verbs with *Too* and *Either*
Auxiliary Verbs in Tag Questions

CONTEXT

Football and Soccer

LESSON FOCUS

We can use auxiliary verbs with *too* and *either*.
I speak French, and the teacher *does too*.
I went to Paris, and my friend *did too*.
We use auxiliary verbs in a tag question.
You speak Italian, *don't you*?
She bought a dictionary, *didn't she*?

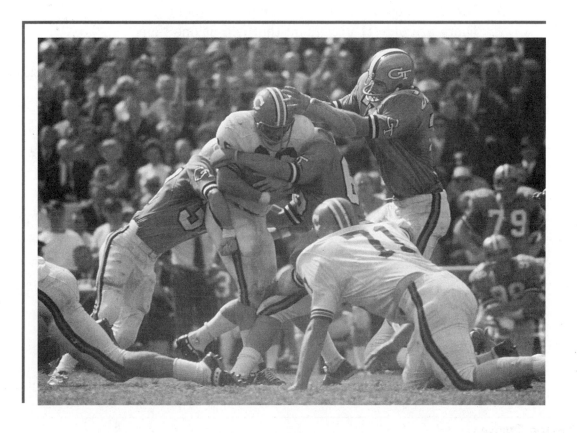

1. What's your favorite sport? Do you like to play it or watch it?
2. Do you ever watch a football game on TV in the U.S.?

football

Read the following conversation between a student from Ecuador (E) and his American friend (A). Pay special attention to auxiliary verbs.

Football and Soccer

E. My favorite sport is football. In my country, Ecuador, everyone likes football.

A. I think you mean soccer, **don't** you?

E. In Ecuador we say football, but football means something different for you, **doesn't** it?

A. Yes.

E. What exactly is the difference between football and soccer?

A. Well, for one thing, the ball is different. A soccer ball is round. A football **isn't**. A football player can carry or throw the ball, but a soccer player **can't**.

E. A football team has the same number of players as a soccer team, **doesn't** it?

A. Yes. They both have 11 players, but a football team really has 22 players. There are only 11 players on the field at one time.

E. There are other differences, **aren't there**?

A. Oh, yes. A soccer game lasts 90 minutes, but a football game **doesn't**. A football game lasts 60 minutes.

E. I don't like football very much.

A. I **don't** either.

E. I prefer soccer.

A. I **do** too.

E. That's strange. I thought all Americans love football.

A. Maybe most **do**, but I **don't**.

soccer

13.1 Auxiliary Verbs with *Too* and *Either*

Affirmative Statements	
A soccer team has 11 players,	and a football team **does too**.
My brother plays soccer,	and I **do too**.
Baseball is popular in the U.S.,	and basketball **is too**.
I like baseball.	I **do too**.

Negative Statements	
Football isn't popular in my country,	and baseball **isn't either**.
I don't like football.	My brother **doesn't either**.
He can't play tennis well.	I **can't either**.

LANGUAGE NOTES

1. The auxiliary verbs are *do*, *does*, *did*, the modals, and *be*. We use auxiliary verbs in the above sentences to avoid repetition of the same verb phrase.
2. Use *too* with two affirmative statements. Use *either* with two negative statements. We can connect the sentences with *and*.
3. In informal speech, Americans often say *me too* and *me neither*.
   A. I like soccer.
   B. Me too.
   A. I don't like football.
   B. Me neither.
4. When *have* is the main verb, Americans usually use *do*, *does*, or *did* as a substitute.

AMERICAN:	BRITISH:
A. I have tickets to a game.	A. I have tickets to a game.
B. I *do* too.	B. I *have* too.

EXERCISE 1 Terri and David have some things in common. Finish each affirmative statement with an auxiliary verb (the same tense as the main verb) + *too*.

EXAMPLES: Terri plays volleyball, and David ___*does too.*___

Terri went to a soccer game last night, and David ___*did too.*___

1. Terri is interested in football, and David _____

Auxiliary Verbs with *Too* and *Either*; Auxiliary Verbs in Tag Questions **345**

2. Terri likes to play tennis, and David _____

3. Terri went bowling last week, and David _____

4. Terri will watch a football game on TV next Sunday, and David

    _____

chess

5. Terri can play chess, and David _____

EXERCISE 2 Terri and David have some things in common. Finish each negative statement with an auxiliary verb (the same tense) + *either*.

EXAMPLES: Terri doesn't like hockey, and David ___*doesn't either.*___

Terri didn't go to the hockey game, and David ___*didn't either.*___

1. Terri doesn't know how to swim, and David _____

2. Terri can't ski, and David _____

3. Terri won't go to the game next Sunday, and David _____

4. Terri isn't interested in baseball, and David _____

5. Terri didn't play tennis last summer, and David _____

13.2 Auxiliary Verbs with Opposite Statements

Affirmative	Negative
I like football,	but my brother **doesn't**.
Football is popular in my country,	but baseball **isn't**.

Negative	Affirmative
You didn't see the soccer game,	but I **did**.
Soccer players can't carry the ball,	but football players **can**.

LANGUAGE NOTES

1. The above sentences show opposites. We use auxiliary verbs to avoid repetition of the same verb phrase.
2. We can connect opposite sentences with *but*.

EXERCISE 3 Terri and David are different in some ways. Finish each statement with an auxiliary verb.

EXAMPLES: Terri works downtown, but David _____doesn't._____

Terri isn't interested in classical music, but David _____is._____

1. Terri likes to cook, but David _____

2. Terri doesn't play the guitar, but David _____

3. Terri can't speak Russian, but David _____

4. Terri went to Hawaii for vacation, but David _____

5. Terri won't work next Sunday, but David _____

EXERCISE 4 Fill in the blanks to compare the U.S. and another country you know. Use *and . . . too* or *and . . . either* for similarities between the U.S. and the other country. Use *but* for differences. Use an auxiliary verb in all cases.

EXAMPLE: The U.S. is a big country, _____and Russia is too._____

OR

The U.S. is a big country, _____but Cuba isn't._____

1. The U.S. has more than 270 million people, _____

2. The U.S. is in North America, _____

3. The U.S. has a president, _____

4. The U.S. doesn't have a socialist government, _____

5. The U.S. fought in World War II, _____

6. The U.S. was a colony of England, _____

7. Americans like football, _____

8. Americans don't celebrate Labor Day in May, _____

9. American schools are closed on December 25, _____

_____

10. The U.S. has a presidential election every four years, _____

_____

EXERCISE 5   Check (√) *yes* or *no* to tell what is true for you. Exchange your book with another student. Make statements about you and the other student.

EXAMPLE: I don't speak Spanish, but Luis does.

	Yes	No
1. I speak Spanish.		
2. I'm interested in football.		
3. I'm interested in soccer.		
4. I have a car.		
5. I use the Internet.		
6. I can drive.		
7. I plan to go back to my native country.		
8. I'm going to buy a computer this year.		
9. I would like to live in a small American town.		
10. I exercise every day.		
11. I'm studying math this semester.		
12. I studied English when I was in my native country.		
13. I came to the U.S. directly from my native country.		
14. I finished college in my native country.		
15. I'm a vegetarian.		
16. I have a cell phone.		

EXERCISE 6   Fill in the blanks in the conversation below. Use an auxiliary verb and *too* or *either* when necessary.

A.   I'm moving on Saturday. Maybe you and your brother can help me. Are you working on Saturday?

B.   My brother is working on Saturday, but I __'m not__ . I can
           (example)
help you.

A.   I need a van. Do you have one?

B.   I don't have one, but my brother _____ . I'll ask him if
                                    (1)
we can use it. By the way, why are you moving?

A.   There are a couple of reasons. I don't like the apartment, and my

wife _____ . She says it's too small for two people.
       (2)

B. How many rooms does your new apartment have?

A. The old apartment has two bedrooms, and the new one _____

    _____. But the rooms are much bigger in the new one,
    (3)
    and there are more closets. Also, we'd like to live near the lake.

B. I _____, but apartments there are very expensive.
       (4)

A. We found a nice apartment that isn't so expensive. Also, I'd like to
    own a dog, but my present landlord doesn't permit pets.

B. Mine doesn't _____. What kind of dog do you plan to
                     (5)
    get?

A. I like big watchdogs. Maybe a German shepherd or a doberman. I
    don't like small dogs.

B. I _____. They just make a lot of noise.
         (6)

A. So now you know my reasons for moving. Can I count on you for
    Saturday?

B. Of course you can.

13.3 Auxiliary Verbs in Tag Questions

Affirmative Statements	Negative Tag Questions	Answers
A football team has 11 players,	**doesn't** it?	Yes, it does.
You can play football,	**can't** you?	Yes, I can.
This is your football,	**isn't** it?	Yes, it is.
There are 11 players on a baseball team,	**aren't** there?	No, there aren't.
I'm right,	**am** I not? /**aren't** I?	Yes, you are.

Negative Statements	Affirmative Tag Questions	Answers
Soccer isn't the same as football,	**is** it?	No, it isn't.
Football players don't wear a helmet,	**do** they?	Yes, they do.
Soccer players can't carry the ball,	**can** they?	No, they can't.

LANGUAGE NOTES

1. A tag question is a short question that we put at the end of a statement. You can use a tag question to ask if your statement is correct or if the listener agrees with you.
2. A tag question uses the auxiliary verb + a subject pronoun (*I, you, we, they, he, she, it*). If the subject is *this* or *that*, use *it* in the tag. If the subject is *these* or *those*, use *they* in the tag. If *there* introduces the subject, use *there* in the tag.
3. The tag question uses the same tense as the main verb.
4. An affirmative statement uses a negative tag. A negative statement uses an affirmative tag.
5. *Am I not?* is a very formal tag. We often say *aren't I?*
6. When *have* is the main verb, Americans usually use *do, does,* or *did* in the tag question.
    > AMERICAN:
    > You have tickets to the game, *don't* you?
    > BRITISH:
    > You have tickets to the game, *haven't* you?

EXERCISE 7   Add a tag question. All the statements are affirmative and have an auxiliary verb.

EXAMPLE: This class is large, _isn't it?_____

1. You're a foreign student, _____
2. You can understand English, _____
3. We'll have a test soon, _____
4. We should study, _____
5. There's a library at this school, _____
6. You'd like to improve your English, _____
7. This is an easy lesson, _____
8. I'm asking too many questions, _____

EXERCISE 8   Add a tag question. All the statements are negative and have an auxiliary verb.

EXAMPLE: You can't speak Italian, _can you?_____

1. You aren't an American citizen, _____
2. The teacher can't speak your language, _____

3. We shouldn't talk in the library, _____

4. You weren't absent yesterday, _____

5. There aren't any Japanese students in this class, _____

6. This exercise isn't hard, _____

EXERCISE 9 Add a tag question. All the statements are affirmative. Substitute the main verb with an auxiliary verb in the tag question.

EXAMPLE: You have the textbook, _don't you?_____

1. English has a lot of irregular verbs, _____

2. You want to speak English well, _____

3. You understood the explanation, _____

4. A soccer team has 11 players, _____

5. They went to a soccer game last week, _____

6. We had a test last week, _____

EXERCISE 10 Add a tag question. All the statements are negative.

EXAMPLE: We don't have class on Saturday, _do we?_____

1. The teacher doesn't pronounce your name correctly, _____

2. Your brother didn't take the last test, _____

3. You didn't bring your dictionary today, _____

4. We don't always have homework, _____

5. I don't have your phone number, _____

6. Your mother doesn't speak English, _____

EXERCISE 11 This is a conversation between two acquaintances,[1] Bob (B) and Sam (S). Sam can't remember where he met Bob. Fill in the blanks with a tag question.

B. Hi, Sam.

S. Uh, hi. . . .

---

[1] An *acquaintance* is a person you don't know well.

B.   You don't remember me, _____*do you?*_____
                                        (example)

S.   You look familiar, but I can't remember your name. We were in the

same chemistry class last semester, _____
                                                (1)

B.   No.

S.   Then we probably met in math class, _____
                                                    (2)

B.   Wrong again. I'm Linda Wilson's brother.

S.   Now I remember you. Linda introduced us at a party last summer,

_____ And your name is Bob, _____
         (3)   (4)

B.   That's right.

S.   How are you, Bob? You graduated last year, _____
                                                            (5)

B.   Yes. And I've got a good job now.

S.   You majored in computers, _____
                                          (6)

B.   Yes. But I decided to go into real estate.

S.   And how's your sister Linda? I never see her anymore. She moved

back to California, _____
                             (7)

B.   No. She's still here. But she's married now, and she's expecting a baby.

S.   That's wonderful. Say hello to Linda when you see her. It was great
     seeing you again, Bob.

EXERCISE 12 A mother (M) is talking to her daughter (D). Fill in the blanks
with a tag question.

M.   You didn't get your scholarship, _____*did you?*_____
                                                   (example)

D.   How did you know?

M.   Well, you look very disappointed. You can apply again next year,
     _____?
            (1)

D.   Yes. But what will I do this year?

M. There are government loans, _____?
(2)

D. Yes.

M. And you don't have to pay them back until you graduate,

_____?
(3)

D. No.

M. And your professors will give you letters of recommendation,

_____?
(4)

D. I'm sure they will.

M. So don't worry. Just try to get a loan, and you can apply again next
year for a scholarship.

13.4 Answering a Tag Question

Right Information	Agreement
California is a big state, isn't it?	**Yes, it is**.
New Jersey isn't a big state, is it?	**No, it isn't**. It's small.

Wrong Information	Disagreement or Correction
California isn't a big state, is it?	**Yes, it is**. It's very big.
New Jersey is a big state, isn't it?	**No, it isn't**. It's small.

LANGUAGE NOTES

1. When we use a tag question, we expect the listener to agree.
2. When we add a negative tag question, we expect the answer to be
   yes. *No* means the information is incorrect or the listener does not
   agree.
3. When we add an affirmative tag question, we expect the answer to
   be *no*. *Yes* means the information is incorrect or the listener does
   not agree.

EXERCISE **13** Complete the answer in the left column. Then check the
meaning of the answer in the right column. (You may work with
a partner.)

A. You don't have a car, do you? B. Yes, _____I do._____	✓Person B has a car. Person B doesn't have a car.
A. You aren't American, are you? B. No, I _____	Person B is American. Person B isn't American.
A. You don't like this city, do you? B. No, _____	Person B likes this city. Person B doesn't like the city.
A. The U.S. is the best country in the world, isn't it? B. No, _____	Person B agrees with the statement. Person B doesn't agree with the statement.
A. You don't speak Russian, do you? B. No, _____	Person B speaks Russian. Person B doesn't speak Russian.
A. You can drive, can't you? B. No, _____	Person B can drive. Person B can't drive.
A. You don't have a watch, do you? B. Yes, _____	Person B has a watch. Person B doesn't have a watch.
A. You work on Saturday, don't you? B. Yes, _____	Person B works on Saturday. Person B doesn't work on Saturday.

EXERCISE 14 Read a statement to another student and add a tag question. The other student will tell you if this information is correct or not.

EXAMPLES: You speak Polish, _____don't you?_____
No, I don't. I speak Ukrainian.

You aren't from Poland, _____are you?_____
No, I'm not. I'm from Ukraine.

You came to the U.S. two years ago, _____didn't you?_____
Yes, I did.

1. You're married, _____

2. You have children, _____

3. You didn't study English in your country, _____

4. You have a car, _____

5. You don't live alone, _____

6. You'll take another English course next semester, _____

7. You won't return to your native country, _____

8. You took the last test, _____

9. You have to work on Saturdays, _____

10. The teacher doesn't speak your language, _____

11. You can type, _____

12. This class isn't too hard for you, _____

13. There was a test last Friday, _____

14. You don't speak German, _____

15. I'm asking you a lot of personal questions, _____

EXERCISE 15 Fill in the blanks with a tag question and an answer that tells if the information is true or not.

A. You come from Russia, _____*don't you?*_____
    (example)

B. _____. I come from Ukraine.
    (1)

A. They speak Polish in Ukraine, _____
    (2)

B. _____. They speak Ukrainian and Russian.
    (3)

A. Ukraine isn't part of Russia, _____
    (4)

B. _____. Ukraine and Russia are different. They were
    (5)

both part of the former Soviet Union.

A. You come from a big city, _____
    (6)

B. _____. I come from Kiev. It's the capital of Ukraine.
    (7)

It's very big.

A. Your parents aren't here, _____
    (8)

B. _____. We came together two years ago. I live with
    (9)

my parents.

A. You studied English in your country, _____
    (10)

B. _____. I only studied Russian and German. I never
    (11)

studied English there.

A. You're not going to go back to live in your country,

_____
(12)

B. _____. I'm an immigrant here. I plan to become an
(13)
American citizen.

Uses of Auxiliary Verbs

1. To avoid repetition of the same verb phrase:

Affirmative Sentence	*and*	Shortened Affirmative Sentence + *Too*
I *like* football,	and	my friend *does too*.
Football *is* fun,	and	soccer *is too*.

Negative Sentence	*and*	Shortened Negative Sentence + *Either*
I *don't like* baseball,	and	she *doesn't either*.
I *didn't watch* the game,	and	she *didn't either*.

Negative Sentence	*but*	Shortened Affirmative Sentence
I *didn't watch* the game,	but	you *did*.
I *can't go* to the game,	but	you *can*.

Affirmative Sentence	*but*	Shortened Negative Sentence
My brother *likes* baseball,	but	I *don't*.
I *have* tickets to the game,	but	my friend *doesn't*.

2. To form tag questions:

Affirmative Sentence	Negative Tag
Soccer *is* fun,	*isn't* it?
You *like* soccer,	*don't* you?

Negative Sentence	Affirmative Tag
He *can't* swim,	*can* he?
She *didn't* go,	*did* she?

1. Don't omit the auxiliary from a shortened sentence with *too* or *either*.

    My brother has a new house, and I ⌃*do* too.

    John didn't take the test, and I *didn't* ⌃ either.

2. Don't confuse *too* and *either*.

    Jack doesn't speak French, and his wife doesn't ~~too~~ *either*.

3. If half your sentence is negative and half is affirmative, the connecting word is *but*, not *and*.

    He doesn't speak French, ~~and~~ *but* his wife does.

4. Be careful to answer a tag question correctly.

    New York isn't the capital of the U.S., is it? ~~Yes~~ *No*, it isn't.

5. Use a pronoun (or *there*) in the tag question.

    That's your hat, isn't ~~that~~ *it*?

    There's some milk in the refrigerator, isn't ~~it~~ *there*?

6. Be careful to use the correct auxiliary verb and the correct tense.

    Her sister didn't go to the party, ~~does~~ *did* she?

    She won't go back to her country, ~~does~~ *will* she?

LESSON 13 TEST / REVIEW

PART 1 Find the mistakes with the underlined words and correct them. Not every sentence has a mistake. If the sentence is correct, write C.

EXAMPLES: Today is Friday, isn't ~~today~~ *it*?

My friend doesn't like soccer, and I <u>don't either</u>. C

1. My mother speaks English well, <u>and</u> my father doesn't.

2. My mother speaks English well, and my brother <u>does too</u>.

3. The Vice President doesn't live in the White House, does he? <u>Yes</u>, he doesn't.

4. A soccer team has 11 players, and a football team <u>too</u>.

5. Bob doesn't have a car, and Mary doesn't <u>too</u>.

6. You're not an American citizen, <u>do</u> you?

7. You didn't finish your dinner, <u>do</u> you?

8. There will be a test next week, <u>won't there</u>?

9. Your father can't come to the U.S., <u>can he</u>?

10. This is the last question, <u>isn't this</u>?

PART 2

This is a conversation between two students who meet for the first time. Fill in the blanks with an auxiliary verb to complete this conversation. Use *either* or *too* when necessary.

C. Hi. My name is Carlos. I'm a new student.

E. I ___*am too*___. My name is Elena.
   (example)

C. I come from Mexico.

E. Oh, really? I _____. I come from a small town in the northern
   (1)
   part of Mexico.

C. I come from Mexico City. I love big cities.

E. I _____. I prefer small towns.
   (2)

C. How do you like living here in Los Angeles?

E. I don't like it much, but my sister _____. She has a good job,
   (3)
   but I _____. I miss my job back home.
   (4)

C. I love it here, and my family _____. The climate is similar to
   (5)
   the climate of Mexico City.

E. What about the air quality? Mexico City doesn't have clean air, and Los

   Angeles _____, so you probably feel right at home.
   (6)

C. Ha! You're right about the air quality, but there are many nice things about Los
   Angeles. Do you want to get a cup of coffee and continue this conversation? I
   don't have any more classes today.

E. I _____, but I have to go home now. I enjoyed our talk.
    (7)

C. I _____. Maybe we can continue it some other time. Well, see
    (8)
    you in class tomorrow.

In this conversation, a new student is trying to find out
information about the school and class. Add a tag question.

A. There's a parking lot at the school, __*isn't there?*__
                                          (example)

B. Yes. It's east of the building.

A. The teacher's American, _____
                            (1)

B. Yes, she is.

A. She doesn't give hard tests, _____
                                 (2)

B. Not too easy, not too hard.

A. We'll have a day off for Christmas, _____
                                        (3)

B. We'll have a whole week off.

A. We have to write compositions, _____
                                   (4)

B. A few.

A. And we can't use a dictionary when we write a composition,

   _____
   (5)

B. Who told you that? Of course we can. You're very nervous about

   school, _____
           (6)

A. Yes, I am. It isn't easy to learn a new language, _____
                                                      (7)

B. No.

A. And I should ask questions about things I want to know, _____
                                                            (8)

B. Yes, of course. You don't have any more questions, _____
                                                       (9)

A. No.

B. Well, I'll see you in the next class. Bye.

EXPANSION ACTIVITIES

1. Complete each statement. Then find a partner and compare yourself to your partner by using an auxiliary verb.

EXAMPLES:

    A. I speak _Chinese_ .
    B. I do too. OR I don't.

    A. I don't speak _Spanish_ .
    B. I don't either. OR I do.

  a. I speak _____ .

  b. I don't speak _____ .

  c. I can _____ .

  d. I have _____ .

  e. I don't have _____ .

  f. I'm _____ .

  g. I usually drink _____ every day.

  h. I'm going to _____ next week.

  i. I come from _____ .

  j. I'm wearing _____ today.

  k. I bought _____ last week.

  l. I went _____ last week.

  m. I don't like _____ .

  n. I brought _____ to the U.S.

  o. I don't like to eat _____ .

  p. I can't _____ very well.

  q. I should _____ more.

2. Find a partner. Tell your partner some things that you think you know about him or her and about his or her native culture or country. Your partner will tell you if you are right or wrong.

The capital of your country is New Delhi, isn't it?
Hindus don't eat meat, do they?
You're studying engineering, aren't you?

3. Work with a partner to match Column A with Column B.
    (Alternate activity: Teacher, copy this page. Cut the copied page along the lines. Give half the class statements from Column A and half the class tag questions from Column B. The students walk around the room to match the statement to the tag question.)

Column A	Column B
Washington is the capital of the U.S.,	is it?
Los Angeles isn't the biggest city,	isn't there?
Puerto Ricans are American citizens,	don't they?
Americans have freedom of speech,	does it?
There's an election every four years,	are you?
Americans fought in World War II,	wasn't she?
There will be a presidential election in 2012,	isn't it?
The President lives in the White House,	doesn't he?
George Washington was the first American president,	won't there?
You're not an American citizen,	did she?
Amelia Earhart didn't come back from her last flight,	aren't they?
Florida doesn't have cold winters,	wasn't he?
Helen Keller was a great woman,	didn't they?

4. The teacher will read each statement. If the statement is true for you, stand up. Students will take turns making statements about two people.

EXAMPLE:

Teacher: Stand up if you drank coffee this morning.
Student: I drank coffee this morning, and Tom did too.
          Mario didn't drink coffee this morning, and Sofia didn't either.
          I drank coffee this morning, but Lisa didn't.

Stand up if you . . .

*   have more than five sisters and brothers
*   walked to class today
*   will buy a house in the next two years
*   are wearing running shoes
*   have a photo of a family member in your pocket or bag

- want to review this lesson
- went to a movie last week
- can't swim
- plan to buy a car soon
- are tired now
- aren't married
- ate pizza today
- speak Polish
- don't like this game
- can understand American TV
- didn't take the last test

5. Tell the teacher what you think you know about the U.S. or Americans. You may work with a partner. The teacher will tell you if you're right or wrong.

EXAMPLES: Most Americans don't speak a foreign language, do they?
Alaska is the largest state, isn't it?

WRITING

1. Choose two sports, religions, countries, people, or stores, and write sentences comparing them.

EXAMPLE: my mother and my father
My father speaks English well, but my mother doesn't.
My father isn't an American citizen, and my mother
isn't either.
My father was born in 1938, and my mother was too.

2. Find a partner. Write a list of some things you have in common and some differences you have.

EXAMPLE: *Alex plays the violin, and I do too.*
Alex is majoring in chemistry, but I'm not.
Alex doesn't have a computer, and I don't either.

_____

_____

_____

Internet Activity

Find information on the Internet about a sport you like or would like to know more about. Write a list of facts about this sport. Bring your list to class. Other students can ask you about this sport using tag questions. Tell them if they're right or wrong.

EXAMPLE: A baseball team has nine players, doesn't it?
Baseball is popular in Japan, isn't it?

Lesson Fourteen

GRAMMAR
Verb Review

CONTEXT
Letter from Puerto Rico

LESSON FOCUS
We are going to compare the tenses presented in this book.

SIMPLE PRESENT	We usually *study* hard.
PRESENT CONTINUOUS	We *are studying* four tenses now.
SIMPLE PAST	We *studied* the simple past last week.
FUTURE	We *are going to study* Book 2 next semester.
FUTURE	We *will study* Book 2 next semester.

1. Do you like to vacation in warm, sunny places?
2. Where did you go on your last vacation?

Letter from Puerto Rico

Jane, her husband Ed, and their two children are on vacation now. Jane is writing a letter to her friend, Rosemary. Read the following letter. Pay special attention to verb tenses.

Dear Rosemary,

*We **arrived** in Puerto Rico last Monday. Our flight **was** smooth and comfortable. We **are staying** at a beautiful hotel in San Juan this week. (San Juan **is** the capital of Puerto Rico.) Our hotel **has** tennis courts and two big swimming pools. Ed **plays** tennis every morning. I usually **sleep** late in the morning. In the afternoon, we usually **go** to the beach or to the pool. The children **love** to swim. Sometimes I **go** shopping in the early evening. At night we usually **eat** at a restaurant. Last night we **had** dinner in a lovely Puerto Rican restaurant. The dinner **was** delicious. Tomorrow we **are going to try** another restaurant.*

*Now I **am sitting** on the beach. I **am getting** a good suntan. The children **are playing** in the water. Ed **is reading** the newspaper in the shade. He always **likes** the shade, but I **prefer** the sun.*

*Next week we **are going to visit** another island nearby, Saint Thomas. We **are going to leave** at 7 o'clock on Friday morning. We **are going to be** there for three days. If I **have** time, I'll **write** you a postcard from St. Thomas. After that, we **are going to return** home. I **will call** you when I **get** home. I **will tell** you all about our vacation.*

Take care,
Jane

Verb Tenses—Uses

SIMPLE PRESENT TENSE

Examples	Uses
Puerto Rico **is** an island. Puerto Rico **has** a tropical climate.	• Facts
Most Americans **wear** a bathing suit at the beach.	• Customs and Habits
Ed and Jane **visit** Puerto Rico once a year. Jane sometimes **writes** letters.	• Regular activities
Ed **wants** to sit in the shade now. Jane **needs** a stamp now.	• With nonaction verbs
I will call you when I **return**.	• In a future time clause
If I **have** time, I will write you again.	• In a future *if* clause
I **come** from Mexico.	• With place of origin

PRESENT CONTINUOUS TENSE

Examples	Uses
Jane **is sitting** on the beach. Her husband **is sitting** in the shade.	• Actions that are happening now
They **are vacationing** in Puerto Rico this week. They **are staying** in a beautiful hotel.	• Actions that are happening in a present time period

NOTE: Do not use the continuous tense with nonaction verbs: *believe, cost, have, hear, know, like, love, need, own, prefer, remember, see, seem, understand, want*

FUTURE TENSE

Examples	Uses
Next week they **are going to** travel to St. Thomas.	Actions that will happen later • Plans (Use *be going to*)
I hear the weather **will be** warm next week.	• Predictions (Use *will* or *be going to*)
I **will call** you next week when I get home.	• Promises and offers (Use *will*)

PAST TENSE

Examples	Uses
The flight **was** smooth and comfortable. They **went** to Puerto Rico last Monday. They **ate** in a Puerto Rican restaurant last night. They **bought** their plane ticket one month ago.	• Actions that happened at a specific time in the past

BE

Examples	Uses
Puerto Rico **is** an island. Puerto Rico **is** beautiful. Puerto Rico **is** in the Caribbean Sea. I **am** from Puerto Rico. I **was** born in Ponce. There **are** many beautiful beaches in Puerto Rico.	• To classify or define the subject • To describe the subject • To tell the location of the subject • With a place of origin • With *born* • With *there*

EXERCISE 1 Fill in the blanks with the correct tense of the verb in parentheses ( ) to complete this letter. Use the simple present, the present continuous, the future, or the simple past.

Dear Rosemary,

We _____*arrived*_____ in Puerto Rico last Monday. Our flight
     (example: arrive)

_____ smooth and comfortable. We _____ at a
     (1 be)   (2 stay)

beautiful hotel in San Juan this week. (San Juan _____ the
                                                      (3 be)

capital of Puerto Rico.) Our hotel _____ tennis courts and two
                                          (4 have)

big swimming pools. Ed _____ tennis every morning. I usually
                            (5 play)

_____ late in the morning. In the afternoon, we usually _____
     (6 sleep)   (7 go)

to the beach or to the pool. The children _____ to swim. Sometimes
                                            (8 love)

I _____ shopping in the early evening. At night we usually
     (9 go)

_____ at a restaurant. Last night we _____ dinner
    (10 eat)   (11 have)

in a lovely Puerto Rican restaurant. The dinner _____ delicious.
                                                    (12 be)

Tomorrow we _____ another restaurant.
                (13 try)

Now I _____ on the beach. I _____ a good
          (14 sit)   (15 get)

suntan. The children _____ in the water. Ed _____
                         (16 play)   (17 read)

the newspaper in the shade. He always _____ the shade, but
                                          (18 like)

I _____ the sun.
    (19 prefer)

Next week we _____ another island nearby, Saint Thomas.
                 (20 visit)

We _____ at 7 o'clock on Friday morning. We _____
      (21 leave)   (22 be)

there for three days. If I _____ time, I _____ you
                              (23 have)   (24 write)

a postcard from St. Thomas. After that, we _____ home. I
                                               (25 return)

_____ you when I _____ home. I _____
    (26 call)   (27 get)   (28 tell)

you all about our vacation.

Take care,

Jane

14.2   Statements and Questions

Simple Present Tense

-s Form	Base Form
Ed **plays** tennis every day.	They **like** Puerto Rico.
He **doesn't play** soccer.	They **don't like** cold weather.
Does he **play** handball?	**Do** they **like** St. Thomas?
No, he **doesn't**.	Yes, they **do**.
When **does** he **play** tennis?	Why **do** they **like** Puerto Rico?
Why **doesn't** he **play** handball?	Why **don't** they **like** cold weather?
Who **plays** handball?	How many people **like** cold weather?

PRESENT CONTINUOUS TENSE

They **are sitting** on the beach.	She **is writing** a letter.
They **aren't sitting** in a restaurant.	She **isn't writing** a post card.
Are they **sitting** in the shade?	**Is** she **writing** a long letter?
No, they **aren't**.	Yes, she **is**.
Where **are** they **sitting**?	To whom **is** she **writing** a letter?
Why **aren't** they **sitting** in the shade?	Why **isn't** she **writing** a postcard?
Who **is sitting** in the shade?	Who **is writing** a postcard?

FUTURE TENSE

Will	Be Going To
She **will call** her friend next week.	They **are going to visit** St. Thomas.
She **won't call** her tomorrow.	They **aren't going to visit** St. John.
Will she **call** her on Friday?	**Are** they **going to visit** Cuba?
No, she **won't**.	No, they **aren't**.
When **will** she **call** her?	When **are** they **going to visit** St. Thomas?
Why **won't** she **call** her on Friday?	Why **aren't** they **going to visit** Cuba?
Who **will call** her on Friday?	Who **is going to visit** Cuba?

SIMPLE PAST TENSE

Regular Verb	Irregular Verb
They **arrived** on Monday.	They **ate** in a restaurant last night.
They **didn't arrive** on Sunday.	They **didn't eat** at home.
Did they **arrive** in the morning?	**Did** they **eat** in a Chinese restaurant?
Yes they **did**.	No, they **didn't**.
What time **did** they **arrive**?	Where **did** they **eat**?
Why **didn't** they **arrive** on Monday?	Why **didn't** they **eat** at home?
Who **arrived** on Monday?	Who **ate** at home?

BE

Present	Past
She **is** in Puerto Rico.	They **were** in a restaurant last night.
She **isn't** at home.	They **weren't** at the pool.
Is she in San Juan?	**Were** they in an American restaurant?
Yes, she **is**.	No, they **weren't**.
Why **is** she in San Juan?	When **were** they in a restaurant?
Why **isn't** she at home?	Why **weren't** they at the pool?
Who **is** at home?	Who **was** at the pool?

Future (*will*)	Future (*Be Going To*)
There **will be** a review tomorrow.	She **is going to be** late.
There **won't be** a test.	She **isn't going to be** on time.
Will there **be** any questions?	**Is** she **going to be** here soon?
Yes, there **will**.	No, she **isn't**.
How many questions **will** there **be**?	When **is** she **going to be** here?
Why **won't** there **be** a test?	Why **isn't** she **going to be** on time?
	Who **is going to be** on time?

EXERCISE 2 Fill in the blanks with the negative form of the underlined verb.

EXAMPLE: They <u>ate</u> in a Puerto Rican restaurant. They ___*didn't eat*___ in a French restaurant.

1. They <u>went</u> to Puerto Rico. They _____ to Hawaii.

2. They're <u>staying</u> in a hotel. They _____ with friends.

3. The hotel <u>has</u> tennis courts. It _____ a golf course.

4. They're <u>at</u> the beach now. They _____ at the hotel.

5. Ed <u>plays</u> tennis every day. Jane _____ tennis.

6. They'll <u>be</u> home in a few weeks. They _____ home this week.

7. Jane <u>likes</u> the sun. Ed _____ the sun.

8. They're <u>going</u> to St. Thomas. They _____ to St. John.

9. They're going to spend three days in St. Thomas. They
_____ a week there.

EXERCISE 3 Read each statement. Then write a *yes/no* question about the words in parentheses ( ). Write a short answer.

EXAMPLE: Jane went to Puerto Rico. (her husband)
Did her husband go to Puerto Rico? Yes, he did.

1. Jane likes to swim. (her husband)
_____

2. Jane's getting a suntan now. (her husband)
_____

3. Jane prefers the sun. (her husband)
_____

4. Ed gets up early every day. (Jane)
_____

5. They ate dinner in a restaurant. (in a French restaurant)
_____

6. The hotel has a pool. (tennis courts)
_____

7. The flight was smooth. (comfortable)
_____

8. They'll visit Saint Thomas. (Saint John)
_____

9. There are a lot of adults at the beach. (a lot of children)
_____

EXERCISE 4 Read each statement. Then write a *wh*- question about the words in parentheses ( ). Answer with a complete sentence.

EXAMPLE: Ed plays tennis. (when)
A. *When does he play tennis?*
B. *He plays tennis in the morning.*

---

1. They went to Puerto Rico. (how)

   A. _____

   B. _____

2. Ed isn't sitting in the sun. (why)

   A. _____

   B. _____

3. They ate dinner last night. (where)

   A. _____

   B. _____

4. Jane will call Rosemary. (when)

   A. _____

   B. _____

5. The children are playing now. (where)

   A. _____

   B. _____

6. They're going to leave on Friday. (what time)

   A. _____

   B. _____

7. Someone plays tennis every morning. (who)

   A. _____

   B. _____

8. Jane doesn't go shopping in the morning. (why)

   A. _____

   B. _____

9. There are swimming pools at the hotel. (how many)

   A. _____

   B. _____

14.3 Modals and Infinitives

Modals

He **can** play volleyball.	She **should** speak English.
He **can't** play tennis.	She **shouldn't** speak Spanish in class.
Can he play soccer?	**Should** she speak English with her classmates?
Yes, he **can**.	Yes, she **should**.
When **can** he play soccer?	Why **should** she speak English in class?
Why **can't** he play tennis?	Why **shouldn't** she speak Spanish?
Who **can** play tennis?	Who **should** speak Spanish?

Infinitives

I want **to leave** now.	• An infinitive doesn't show tense.
I tried **to call** you last night.	• Always use the base form after *to*.
It was hard **to get** a visa.	
I'm happy **to be** in the U.S.	

EXERCISE 5   Fill in the blanks with the correct tense or form of the words in parentheses ( ).

I _____*come*_____ from India. I _____ to the U.S. ten
   (example: come)   *(1 decide/move)*

months ago. It was difficult _____ my friends and family, but I
                                (2 leave)

_____ to the U.S. and have more opportunities.
   (3 want/come)

When I _____ in India, I was a draftsman. When I _____
         (4 live)   *(5 come)*

to the U.S. in July, I _____ a job at first because my English
                     (6 not/find)

wasn't good enough. Last September, I _____ a job in a laundromat.
                                     (7 find)

I don't like my job at all. I _____ a better job soon. I know
                          (8 want/find)

I _____ a better job when I _____ English better.
   (9 get)   *(10 speak)*

I _____ my money now. When I _____ enough
   (11 save)   *(12 have)*

money, I _____ engineering courses at the university. My
       (13 begin/take)

parents _____ proud of me when I _____.
      (14 be)   *(15 graduate)*

Right now, I _____ ESL courses at a college near my house.
    (16 take)

I _____ English in India, but it was different from American English.
  (17 study)

When I listen to Americans at my job or on TV, I _____
                                              (18 can/not/understand)

a lot of things they say. Sometimes when I _____ with Americans
                                          (19 speak)

at my job, they _____ me. They sometimes _____
              (20 not/understand)   (21 laugh)

at my pronunciation. They aren't bad people, but they _____
                                                    (22 not/understand)

that it is hard _____ another language and live in another country.
              (23 learn)

I usually _____ by myself at work. I _____
        (24 stay)   (25 know)

I _____ more, but I'm very shy.
 (26 should/practice)

When I _____ in India, I _____ in a big house
     (27 be)   (28 live)

with my parents, sisters and brothers, and grandparents. Now I _____
                                                            (29 have)

a small apartment and live alone. Sometimes I _____ lonely. I
                                            (30 be)

would like _____ married someday, but first I want _____
         (31 get)   (32 earn)

some money and _____ for my future.
             (33 save)

EXERCISE 6   Write the negative form of the underlined words.

EXAMPLE: He <u>moved</u> to the U.S. He ___*didn't move*___ to England.

1. He <u>studied</u> English in India. He _____ German.

2. He <u>wants to work</u> as an engineer. He _____ in a laundromat.

3. He <u>is going to study</u> engineering. He _____ art.

4. He <u>is taking</u> courses at a community college now. He _____ _____ courses at a university.

5. He's <u>saving</u> his money to get married. He _____ his money to go back to his country.

6. His coworkers <u>know</u> that he is a foreigner. They _____ how difficult his life is.

7. He <u>should</u> practice English with Americans. He _____ be shy.

8. He <u>can understand</u> some TV programs. He _____ all TV programs.

Read each statement. Then write a *yes/no* question about the words in parentheses ( ). Write a short answer.

EXAMPLE: He <u>studied</u> English in India. (American English)
Did he study American English? No, he didn't.

1. He'll <u>study</u> engineering. (accounting)

2. Americans <u>don't understand</u> him. (Indians)

3. He's <u>studying</u> American English now. (American history)

4. He <u>lives</u> in a small apartment. (with his family)

5. He <u>can understand</u> British English. (American English)

6. It <u>is hard to learn</u> another language. (live in another country)

7. He <u>wants to get</u> married. (next year)

8. He <u>lived</u> with his parents in India. (with his grandparents)

EXERCISE 8   Read each statement. Then write a *wh-* question with the words in parentheses ( ). (An answer is not necessary.)

EXAMPLE: He <u>left</u> India. (why)
Why did he leave India?

1. He <u>is saving</u> his money. (why)

2. He <u>is going to get</u> married. (when)

3. Some people <u>laugh</u> at him. (who)

4. He <u>is</u> lonely. (why)

_____

5. His parents <u>aren't</u> in the U.S. (why)

_____

6. He <u>didn't find</u> a job at first. (why)

_____

7. He <u>will graduate</u> from the university. (when)

_____

8. He <u>came</u> to the U.S. alone. (why)

_____

9. His coworkers <u>don't understand</u> his accent. (why)

_____

10. He <u>lived</u> in a big house. (when)

_____

EXERCISE 9 Write a question with the *wh-* word given. (You may answer the question.)

EXAMPLE: We had a test last week. What kind of test _*did we have?*_____

1. We often have a test. How often _____

2. We're reviewing tenses now. Why _____

3. We need more practice with verbs. Why _____

4. We'll have a final exam soon. When _____

5. The teacher doesn't speak fast in class. Why _____

6. The teacher usually comes to class on time. What time _____

_____

7. We studied the present tense. When _____

8. We should study every day. Why _____

9. We're going to finish this lesson. When _____

10. The school is closed on January 1. Why _____

11. The teacher is helping the students. How _____

12. We're doing an exercise. What kind _____

13. We read a story about Helen Keller. When _____

14. Vacation is going to start soon. When _____

15. This class has many students. How many students _____

16. The teacher explains the grammar. How _____

17. The classroom doesn't have a computer. Why _____

18. We had a test on modals. When _____

19. You should register for classes early. Why _____

20. It's important to learn English. Why _____

21. There are a lot of questions in this exercise. How many _____

_____

22. The teacher shouldn't speak our language in class. Why _____

_____

23. Some students will get an A. Who _____

24. One student went back to his country. Who _____

25. One student sits near the door. Who _____

26. Some students come from Mexico. How many students _____

_____

27. You won't be our teacher next semester. Who _____

_____

EXPANSION ACTIVITIES

CLASSROOM ACTIVITY

1. Find a partner. Use the words below to ask and answer questions with your partner. Practice the simple present, the present continuous, the future, and the simple past.

EXAMPLES:

you/from Asia
A. Are you from Asia?
B. Yes, I am. OR No, I'm not.

where/you/from
A. Where are you from?
B. I'm from Pakistan.

1. when/you/leave your hometown
2. how/you/come to the U.S.
3. you/come/to the U.S. alone
4. where/you/born

5. what language(s)/you speak
6. you/return to your hometown next year
7. you/have a job now
8. you/have a job in your hometown
9. how many brothers and sisters/you/have
10. your country/big
11. your country/have a lot of petroleum
12. you/live in an apartment in your hometown
13. you/study English in your country
14. what/you/study this semester
15. what/you/study next semester
16. you/like this class
17. the teacher/speak your language
18. this class/hard for you
19. who/your teacher last semester
20. who/your teacher next semester

2. Write sentences in each category, if you can. Write one for simple present, one for present continuous, one for future, and one for simple past.

	Simple Present	Present Continuous	Future	Simple Past
Job	I work in a factory.	I'm looking for a new job.	Next week I'm going to have an interview.	In my country, I was a taxi driver.
School				
Family				
Weather				
Apartment				
Job				

OUTSIDE ACTIVITY

Use the words below to interview an American student at this college. Practice the simple present, the present continuous, the future, and the simple past. Report something interesting to the class about this student.

EXAMPLE: have a car (what kind)
A. Do you have a car?
B. Yes, I do.
A. What kind of car do you have?
B. I have a Honda.

1. you/study another language now (what language)
2. you/live alone (who . . . with)
3. your family/live in this city
4. you/like this city (why/why not)
5. you/go to high school in this city (where)
6. what/your major
7. you/graduate soon (when)
8. what/you do/after/you/graduate
9. you/like to travel (when . . . your last vacation) (where . . . go)
10. you/own a computer (what kind) (when . . . buy it)
11. you/eat in a restaurant/last week (where)
12. you/buy something new/in the near future (what)
13. you/do something interesting/last weekend (what . . . do)
14. you/plan to do something interesting/next weekend (what . . . do)

Invite the American to interview you. Write down the questions that he or she asks you.

WRITING

Write a short composition about a big change you made in your life. Use Exercise 5 on pages 372 and 373 as your model.

Internet Activity

Use the Internet to find a hotel in a city that interests you. Find out the price of a room, the location of the hotel, and the facilities the hotel has (such as swimming pool, tennis courts, etc.).

APPENDIX

The Verb *GET*

Get has many meanings. Here is a list of the most common ones:

- get something = receive

  I got a letter from my father.

- get + (to) place = arrive

  I got home at six. What time do you get to school?

- get + object + infinitive = persuade

  She got him to wash the dishes.

- get + past participle = become

get acquainted	get worried	get hurt
get engaged	get lost	get bored
get married	get accustomed to	get confused
get divorced	get used to	get scared
get tired	get dressed	

  They got married in 1989.

- get + adjective = become

get hungry	get sleepy
get rich	get dark
get nervous	get angry
get well	get old
get upset	get fat

  It gets dark at 6:30.

- get an illness = catch

  While I was traveling, I got malaria.

- get a joke or an idea = understand

  Everybody except Tom laughed at the joke. He didn't get it.

  The boss explained the project to us, but I didn't get it.

- get ahead = advance

    He works very hard because he wants to get ahead in his job.

- get along (well) (with someone) = have a good relationship

    She doesn't get along with her mother-in-law.

    Do you and your roommate get along well?

- get around to something = find the time to do something

    I wanted to write my brother a letter yesterday, but I didn't get around to it.

- get away = escape

    The police chased the thief, but he got away.

- get away with something = escape punishment

    He cheated on his taxes and got away with it.

- get back = return

    He got back from his vacation last Saturday.

- get back at someone = get revenge

    My brother wants to get back at me for stealing his girlfriend.

- get back to someone = communicate with someone at a later time

    I can't talk to you today. Can I get back to you tomorrow?

- get by = have just enough but nothing more

    On her salary, she's just getting by. She can't afford a car or a vacation.

- get in trouble = be caught and punished for doing something wrong

    They got in trouble for cheating on the test.

- get in(to) = enter a car

    She got in the car and drove away quickly.

- get out (of) = leave a car

    When the taxi arrived at the theater, everyone got out.

- get on = seat yourself on a bicycle, motorcycle, horse

    She got on the motorcycle and left.

- get on = enter a train, bus, airplane

    She got on the bus and took a seat in the back.

- get off = leave a bicycle, motorcycle, horse, train, bus, airplane

    They will get off the train at the next stop.

- get out of something = escape responsibility

    My boss wants me to help him on Saturday, but I'm going to try to get out of it.

- get over something = recover from an illness or disappointment

  She has the flu this week. I hope she gets over it soon.

- get rid of someone or something = free oneself of someone or something undesirable

  My apartment has roaches, and I can't get rid of them.

- get through (to someone) = communicate, often by telephone

  She tried to explain the harm of eating fast food to her son, but she couldn't get through to him.

  I tried to call my mother many times, but her line was busy. I couldn't get through.

- get through with something = finish

  I can meet you after I get through with my homework.

- get together = meet with another person

  I'd like to see you again. When can we get together?

- get up = arise from bed

  He woke up at 6 o'clock, but he didn't get up until 6:30.

APPENDIX B

MAKE and *DO*

Some expressions use **make**. Others use **do**.

Make	**Do**
make a date/an appointment	do (the) homework
make a plan	do an exercise
make a decision	do the dishes
make a telephone call	do the cleaning, laundry, ironing, washing, etc.
make a reservation	do the shopping
make a meal (breakfast, lunch, dinner)	do one's best
make a mistake	do a favor
make an effort	do the right/wrong thing
make an improvement	do a job
make a promise	do business
make money	What do you do for a living? (asks about a job)
make noise	How do you do? (said when you meet someone for the first time)
make the bed	

Question Formation

1. Statements and Related Questions with a Main Verb.

Wh- Word	*Do/Does/Did (n't)*	Subject	Verb	Complement
When	does	She she	watches watch	TV. TV?
Where	do	My parents your parents	live live?	in Peru.
Who(m)	does	Your sister she	likes like?	someone.
Why	did	They they	left leave	early. early?
How many books	did	She she	found find?	some books.
What kind of car	did	He he	bought buy?	a car.
Why	didn't	She she	didn't go go	home. home?
Why	doesn't	He he	doesn't like like	tomatoes. tomatoes?
		Someone Who	has has	my book. my book?
		Someone Who	needs needs	help. help?
		Someone Who	took took	my pen. my pen?
		One teacher Which teacher	speaks speaks	Spanish. Spanish?
		Some men Which men	have have	a car. a car?
		Some boys How many boys	saw saw	the movie. the movie?

2. Statements and Related Questions with the Verb *Be*.

Wh- Word	*Be*	Subject	*Be*	Complement
Where	is	She she?	is	in California.
Why	were	They they	were	hungry. hungry?
Why	isn't	He he	isn't	tired. tired?
When	was	He he	was	born in England. born?
		One student Who Which student	was was was	late. late? late?
		Some kids How many kids Which kids	were were were	afraid. afraid? afraid?

3. Statements and Related Questions with an Auxiliary (Aux) Verb and a Main Verb.

Wh- Word	Aux	Subject	Aux	Main Verb	Complement
Where	is	She she	is	running. running?	
When	will	They they	will	go go	on a vacation. on a vacation?
What	should	He he	should	do do?	something.
How many pills	can	You you	can	take take?	a pill.
Why	can't	You you	can't	drive drive	a car. a car?
		Someone Who	should should	answer answer	the question. the question?

Alphabetical List of Irregular Past Forms

Base Form	Past Form	Base Form	Past Form
arise	arose	forget	forgot
awake	awoke	forgive	forgave
be	was/were	freeze	froze
bear	bore	get	got
beat	beat	give	gave
become	became	go	went
begin	began	grind	ground
bend	bent	grow	grew
bet	bet	hang	hung[1]
bind	bound	have	had
bite	bit	hear	heard
bleed	bled	hide	hid
blow	blew	hit	hit
break	broke	hold	held
breed	bred	hurt	hurt
bring	brought	keep	kept
broadcast	broadcast	kneel	knelt (or kneeled)
build	built	know	knew
burst	burst	lay	laid
buy	bought	lead	led
cast	cast	leave	left
catch	caught	lend	lent
choose	chose	let	let
cling	clung	lie	lay
come	came	light	lit (or lighted)
cost	cost	lose	lost
creep	crept	make	made
cut	cut	mean	meant
deal	dealt	meet	met
dig	dug	mistake	mistook
do	did	pay	paid
draw	drew	put	put
drink	drank	quit	quit
drive	drove	read	read
eat	ate	ride	rode
fall	fell	ring	rang
feed	fed	rise	rose
feel	felt	run	ran
fight	fought	say	said
find	found	see	saw
fit	fit	seek	sought
flee	fled	sell	sold
fly	flew	send	sent
forbid	forbade	set	set

[1]*Hanged* is used as the past form to refer to punishment by death. *Hung* is used in other situations: She *hung* the picture on the wall.

Base Form	Past Form	Base Form	Past Form
shake	shook	stink	stank
shed	shed	strike	struck
shine	shone (or shined)	strive	strove
shoot	shot	swear	swore
shrink	shrank	sweep	swept
shut	shut	swim	swam
sing	sang	swing	swung
sink	sank	take	took
sit	sat	teach	taught
sleep	slept	tear	tore
slide	slid	tell	told
slit	slit	think	thought
speak	spoke	throw	threw
speed	sped	understand	understood
spend	spent	upset	upset
spin	spun	wake	woke
spit	spit	wear	wore
split	split	weave	wove
spread	spread	weep	wept
spring	sprang	win	won
stand	stood	wind	wound
steal	stole	withdraw	withdrew
stick	stuck	wring	wrung
sting	stung	write	wrote

APPENDIX E

Meanings of Modals and Related Words

- Ability, Possibility

    Can you drive a truck?

    You *can* get a ticket for speeding.

- Necessity, Obligation

    A driver *must* have a license.

    I *have to* buy a new car.

- Permission

    You *can* park at a meter.

    You *can't* park at a bus stop.

- Possibility

    I *may* buy a new car soon.

    I *might* buy a Japanese car.

- Advice

    You *should* buy a new car. Your old car is in terrible condition.

- Permission Request

    May I borrow your car?

    Can I have the keys, please?

    Could I have the keys, please?

- Polite Request

    Would you teach me to drive?

    Could you show me your new car?

- Want

    What *would* you *like* to eat?

    I'd *like* a turkey sandwich.

APPENDIX F

Capitalization Rules

- The first word in a sentence: **My** friends are helpful.

- The word "I": My sister and **I** took a trip together.

- Names of people: **M**ichael **J**ackson; **G**eorge **W**ashington

- Titles preceding names of people: **D**octor (**Dr.**) **S**mith; **P**resident **L**incoln; **Q**ueen **E**lizabeth; **Mr. R**ogers; **Mrs. C**arter

- Geographic names: the **U**nited **S**tates; **L**ake **S**uperior; **C**alifornia; the **R**ocky **M**ountains; the **M**ississippi **R**iver

    NOTE: The word "the" in a geographic name is not capitalized.

- Street names: **P**ennsylvania **A**venue (**A**ve.); **W**all **S**treet (**S**t.); **A**bbey **R**oad (**R**d.)

- Names of organizations, companies, colleges, buildings, stores, hotels: the **R**epublican **P**arty; **H**einle and **H**einle **P**ublishers; **D**artmouth **C**ollege; the **U**niversity of **W**isconsin; the **W**hite **H**ouse; **B**loomingdale's; the **H**ilton **H**otel

- Nationalities and ethnic groups: **M**exicans; **C**anadians; **S**paniards; **A**mericans; **J**ews; **K**urds; **E**skimos

- Languages: **E**nglish; **S**panish; **P**olish; **V**ietnamese; **R**ussian

- Months: **J**anuary; **F**ebruary

- Days: **S**unday; **M**onday

- Holidays: **C**hristmas; **I**ndependence **D**ay

- Important words in a title: **G**rammar in **C**ontext; **T**he **O**ld **M**an and the **S**ea; **R**omeo and **J**uliet; **T**he **S**ound of **M**usic

    NOTE: Capitalize "the" as the first word of a title.

Metric Conversion Chart

LENGTH

When You Know	Symbol	Multiply by	To Find	Symbol
inches	in	2.54	centimeters	cm
feet	ft	30.5	centimeters	cm
feet	ft	0.3	meters	m
yards	yd	0.91	meters	m
miles	mi	1.6	kilometers	km

When You Know	Symbol	Multiply by	To Find	Symbol
centimeters	cm	0.39	inches	in
centimeters	cm	0.32	feet	ft
meter	m	3.28	feet	ft
meters	m	1.09	yards	yd
kilometers	km	0.62	miles	mi

NOTE:

1 foot = 12 inches

1 yard = 3 feet or 36 inches

AREA

When You Know	Symbol	Multiply by	To Find	Symbol
square inches	in^2	6.5	square centimeters	cm^2
square feet	ft^2	0.09	square meters	m^2
square yards	yd^2	0.8	square meters	m^2
square miles	mi^2	2.6	square kilometers	km^2

When You Know	Symbol	Multiply by	To Find	Symbol
square centimeters	cm^2	0.16	square inches	in^2
square meters	m^2	10.76	square feet	ft^2
square meters	m^2	1.2	square yards	yd^2
square kilometers	km^2	0.39	square miles	mi^2

WEIGHT (Mass)

When You Know	Symbol	Multiply by	To Find	Symbol
ounces	oz	28.35	grams	g
pounds	lb	0.45	kilograms	kg

When You Know	Symbol	Multiply by	To Find	Symbol
grams	g	0.04	ounces	oz
kilograms	kg	2.2	pounds	lb

> NOTE:
> 16 ounces = 1 pound

VOLUME

When You Know	Symbol	Multiply by	To Find	Symbol
fluid ounces	fl oz	30.0	milliliters	mL
pints	pt	0.47	liters	L
quarts	qt	0.95	liters	L
gallons	gal	3.8	liters	L

When You Know	Symbol	Multiply by	To Find	Symbol
milliliters	mL	0.03	fluid ounces	fl oz
liters	L	2.11	pints	pt
liters	L	1.05	quarts	qt
liters	L	0.26	gallons	gal

TEMPERATURE

When You Know	Symbol	Do this	To Find	Symbol
degrees Fahrenheit	°F	Subtract 32, then multiply by 5/9	degrees Celsius	°C

When You Know	Symbol	Do this	To Find	Symbol
degrees Celsius	°C	Multiply by 9/5, then add 32	degrees Fahrenheit	°F

Sample temperatures:

Fahrenheit	Celsius
0	−18
10	−12
20	−7
30	−1
40	4
50	10
60	16
70	21
80	27
90	32
100	38

APPENDIX **H**

Prepositions of Time

- **in** the morning: He takes a shower *in* the morning.

- **in** the afternoon: He takes a shower *in* the afternoon.

- **in** the evening: He takes a shower *in* the evening.

- **at** night: He takes a shower *at* night.

- **in** the summer, fall, winter, spring: He takes classes *in* the summer.

- **on** that/this day: October 10 is my birthday. I became a citizen *on* that day.

- **on** the weekend: He studies *on* the weekend.

- **on** a specific day: His birthday is *on* March 5.

- **in** a month: His birthday is *in* March.

- **in** a year: He was born *in* 1978.

- **in** a century: People didn't use cars *in* the 19th century.

- **on** a day: I don't have class *on* Monday.

- **at** a specific time: My class begins *at* 12:30.

- **from** a time **to** another time: My class is *from* 12:30 *to* 3:30.

- **in** a number of hours, days, weeks, months, years: She will graduate *in* 3 weeks. (This means "after 3 weeks.")

- **for** a number of hours, days, weeks, months, years: She was in Mexico *for* 3 weeks. (This means during the period of 3 weeks.)

- **by** a time: Please finish your test *by* 6 o'clock. (This means "no later than 6 o'clock.)

- **until** a time: I lived with my parents *until* I came to the U.S. (This means "all the time before.")

- **during** the movie, class, meeting: He slept *during* the meeting.

- **about/around** 6 o'clock: The movie will begin *about* 6 o'clock. People will arrive *around* 5:45.

- **in** the past/future: *In* the past, she never exercised.

- **at** present: *At* present, the days are getting longer.

- **in** the beginning/end: *In* the beginning, she didn't understand the teacher at all.

- **at** the beginning/end of something: The semester begins *at* the beginning of September. My birthday is *at* the end of June.

- **before/after** a time: You should finish the job *before* Friday. The library will be closed *after* 6:00.

- **before/after** an action takes place: Turn off the lights *before* you leave. Wash the dishes *after* you finish dinner.

APPENDIX I

Glossary of Grammatical Terms

- **Adjective** An adjective gives a description of a noun.

  It's a *tall* tree.   He's an *old* man.   My neighbors are *nice*.

- **Adverb** An adverb describes the action of a sentence or an adjective or another adverb.

  She speaks English *fluently*.   I drive *carefully*.
  She speaks English *extremely* well.   She is *very* intelligent.

- **Adverb of Frequency** An adverb of frequency tells how often the action happens.

  I *never* drink coffee.   They *usually* take the bus.

- **Affirmative** means *yes*.

- **Apostrophe** '

- **Article** The definite article is *the*. The indefinite articles are *a* and *an*.

  I have *a* cat.   I ate *an* apple.   *The* President was in New York last weekend.

- **Auxiliary Verb** Some verbs have two parts: an auxiliary verb and a main verb.

  He *can't* study.   We *will* return.

- **Base Form** The base form of the verb has no tense. It has no ending (*-s* or *-ed*):
  be, go, eat, take, write

  I didn't *go* out.   He doesn't *know* the answer.   You shouldn't *talk* loud.

- **Capital Letter** A B C D E F G . . .

- **Clause** A clause is a group of words that has a subject and a verb. Some sentences have only one clause.

  She speaks Spanish.

  Some sentences have a **main clause** and a **dependent clause.**

MAIN CLAUSE	DEPENDENT CLAUSE (reason clause)
She found a good job	because she has computer skills.
MAIN CLAUSE	DEPENDENT CLAUSE (time clause)
She'll turn off the light	before she goes to bed.
MAIN CLAUSE	DEPENDENT CLAUSE (*if* clause)
I'll take you to the doctor	if you don't have your car on Saturday.

- **Colon :**

- **Comma ,**

- **Comparative Form** A comparative form of an adjective or adverb is used to compare two things.

  My house is *bigger* than your house.

  Her husband drives *faster* than she does.

- **Complement** The complement of the sentence is the information after the verb. It completes the verb phrase.

  He works *hard*.   I slept *for five hours*.   They are *late*.

- **Consonant** The following letters are consonants: *b, c, d, f, g, h, j, k, l, m, n, p, q, r, s, t, v, w, x, y, z.*

  NOTE: *y* is sometimes considered a vowel.

- **Contraction** A contraction is made up of two words put together with an apostrophe.

  | *He's* my brother. | *You're* late. | They *won't* talk to me. |
  | (*He's = he is*) | (*You're = you are*) | (*won't = will not*) |

- **Count Noun** Count nouns are nouns that we can count. They have a singular and a plural form.

  1 pen / 3 pens   1 table / 4 tables

- **Dependent Clause** See **Clause.**

- **Direct Object** A direct object is a noun (phrase) or pronoun that receives the action of the verb.

    We saw *the movie*.   You have *a nice car*.   I love *you*.

- **Exclamation Mark !**

- **Hyphen -**

- **Imperative** An imperative sentence gives a command or instructions. An imperative sentence omits the word *you*.

    Come here.   *Don't be* late.   Please *sit* down.

- **Infinitive** An infinitive is *to* + base form.

    I want *to leave*.   You need *to be* here on time.

- **Linking Verb** A linking verb is a verb that links the subject to the noun or adjective after it. Linking verbs include *be, seem, feel, smell, sound, look, appear, taste*.

    She *is* a doctor.   She *seems* very intelligent.   She *looks* tired.

- **Modal** The modal verbs are *can, could, shall, should, will, would, may, might, must*.

    They *should* leave.   I *must* go.

- **Negative** means no.

- **Nonaction Verb** A nonaction verb has no action. We do not use a continuous tense (*be* + verb *-ing*) with a nonaction verb. The nonaction verbs are: *believe, cost, care, have, hear, know, like, love, matter, mean, need, own, prefer, remember, see, seem, think, understand, want*

- **Noncount Noun** A noncount noun is a noun that we don't count. It has no plural form.

    She drank some *water*.   He prepared some *rice*.   Do you need any *money*?

- **Noun** A noun is a person (*brother*), a place (*kitchen*) or a thing (*table*). Nouns can be either count (1 *table*, 2 *tables*) or noncount (*money, water*).

    My *brother* lives in California. My *sisters* live in New York. I get *mail* from them.

- **Noun Modifier** A noun modifier makes a noun more specific.

    fire department   *Independence* Day   *can* opener

- **Noun Phrase** A noun phrase is a group of words that form the subject or object of the sentence.

    A very nice woman helped me at registration.

    I bought *a big box of candy*.

- **Object** The object of the sentence follows the verb. It receives the action of the verb.

    He bought *a car*.   I saw *a movie*.   I met *your brother*.

- **Object Pronoun** Use object pronouns (*me, you, him, her, it, us, them*) after the verb or preposition.

    He likes *her*.   I saw the movie. Did you see *it*?

- **Parentheses** ( )

- **Paragraph** A paragraph is a group of sentences about one topic.

- **Participle, Present** The present participle is verb + *-ing*.

    She is *sleeping*.   They were *laughing*.

- **Period** .

- **Phrase** A group of words that go together.

    Last month my sister came to visit.

    There is a strange car *in front of my house*.

- **Plural** Plural means more than one. A plural noun usually ends with *-s*.

    She has beautiful *eyes*.

- **Possessive Form** Possessive forms show ownership or relationship.

    Mary's coat is in the closet.   *My* brother lives in Miami.

- **Preposition** A preposition is a short connecting word: *about, above, across, after, around, as, at, away, back, before, behind, below, by, down, for, from, in, into, like, of, off, on, out, over, to, under, up, with.*

- **Pronoun** A pronoun takes the place of a noun.

    I have a new car. I bought *it* last week.

    John likes Mary, but *she* doesn't like *him*.

- **Punctuation** Period . Comma , Colon : Semicolon ; Question Mark ? Exclamation Mark !

- **Question Mark** ?

- **Quotation Marks** " "

- **Regular Verb** A regular verb forms its past tense with *-ed*.

    He *worked* yesterday.   I *laughed* at the joke.

- **Sense-Perception Verb** A sense-perception verb has no action. It describes a sense.

    She *feels* fine.   The coffee *smells* fresh.   The milk *tastes* sour.

- **Sentence** A sentence is a group of words that contains a subject[1] and a verb (at least) and gives a complete thought.

    Sentence: She came home.

    Not a sentence: When she came home

---

[1]In an imperative sentence, the subject *you* is omitted: *Sit down. Come here.*

- **Simple Form of Verb** The simple form of the verb has no tense; it never has an *-s*, *-ed*, or *-ing* ending.

    Did you *see* the movie?

    I couldn't *find* your phone number.

- **Singular** Singular means one.

    She ate *a sandwich*.   I have one *television*.

- **Subject** The subject of the sentence tells who or what the sentence is about.

    My sister got married last April. *The wedding* was beautiful.

- **Subject Pronouns** Use subject pronouns (*I, you, he, she, it, we, you, they*) before a verb.

    They speak Japanese.   *We* speak Spanish.

- **Superlative Form** A superlative form of an adjective or adverb shows the number one item in a group of three or more.

    January is the *coldest* month of the year.

    My brother speaks English the *best* in my family.

- **Syllable** A syllable is a part of a word that has only one vowel sound. (Some words have only one syllable.)

    change (one syllable)   after (af·ter = 2 syllables)
    look (one syllable)   responsible (re·spon·si·ble = 4 syllables)

- **Tag Question** A tag question is a short question at the end of a sentence. It is used in conversation.

    You speak Spanish, *don't you?*

    He's not happy, *is he?*

- **Tense** A verb has tense. Tense shows when the action of the sentence happened.

    SIMPLE PRESENT: She usually *works* hard.

    FUTURE: She *will work* tomorrow.

    PRESENT CONTINUOUS: She *is working* now.

    SIMPLE PAST: She *worked* yesterday.

- **Verb** A verb is the action of the sentence:

    He *runs* fast.   I *speak* English.

    Some verbs have no action. They are linking verbs. They connect the subject to the rest of the sentence:

    He *is* tall.   She *looks* beautiful.   You *seem* tired.

- **Vowel** The following letters are vowels: *a, e, i, o, u. Y* is sometimes considered a vowel (for example, in the word *mystery*).

Verbs and Adjectives Followed by a Preposition

(be) accustomed to	forgive someone for	(be) proud of
(be) afraid of	(be) glad about	recover from
agree with	(be) good at	(be) related to
(be) angry about	(be) happy about	rely on/upon
(be) angry at/with	hear about	(be) responsible for
approve of	hear of	(be) sad about
argue about	hope for	(be) satisfied with
(be) ashamed of	(be) incapable of	(be) scared of
(be) aware of	insist on/upon	(be) sick of
believe in	(be) interested in	(be) sorry about
(be) bored with/by	(be) involved in	(be) sorry for
(be) capable of	(be) jealous of	speak about
care about/for	(be) known for	speak to/with
(be) compared to	(be) lazy about	succeed in
complain about	listen to	(be) sure of/about
(be) concerned about	look at	(be) surprised at
concentrate on	look for	take care of
consist of	look forward to	talk about
count on	(be) mad about	talk to/with
deal with	(be) mad at	thank someone for
decide on	(be) made from/of	(be) thankful to someone for
depend on/upon	(be) married to	think about/of
dream about/of	object to	(be) tired of
(be) engaged to	participate in	(be) upset about
(be) excited about	plan on	(be) upset with
(be) familiar with	pray to	(be) used to
(be) famous for	pray for	wait for
feel like	(be) prepared for	warn about
(be) fond of	prohibit from	(be) worried about
forget about	protect from	worry about